This ambitious study offers a radical reassessment of one of the most important concepts of the Romantic period – the imagination. In contrast to traditional accounts, John Whale locates the Romantic imagination within the period's lively and often antagonistic polemics on aesthetics and politics. In particular he focuses on the different versions of imagination produced within British writing in response to the cultural crises of the French Revolution and the ideology of utilitarianism. Through detailed analysis of key texts by Burke, Paine, Wollstonecraft, Bentham, Hazlitt, Cobbett and Coleridge, *Imagination Under Pressure* seeks to restore the role of imagination as a more positive force within cultural critique. The book concludes with a chapter on the afterlife of the Coleridgean imagination in the work of John Stuart Mill and I. A. Richards. As a whole it represents a timely and inventive contribution to the ongoing redefinition of Romantic literary and political culture.

JOHN WHALE is Senior Lecturer in English at the University of Leeds. He is the author of *Thomas De Quincey's Reluctant Autobiography* (1984), co-editor with Stephen Copley of *Beyond Romanticism: New Approaches to Texts and Contexts, 1789–1832* (1992), and editor of Edmund Burke's *Reflections on the Revolution in France*, 'Texts in Culture' series (2000).

CAMBRIDGE STUDIES IN ROMANTICISM 39

IMAGINATION UNDER PRESSURE,
1789–1832

CAMBRIDGE STUDIES IN ROMANTICISM

General editors

Professor Marilyn Butler
University of Oxford

Professor James Chandler
University of Chicago

Editorial board
John Barrell, *University of York*
Paul Hamilton, *University of London*
Mary Jacobus, *Cornell University*
Kenneth Johnston, *Indiana University*
Alan Liu, *University of California, Santa Barbara*
Jerome McGann, *University of Virginia*
David Simpson, *University of California, Davis*

This series aims to foster the best new work in one of the most challenging fields within English literary studies. From the early 1780s to the early 1830s a formidable array of talented men and women took to literary composition, not just in poetry, which some of them famously transformed, but in many modes of writing. The expansion of publishing created new opportunities for writers, and the political stakes of what they wrote were raised again by what Wordsworth called those 'great national events' that were 'almost daily taking place': the French Revolution, the Napoleonic and American wars, urbanization, industrialization, religous revival, an expanded empire abroad and the reform movement at home. This was an enormous ambition, even when it pretended otherwise. The relations between science, philosophy, religion and literature were reworked in texts such as *Frankenstein* and *Biographia Literaria*; gender relation in *A Vindication of the Rights of Woman* and *Don Juan*; journalism by Cobbett and Hazlitt; poetic form, content and style by the Lake School and the Cockney School. Outside Shakespeare studies, probably no body of writing has produced such a wealth of response or done so much to shape the responses of modern criticism. This indeed is the period that saw the emergence of those notions of 'literature' and of literary history, especially national literary history, on which modern scholarship in English has been founded.

The categories produced by Romanticism have also been challenged by recent historicist arguments. The task of the series is to engage both with a challenging corpus of Romantic writings and with the changing field of criticism they have helped to shape. As with other literary series published by Cambridge, this one will represent the work of both younger and more established scholars, on either side of the Atlantic and elsewhere.

For a complete list of titles published see end of book.

IMAGINATION UNDER PRESSURE, 1789–1832

Aesthetics, Politics and Utility

JOHN WHALE

CAMBRIDGE UNIVERSITY PRESS

PUBLISHED BY THE PRESS SYNDICATE OF THE UNIVERSITY OF CAMBRIDGE
The Pitt Building, Trumpington Street, Cambridge, United Kingdom

CAMBRIDGE UNIVERSITY PRESS
The Edinburgh Building, Cambridge CB2 2RU, United Kingdom   www.cup.ac.uk
40 West 20th Street, New York, NY 10011–4211, USA   www.cup.org
10 Stamford Road, Oakleigh, Melbourne 3166, Australia
Ruiz de Alarcón 13, 28014 Madrid, Spain

© John Whale 2000

This book is in copyright. Subject to statutory exception and to the provisions
of relevant collective licensing agreements, no reproduction of any part may
take place without the written permission of Cambridge University Press.

First published 2000

Printed in the United Kingdom at the University Press, Cambridge

Typeset in Baskerville 11/12.5 pt [VN]

A catalogue record for this book is available from the British Library

ISBN 0 521 77219 2 hardback

820.9
W552i

for
John Battle

Contents

Acknowledgements	*page* xi
Introduction	1
PART I IMAGINATION AND REVOLUTION	17
1 Burke and the civic imagination	19
2 Paine's attack on artifice	42
3 Wollstonecraft, imagination, and futurity	68
PART II IMAGINATION AND UTILITY	98
4 Hazlitt and the limits of the sympathetic imagination	110
5 Cobbett's imaginary landscape	140
6 Coleridge and the afterlife of imagination	166
Afterword	194
Notes	197
Bibliography	227
Index	237

Acknowledgements

This book has been some years in the making and, consequently, has incurred a large number of intellectual debts along the way. It had its origins a long time ago when I worked alongside Stephen Copley at University College Cardiff (as it was then called) and grew gradually into a book during the subsequent happy years I have spent here in the School of English at Leeds. And I am indebted to the students who over those years endured my MA course 'Political Prose of the Romantic Period' and my undergraduate option 'Literature of the 1790s'. I am even more indebted to the research students in the Romantic period who (often without knowing it) provided me with an opportunity to try things out and learn from their example. Foremost among these were Amanda Cook, Mandy Young, Tim Burke, Kirsten Daly, Angela Keane, and Richard Turley. (The last four I'm now pleased to know as colleagues at other institutions.) Paul Hamilton read an early version of the project's outline and its first two chapters. His encouragement to pursue it further was timely and much appreciated. The School of English has always been a stimulating, supportive, and humane environment in which to work. Former colleagues and friends Susan Matthews and Stephen Bygrave were extremely helpful in making me form and rethink my ideas on the period 1789–1832. David Fairer has always been encouraging as well as unstinting in his reminders of what came before the 1790s. Angela Keane has recently reversed roles and in that capacity supervised my writing of the introduction with typical acuteness and great good humour. Vivien Jones has been characteristically generous in casting her judicious eye over most of what follows; I hope it matches in some small part the quality of her support and her critical acumen.

Support from the School of English and an award from the British Academy's Leave Extension Scheme enabled me to bring the project to a conclusion. Earlier drafts of parts of chapters two, three, and four have appeared in *British Responses to the French Revolution* (edited by Kelvin Everest), *Reviewing Romanticism* (edited by Philip Martin and Robin Jarvis), *Studies in Romanticism*, and *Romanticism*. I am grateful to the editors and publishers for permission to reprint them here. Early versions of sections of chapters one and two were also given as papers at the inaugural British Association for Romantic Studies conference at King Alfred's College, Winchester (1989) and 'Edmund Burke and Our Present Discontents Conference' held at Goldsmiths College, University of London in 1997. I have been grateful for the opportunity to share ideas at a good number of BARS conferences in recent years with fellow Romanticists; and most particularly to share my interest in Hazlitt and Cobbett with Greg Dart and Kevin Gilmartin.

Sally, Helen, and Lucy have had to live with an imagination under pressure all this while. I thank them all for not exploding – and more. My only regret is that Stephen Copley, who was there at the beginning, and one of the people I most wanted to read the following pages, did not live to see the finished product.

Introduction

The aim of this book is to offer a new understanding of the way in which 'imagination' functions in key texts of the Romantic period and in particular of the way in which it is involved in two moments of cultural crisis: the British response to the French Revolution and the reaction to utilitarianism. Imagination thus figures in this study as a point of access to larger definitions and arguments about aesthetics and 'representation'. My contention is that imagination is an integral and still undervalued component of cultural critique, both in this particular historical period and beyond. My chosen texts, with the possible exception of those by Coleridge and Hazlitt, are not the ones usually mustered to write a sympathetic and celebratory history of the creative faculty. Indeed for some of the writers I focus on, 'imagination' is predominantly a negative term; while for all of them it is problematic. My concentration on non-fictional prose writers in itself offers a revealingly different generic history of Romantic aesthetics, one which depends upon the necessarily discursive nature of such writing and one which avoids a preemptively celebratory account. It is a choice which I hope will implicitly and explicitly challenge some of our accepted notions of 'literariness' through this discursivity of both approach and materials. To see the production of different, often contradictory, notions of imagination in relation to cultural crises will enable us to uncover a sense of 'imagination' as an integral figure in cultural critique and as a complex, often creative, response to cultural change. In this respect, I hope that this study will enable us to see the particularity of different imaginations in the period rather than simply to replicate 'the Romantic Imagination' and its undeniably powerful history of appropriations. What follows then is offered up as a deliberate resistance, a strategic particularity, to the homogenising power of that intellectual, historical, and still active idea of 'the Romantic Imagination' and its associated Romanticism.

This study offers a challenge to Romanticist views of imagination which celebrate it as an essential and humanist creative faculty. My contention is that imagination is an important reflex of cultural crisis. There is also a paradox at the heart of my argument: even when imagination is shown or seen to fail – as it often is in the chapters which follow – it maintains a necessary and vital presence. Even as the authors I focus on bemoan its incapacity or confidently mock its delusiveness, imagination accrues an uncanny power: a power to return in another beguiling form. The historical failures of imagination charted here are also therefore testimonies to its resistance and to its enduring presence as it resurfaces in the language and strategies of its opponents. Imagination is not only produced by a split or fracture in the culture; it reproduces and disseminates itself across that divide.

Imagination is an overdetermined term and one which can be referred to a bewildering variety of historical examples in the hope of definition.[1] For the historian of the Romantic period within literary studies, the problem is compounded by the obvious fact that this faculty has occupied a central and privileged position in the post-hoc formulation of 'Romanticism' which since the Victorian period has served to construct a dominant version of liberal aesthetics and to support an institutionalised version of culture which has consolidated a range of national and imperial identities. Any return to the historical site of imagination in the period 1789–1832 therefore might appear to offer the promise of a release from this overdetermined history, but no such innocence exists. To write a particular history of imagination and its relationship to aesthetics in a selection of key texts and in relation to two very particular crises in representation and cultural value is immediately to invoke (and implicate oneself in) a set of meanings about the term imagination which are at the same time historical and present.

In order to focus my study of the production of different versions of imagination in response to cultural and representational crises I have chosen to divide the book into two sections: the first dealing with responses to the French Revolution, the second dealing with responses to the idea of utility. In part, this is a form of convenience. My hope is that there are as many connections and correspondences as discrete differences between the two sections and the six writers who are studied in detail. In a number of significant ways the writers in the second half of this book revisit and rehearse many of the concerns that had arisen out of the French Revolution. For example, Burke's depiction of the French revolutionaries resurfaces in the castigation of the philosophers of utility carried out by Hazlitt and Coleridge. And Cobbett's determined literalism in response to the corruption of 'the system' in the Regency replays with significant differences Paine's assault on aristocratic culture in the 1790s. Splitting the book into two should not be read as a description of a firm historical divide – more a way of re-focusing the debate from another angle. I certainly do not wish to suggest that one event follows another in any simple progressive way, though certain problems of representation are repeated and inherited to take on a different form in the later section. I am also aware that my selection of six writers, Burke, Paine, Wollstonecraft, Hazlitt, Coleridge, and Cobbett, while representing a range of different political, social, and stylistic positions within English culture, does not represent a complete cross-section or representative picture. New historiographical work in the period has already increased our appreciation of the sheer variety within radical culture, for example.[2]

Retaining a sense of the strategic and multiple nature of 'imaginations' guards us against the temptation to look for a point of origin at which there emerged a clear-cut distinction between the utilitarian and the literary, where the utilitarian is simply mechanistic and the literary is purely noumenal. Indeed, one of my contentions is that the issue of the French Revolution and the question of utility for writers in the period are inextricably linked. It is not a question of addressing a clear-cut binary divide between the utilitarian and the 'imaginative' – another version of the 'two cultures' argument, to use C. P. Snow's mid-twentieth-century formulation. Rather it is a question of seeing the interaction and competition of these terms within specific cultural debates. Since the figure and faculty of imagination is defined so often as a mediatory power, ostensibly healing the breach between categories and dichotomies, it is easy to take the idea of a divided culture for granted and not to see this split itself as a rhetorical feature of many arguments in the field of cultural value. For example, recent studies have shown us that though the organic and the mechanical might feature as polar opposites within the discourse deployed by such writers as Coleridge and De Quincey, this should not lead us to make too easy a separation. Both De Quincey and Coleridge are good examples of writers who retain and value a sense of the mechanical and even of the mechanistic to suit their respective visions of the relationship between language, literature, and society.[3]

Despite the claims made by a range of American critics for the continuities between 'Romantic literature' and the discourse of contemporary criticism,[4] other cultural historians, including Richard Kearney, have claimed more generally that our condition of postmodernity seems to find imagination an anathema; it is a faculty which represents an outmoded and belated belief in originality.[5] For over twenty years critics such as M. H. Abrams, Harold Bloom, and Geoffrey Hartman dominated the literary critical scene with powerful studies which could speak positively – if anxiously and agonistically – of 'imagination' and 'vision'. In Romantic studies it has now become almost unfashionable to refer to the term. In the introduction to his 1991 study *Romantic Ecology: Wordsworth and the Environmental Tradition*, for example, Jonathan Bate claims that 'the buzzwords among Romanticists are now "history" and "politics" – terms like "vision" and "imagination", so central to the previous generation of critics, are now treated with scepticism and often with outright hostility'.[6] In order to avoid what he sees as the false idealism of 'Wordsworthianism', Alan Liu, in his important study of Wordsworth and history, self-consciously provides 'a litany of broken promises' which culminates with: 'Therefore, there is no Imagination.'[7]

This recent engagement with forms of historicism does not represent the whole story, for the demise of the imagination has also coincided with what may be termed the rise of the sublime. Over the last twenty years the latter has, in comparison, proved to be an almost inexhaustible source of critical and historical investigations and even of modern poetics – especially when read in conjunction with contemporary forms of psychoanalysis or as an integral part of an on-going post-Kantian problem of self-representation.[8] The sublime is also, of course, at one with the condition of postmodernity, due largely to the work of Jean-François Lyotard.

This demise in the fortunes of 'imagination' within critical debate has coincided with the recent renewal of interest in questions and practices of competing forms of historicism, what has glibly been termed 'the return to history'. As early as 1981, Marilyn Butler's *Romantics, Rebels, and Reactionaries: English Literature and Its Background, 1760–1830* encouraged, at least in Britain, a new historical perception of the period which questioned the assumptions of 'Romanticism' and along with them the touchstone faculty of imagination. In order to challenge the existence of a single intellectual movement by foregrounding the complex of different cultural responses within the period, her study focused attention away from what she refers to as the 'inwardness', 'internalized imaginative worlds' and 'Mind'[9] informing the poetics of the canonical male Romantic poets.

In this new wave of historicist critiques of Romanticism the idealizing or transcendent 'Imagination' has often figured as an instrument of false consciousness, that which has attempted to occlude history and politics with the delusions of individualism. As a result, it can be legitimately attacked from both sides: it is castigated for disconnecting aesthetics from realpolitik, renouncing its civic responsibilities, and then for empowering itself as a form of private consciousness. Its power can be seen to reside either in its renunciation or in its evasion of power.[10] In this form of the aesthetic exerting but denying power, it came to characterise what Jerome McGann in 1986 famously, and by now infamously, christened 'the romantic ideology'.

Some of the most impressive studies of Romantic aesthetics and imagination in recent years have taken the form of a demystifying materialism, at their best offering a 'cultural materialist' account of the production of would-be transcendent and metaphysical versions of the aesthetic. In line with this demand for 'history' and 'politics' the tendency has been to expose the material ground upon which the aesthetic rests and for imagination to give way to writing as an occupation or a form of socio-economic exchange.[11] 'Literature' has been shown to be the tool of ideology as a specific and focused form of state apparatus working through a process of internalisation. In this respect, Terry Eagleton's *The Ideology of the Aesthetic* represents the most panoptic survey of post-Kantian aesthetics and of the way in which they characteristically operate a paradox of liberal freedom: at once controlling and offering up the affect of 'inner space' at the site of imagination.[12]

On a slightly less grand scale and within more familiar literary boundaries, Peter de Bolla's *The Discourse of the Sublime: Readings in History, Aesthetics and the Subject* is a classic example of the deployment of a discursiveness applied to the conceptually unified, but not simply limited, field of the eighteenth-century sublime which links the production of sublimity to the Seven Years War.[13] Nigel Leask performs a similar and equally impressive task in his *The Politics of Coleridge's Imagination*, where his central concern is to '[insist] upon the materiality of this noumenal quality' and to show 'the progenitor of this current notion of Imagination to have been a thoroughly political animal'.[14] Leask's history takes us back beyond a by now familiar culture split to Coleridge's 'One Life' theory which saw imagination working on behalf of a civic rather than a noumenal mystery. Leask's own argument, in carefully defining itself against uncritical humanists who fall into the trap of replicating a Romantic position, could itself be said to yearn, or at least lean, towards a satisfying imaginative vision of wholeness instead of living with the breaks, fractures, and discontinuities. (Its own vision of wholeness comes from a subscription to a Harringtonian classical republicanism.) And more recently, in *Romantic Discourse and Political Modernity*, Richard Bourke has argued for a similar lost opportunity in the case of Wordsworth's aesthetics and poetical practices. Wordsworth's appropriation by Victorian culture – what Bourke calls Wordsworthianism – becomes the main object of inquiry as he draws attention to the false consolations and serenity offered by the liberal imagination. The aesthetic is reduced to an ineffective realm of immanence from which it rails against the alienation effect of industrialisation and from which it functions as a 'regulative ideal'.[15]

Alan Richardson's 1994 study *Literature, Education, and Romanticism: Reading as Social Practice 1780-1832* outlines the ways in which the production or invention of modern ideas of childhood worked hand in hand with the creation of the category of imaginative literature during the Romantic period. As well as importantly revealing the variety of different forms of writing and the competing varieties of childhood – Lockean and Rousseauist to mention but two – involved in this process, Richardson uncovers the regulatory function played by 'literature': in particular, the ways in which these ideas served to discipline and in many cases to infantilise specific social, ethnic, and gendered groups in the period. For Richardson, the legacy of Romanticism is complex and mixed. Aware of the positive potential of its 'emancipatory and egalitarian practices', his placing of its 'representations and pronouncements on education' leads to a picture of 'social discipline, ideological conformity, and state security'.[16] The expansive human nature and proclaimed individualist human freedom of the Romantic aesthetic is revealed as a dangerously homogenising ideology struggling to keep at bay the threatening particularities of class, ethnicity, and gender. At the bottom of it all and acting, it seems, as the lynch-pin of the system is 'Imagination'. Literature, according to Richardson, 'awake[n]s a common, essential human selfhood, conveying a sense of an ideal mental community to which all readers might belong'. 'Literature could alone perform this function,' he argues (quoting Coleridge) 'because . . . it brought the "whole soul of man into activity", fusing the particular and the general, the individual and the representative, the local and the universal through the "synthetic and magical" power of imagination.'[17]

Two major discursive studies of imagination by Pyle and Heinzelman span the period of renewed and more self-conscious historicism which has characterised the last fifteen years. Heinzelman's pioneering and prescient 1980 study *The Economics of the Imagination* employed a Foucauldian methodology to illuminate the fictive nature of political economy and its relationship to 'literature' from the eighteenth through to the early twentieth century. The significance of Heinzelman's study lies not in defining the nature or characteristics of the literary imagination, but in arguing a case for its involvement and interaction with competing ideas of economy. The effect, again following Coleridge, is to question the assumption of a history of two cultures or the existence of a binary divide between the literary and the economic. Heinzelman's claim for a pervasive 'metaphor of economics' as the 'copula which connects two activities [of Trade and Literature]' leads to an understanding of 'how commerce and literature attempt to transcend and moderate . . . each other'.[18] One might add 'create each other'. Heinzelman's study can now be read alongside more recent work which, equally, has alerted us to the creation of 'literature' in the early nineteenth century by exploring new disciplinary perspectives.[19] For Heinzelman, political economy after Adam Smith is imbued with an imaginative structure which 'has the force of poiesis' and which can be seen almost as a counterpoetics. Although his account is always more concerned to maintain his idea of mutual definition rather than a history of conflicts, he presents the mutations of political economy from Aristotle through to Malthus and Ricardo and is able to focus in particular on the conflicting communitarian and proprietorial aspects of Wordsworth's poetry. Important as it is in establishing the ground on which literature and economics are constituted by the early nineteenth century, the 'imagination' of Heinzelman's study turns out to resist definition. In his concluding chapter on William Carlos Williams he discloses that 'the core of all cures for the economist as well as the poet, lies in the dissatisfied labour of the irrepressible imagination'.[20]

Forest Pyle's more recent study performs a similar function as regards the relationship between imagination and ideology.[21] For Pyle, 'imagination' is the connecting agent which serves to mask contradictions within culture, in particular the gap between individual and society. At the same time as illustrating imagination's role in offering a mystificatory aestheticisation of a familiar dichotomy, Pyle is rightly sensitive to imagination's resistance to definition. Having decided to describe it as a rhetorical figure, the figure he chooses turns out to be catachresis – a misnaming. Like Heinzelman, Pyle is careful to stress the symbiotic or imbricated relationship between imagination and ideology. Through a combination of historical materialism derived from critical Marxism and a formal materialism derived from Paul de Man,[22] he explores the space occupied by the figure of imagination. He is alert to the dangers and temptations of moving outside 'the ideology of imagination' – the lure evident in McGann's attempt to interrogate a Romantic ideology, a project which, in Pyle's view, only serves to replicate the wish-fulfilment of the Romantic aesthetic. Pyle's own definition of the historical subsumes particularity and difference and perhaps even the possibility of discontinuity and fracture. Within the logic of his argument, then, imagination figures as the ineffable. His own figure of catachresis speaks of a longing that can never be satisfied; it is the 'something missing' in the space opened up by imagination's 'failure'. In asking the following question, Pyle could be said to go beyond the examination of a '*particular* figure' and to assume the existence of a common (human) faculty existing in the present. Having announced the wake of imagination, like Kearney, he addresses a figure already presumed dead. It is a reversibility very similar to Heinzelman's:

For after Althusser – indeed, after Marx – how can we imagine a product of language or activity of *mind* that would not be ideological? It is my thesis that a reading of 'the ideology of imagination' not only sheds light on the imagination but in turn reflects upon the very workings of ideology.[23]

In their very different ways, these studies by Heinzelman and Pyle offer valuable cultural histories of imagination. But both also illustrate the power of this figure to resist appropriation at the same time as seeming to offer itself up to it. It can clearly be seen that both Heinzelman and Pyle perform their respective studies of imagination in such a way as to appropriate its opposition: economics and ideology. Both studies are extremely valuable for the way in which they are able to articulate a history of the contest of faculties or discourse within the Romantic period, but both essentially lock imagination into a totalising narrative or at least unescapable reversibility. Having done so they then both invoke another ghostly figure of imagination in order to speculate beyond the impasse. This figure conveniently doubles and manifests itself again outside the terms of critique. For all their sophistication and intelligence both studies manifest the dangers of a holistic approach to imagination.

One is tempted to suggest that the critical history of imagination has been too easily swayed by the qualities ascribed to the faculty. Having been described as a synthesising power, the history of imagination has itself been too synthesising, too willing to incorporate related terms at the expense of cultural and historical difference. Indeed the very ideological power, even hegemonic potential, of 'imagination' could be said to reside in its ability to skip conveniently between the particular and the abstract, between process and product, between cognition and writing. And to separate out a particular history of the imagination from a related sense of a creative human faculty is more difficult than one might initially think. Despite the fact that 'imagination' refers to a bewilderingly diffuse set of ideas, its cultural force has been derived from its ability to articulate opposed, paradoxical, and contradictory ideas. In this sense even the longstanding negative association with the potential synonym 'fancy' or with Hobbes's idea of 'decaying sense' could be seen as an opportunity to be exploited in the Romantic period. This forcing of unity out of contradiction is most strongly associated with Coleridge's acts of Romantic purification, his desynonymisation of the word. As we shall see, the power and pervasiveness of many of Coleridge's articulations of the imagination lie in this double appeal: recognition of a cultural schism simultaneous with a healing synthesis. And, even today, 'imagination' possesses different and sometimes radically opposed identities as it appears at different levels of cultural production and within different disciplinary boundaries. The aggressive demystification it has received within Romantic aesthetics stands in marked contrast to the power and potential it still enjoys in the areas of creative writing, educational psychology, and philosophical individualism.

In the face of this cluttered and apparently overdetermined literary critical field of Romantic aesthetics, recent work in the disciplines of philosophy and education could easily be viewed as surprisingly idealistic, even naive. But it should serve as a salutary reminder to the literary historian of the way in which it might still be possible to formulate positive contemporary accounts of imagination. At the very least it provides a good illustration of how new versions of imagination are still being produced to serve as possible solutions to ontological, pedagogic, and sociological problems. Foremost among recent British accounts is Mary Warnock's *Imagination and Time*, a passionate defence of the ethical possibilities available in the philosophical and Romantic aesthetic ideas of imagination.[24] Aggressively disposed to what she sees as the chaotic and anarchic relativism of postmodernism, she argues forcefully for a materialist (at times positively biological) humanism which can overcome, with the help of Hume and Kant, the threat of Cartesian dualism. By charting her own narrative of the correlation of memory and imagination Warnock (rather like Hume) ruthlessly avoids what she sees as the false premises and metaphysics of religion (particularly Christianity). According to her argument, memory in conjunction with imagination is able to link us not only with the past, but with the future. From this neo-Wordsworthian perspective she offers us a vision of consensus and continuity contained within a sense of unfinished and ever-changing narrative. Imagination is thus seen to guarantee a sense of identity through history and story-telling despite being open to revision and despite having to take account of cultural difference in a multi-ethnic society.[25] And in their introduction to a recent collection of essays entitled *Imagination and Education*,[26] the editors make a plea for the clarification of the very term imagination which is familiar to a literary historian of the eighteenth and nineteenth centuries; and within the volume itself the contradictory and multifarious history of the term is well illustrated. Despite all these problems of definition however there seems to be no difficulty in believing in the psychological reality of something called 'imagination' and in urging its application and exercise in the classroom. What comes across from both these books is the need in their authors for a space labelled 'imagination'. In the latter case, this seems to be almost desperate. Unlike Warnock, they do not seem to see the need to select and construct a particular version of imagination which can be justified, defended, and articulated. And to my mind, the abiding contradiction in this need is the way in which that space of imagination is characterised by alterity/ creativity/ transgression/ freedom and at the same time must be subject to normative notions of development and pedagogy.

If these examples of work in other disciplinary areas seem to replicate many of the problems which literary critics have located historically in the field of Romanticism and its literary legacies, they also provide a contemporary example of how the 'imagination' can be produced to fill a gap in culture. It clearly remains a figure which can be drawn upon to solve a problem in a crisis of representation spanning theory and practice – much as it did in the period 1789–1832.

It is my contention that the discursive analysis of imagination which I offer in the following chapters will provide a more representative history of the term than that which has previously prevailed in Romantic criticism. Only by situating imagination within specific contexts of usage, including those which are critical and even derogatory, can we hope to escape the power of the term as it has been purified and reified in high Romantic discourse. By working discursively and outside the privileged genre of poetry my account attempts a demystification of the term. We need to pay more careful attention to the different ways in which imagination connects with other competing terms in the matrix of the aesthetic and ideological debates of the time. Only by observing how imagination is offered up in the face of a particular crisis – how it is produced under pressure – can we articulate its resistant history in the context of a prevailing 'Romanticism' which pervades not only the wider cultural sphere of literary creativity, but also the more particular activity of literary criticism itself.

Imaginations are culturally and historically specific. We should avoid thinking of the term as a human constant or as an essence. Acknowledging the power and validity of recent political critiques of the mystifying power of the agent of the aesthetic, I would like to argue for the imagination as a strategically deployed category: to see it as reactive – as a reflex or a reaction to an epistemological, cultural, or representational crisis rather than always invoking its hegemonic control or potential. I would like to recover some of its desperation, anxiety, and unhappiness (following Bloom and Hartman) in order to focus on its capacity to reveal an urgent need. Even in the Romantic period itself the 'imagination' (above all else) is forced to compete with other would-be hegemonic discourses and subject positions. To see imagination as a sign of crisis rather than a faculty of truth, to focus on its production rather than its content, might reveal a different history and a more helpful potential in the term. Imagination is here not just a form of evasion or an ideological illusion, it is a means of articulating resistance. To invest imagination with some of the excitement, strangeness, and force that has recently been assigned to the idea of the 'in-between' might enable us to see more of the dynamic competition for representation which took place at this historical moment, more of the inherent instability of 'Romanticism', and more of the competing and conflicting varieties of imagination in the writings of the period.

My choice of authors also reflects my particular interest in the relationship between different forms of literalism and the symbolic in the period. This is a contest which exists at both the wider cultural level and within the work of an individual writer. For example, my analyses of the writings of Paine and Cobbett focus on their literalism: the supposed 'transparency' or plainness of their respective styles. By analysing their work in detail my aim is to reveal not only the specific nature of their different literalisms, but also the extent to which this very quality depends on and cannot avoid a sense of aesthetic excess. In Paine and

Cobbett this can take the form of a rationalist revolutionary sublime and an Edenic Tory nostalgia. From this perspective, Wollstonecraft and Hazlitt can be seen to inhabit a problematic middle ground as polite radical or 'liberal' writers whose work in different ways is more evenly struck between aesthetic excess and rationalist empiricism. On the other side of the equation, Coleridge's more famous definitions of the symbol and of the 'Idea' can be compared with Burke's organicism in terms of an ideologically powerful mode of representation which can switch with ease between the particular and the abstract and at the same time claim to absorb within its articulations the isolated and discrete units of mere particularity. This dynamic competition between forms of representational plainness underscores my concern to trace the various projections of imagination produced by Romantic period writers in response to revolution and utility. Some of these larger debates about transparency and symbolic modes of representation which my study defines have a wide-ranging and pervasive significance not only for the literary culture of the period, but also for our appreciation of it at the end of the twentieth century. My examination of imagination's embattled involvement with competing forms of literalism within the prose of the period provides a new foundation for rethinking the history of the Romantic symbol and a starting-point for a reconsideration of our assumptions about the stylistic and generic polarities of Romantic literary texts – the relationship between the 'simplicity' of the ballad and the discursiveness of blank verse in *Lyrical Ballads*, for example.

The story of imagination which emerges from my detailed analysis of six selected authors challenges the still widely-held assumption that 'imagination' inhabits an autonomous aesthetic realm. Imagination here is not simply waged against its cultural opponents – literalism, revolutionary rationalism, utility – it is produced in conjunction and collusion with them. Imagination inhabits the gaps, the fractures, in culture which are produced by the French Revolution and the ideology of utility. And from this position it provides the means for articulating and responding to the dominant forms of culture.

For these reasons, my account of imaginations attempts to address not only the advocates of imagination, but also its opponents. In my chapters on Burke, Wollstonecraft, Hazlitt, and Coleridge I analyze a variety of different constructions of imagination, but all of them are reactive and embattled. In the cases of Wollstonecraft and Hazlitt, imagination has, at times, to be kept at bay, even renounced. But in my chapters on Paine and Cobbett I focus deliberately on the professed absence of imagination in two writers who oppose themselves to what they see as the corrupt, dominant mode of aesthetics in British society. As we shall see, their different attempts to escape or repress imagination actually serve to facilitate its return as an integral component of radical cultural critique.

In my final chapter I devote a considerable amount of attention to the afterlife of the Coleridgean imagination as it manifests itself in the work of John Stuart Mill and I. A. Richards. In Mill's intellectual history we witness the necessary return of imagination after the perceived psychological inadequacy of the ideology of utility. In Richards we are able to see, within the discipline of literary criticism and linguistics, a demonstration of the interaction of imagination and utility. The Coleridgean imagination is a necessary component of Richards's brand of utilitarianism, his dream of a scientific criticism, even as it is construed as supplementary. Richards's ambitious project to accommodate the Coleridgean imagination thus exemplifies my argument about the essential role played by imagination in the formation of critique even when it has apparently been relegated to the realm of the aesthetic. It functions even as it is dismissed. In this Richards's example is salutary. At least a generation before the criticism of the Romantic period which now repeatedly construes imagination as false consciousness – the idealist mask behind which materialist interests operate – Richards's engagement with Coleridge is symptomatic of the need to encounter and engage with the figure of imagination even when in the business of transcending it. In Richards's career, then, we see not only the afterlife of the Coleridgean imagination as it has been constructed in opposition to utilitarianism, but also the ghost within the current critical debate on Romantic aesthetics.

In this final chapter there is a line of continuity, a history of imagination, but the narrative might better be described, at each stage, as a violent rewriting of imagination. Imagination here figures as the term which inhabits the crisis: not the essence or content of the schism, but the name given to the schism itself, a way at once urgent and convenient of naming and describing that which won't hold. Throughout this book I reserve a space within critique for the reactive and constantly changing figure of imagination.

Similarly, my strategy of addressing the opposition to and, more particularly, the absence of imagination might be seen as falling into the kind of reification that I have already explicitly sought to avoid. Another version of the transcendent Romantic Imagination – or at least a notion of the essential entity of imagination – might be construed as entering through the back door. But the reactive and conflictual nature of imagination in these debates is such that one is forced to address its absence as much as its presence: its very identity may be said to be produced through repressions and erasures alongside its opponent utility.

In what follows I have addressed imagination sometimes as a key word in the discourse of aesthetics and perception and sometimes as a concept underpinning such a key term. This is not to suppose or endorse its inherent reality outside of its deployment by writers and audiences who are themselves engaged in important acts of idealisation and reification. But the historically located account of imagination which I'm offering must engage with these different manifestations of the relationship between the word and idea of 'imagination' even as it addresses its contradictions and uncovers its multiplicity of identities. In the chapters which follow I treat and follow imagination through its historical manifestations as a key word, a concept, and as a historically conveyed idea capable of influencing, determining, and reacting with subsequent critical and creative crises in the early and late twentieth century. In following such transmutations of imagination I am aware as much of the act of transforming appropriation, of the difference necessarily involved in a history of influence, as I am of the continuity in the terminology employed. It is therefore not only strategic, but historically appropriate that in the account of imagination which follows its multiple fractures are read alongside its idealisations and its production as an essential and inherent entity. I will be as interested in analysing the appearance of the linguistic sign 'imagination' as in tracing its role and presence as a concept, idea, and speculative possibility. In explaining the very discursivity of imagination, I do not wish to limit myself to its specifically linguistic or philological character.

In the first three chapters of this book I am not so much interested in the French Revolution itself as in what it elicits in these most famous of British responses.[27] In very different ways from their French counterparts, Burke, Paine, and Wollstonecraft are forced to rethink, revise, and re-imagine their most cherished beliefs in the structure of British society given the tumultuous events taking place across the Channel. Burke's negative response to the revolution begins the sequence not simply because it was the first to significantly address the subject, but because, as many commentators have pointed out, it rather ironically set the terms of the debate (or the 'revolution controversy')[28] by crediting the French experiment with the status of a new epistemology. In its rhetorical deployment of fear, Burke's *Reflections* constructs the British response as a problem of cultural and philosophical understanding, what we now perceive to be a crisis of representation. Burke's fierce rearguard defence of English aristocratic culture as a sign, more generally, of European chivalry marks the change threatened from revolutionary France as an event of world historical importance: even as the end of culture or the end of history.[29] But even amidst Burke's representations of fear, chaos, and ferocious contempt he holds up as his damsel in distress the civilised liberty of his culture, the compliment paid by that culture to the imaginations of its enfranchised and disenfranchised subjects. In the reciprocal labour of aristocratic culture – its 'armorial ensigns and bearings' – Burke locates that self-reflective respect which generates a society which, it is claimed, transcends the atomism of individualism, the arithmetic of utilitarian calculations, and the raw economics of commerce. That he does so in the antiquated terms of chivalry suggests the belatedness of the very aristocratic culture he defends.[30] Despite the danger of being historically marked by romance, imagination in Burke's *Reflections* figures as the agent of civic self-consciousness at the same time as it serves the purpose of hegemonic control, of false consciousness.

In their different responses to Burke, Paine and Wollstonecraft traverse much of the same territory of historical self-consciousness addressed by Burke. Confronting the change of revolutionary France and addressing their own very specific English and differently gendered goals, they too are forced to question the bases of their belief in individualism and the polity in which it is situated. Both address the imagination as a key component of these systems of belief. For Paine, it is a question of mounting an assault upon the imagination as the historically imposed barrier to truth. For his dream of transparency there is, he thinks, no longer any need for such an obfuscatory middle-agent. His rational sublimity attempts to collapse the exiled space between language and truth. For Wollstonecraft, on the other hand, the imagination retains its importance as a mediatory agent. Its discursive potential allows at least for the possibility of negotiating between instinct and self-consciousness; between feeling and reason; between ethics and materiality. It has a powerful role to play once redeemed and purified of its associations with a falsely consoling and libertine aesthetic. As well as taking part in a battle of origins,[31] Paine and Wollstonecraft are engaged in a reformulation of the subjectivity which must undergo revolutionary change. Not surprisingly therefore, they are both engaged in debates about the nature of change as it affects the body. Both use images of the dying body to rearticulate their notions of the state and of the soul. This in turn generates a series of moral discourses which articulate themselves around other competing ideas of change: commerce, progress, and belief in a divine creator. The narrative of social change inevitably engages with the question of religious faith: the utopian dream of a better society knocks against the promise of the hereafter and the reassuring assumption of a beneficent creation. As will be seen, Paine and Wollstonecraft are diametrically opposed on the subject of commerce and, as proponents of social change, adopt very different concepts of narrative transcendence in order to compensate for the limits of physical individuality and the self-abnegation suffered by many in the service of utopian struggle. Paine adopts a commonsense rationality to match Burke's sublimity both in its awe-inspiring claim to truth and in its capacity for terror.[32] Wollstonecraft, on the other hand, argues for a morally purified version of sensibility to complement her confrontational rationalism.[33] In these various debates and arguments about the meaning of the self in relation to the process of history and social change imagination figures both as the agent of self-representation and the familiar psychological component of the mind which is most susceptible to traditional aesthetics: to art, beauty, and the compensatory realm of the soul when it is imagined no soul exists. In my account, therefore, imagination is by turns both agent and victim, both hero and villain of the piece as these writers articulate the self in relation to revolution.

PART I

Imagination and revolution

CHAPTER I

Burke and the civic imagination

I

In his *Reflections on the Revolution in France* Burke politicises and depoliticises the imagination. Imagination is depicted as obscuring the power relations which underpin the workings of the state and as maintaining the status quo through a pleasing state of false consciousness. In his defence of British liberty and in his attack upon the new French constitution, Burke highlights imagination's central role in the formation of ideology.[1] In its famous aestheticisation of politics the *Reflections* at the same time exposes and celebrates the mechanism of a faculty which keeps the naked workings of power from the ordinary citizen.[2] In this sense, imagination for Burke may be said to be symptomatic of civil society itself. It is the faculty which provides the citizen's perception of the benefits of being in civil society as distinct from a state of nature. And in this peculiarly powerful double-take imagination is charged with carrying out a seemingly impossible task: of providing the subject with a sense of self-consciousness of his role in the body politic at the same time as pleasingly hiding from him the stark nature of the contract he has made with the state in order to enjoy the benefits of civil society.[3] This ideological doubling of imagination in Burke's *Reflections* is, of course, further complicated by the fact that the text's strategic epistolary rhetoric, as well as its most famous scenes of violation, at the same time appeal graphically to the imagination of its reader.

At the outset of his career, Burke's *A Philosophical Enquiry into the Origin of Our Ideas of the Sublime and Beautiful* (1757) places a Lockean restriction on 'imagination': 'this power of the imagination is incapable of producing any thing absolutely new; it can only vary the disposition of those ideas which it has received from the senses',[4] but this is immediately followed by an admission of the vast cultural territory available to this most ambivalent of faculties: 'Now the imagination is the most extensive province of pleasure and pain, as it is the region of our fears and our hopes, and of all our passions that are connected with them.'[5] Burke's writings of the 1790s place severe restrictions on those advocates of the rights of men who would attempt to rewrite government and social contracts – those artist revolutionaries who wish to create 'any thing absolutely new' or vary the disposition of prevailing ideas. At the same time these writings engage substantially with both ennobling and lurid forms of imagination.

For these reasons, Burke provides a good starting-point from which to reassess the deployment of imaginations in the literature of the Romantic period. Over the last fifteen years or so the workings of the literary imagination and their nineteenth- and twentieth-century constructions have been subject to a severe critique on the grounds that they represent a masking or repression of the workings of ideology. Burke, however, provides a powerful and resistant example of the way in which ideology functions in the same text through a combination of exposure and disclosure. Burke's text does not so easily accommodate itself to the charge laid against many texts of the English Romantic poets: that they compose an aesthetic or Romantic ideology,[6] whose defining characteristic is that they claim to be non-ideological. Nor can it so easily be fitted to an act of contemporary historical criticism which too easily assumes that it can redeem the past's bad faith or expose its repressed unconscious.

II

> All the pleasing illusions, which made power gentle, and obedience liberal, which harmonized the different shades of life, and which, by a bland assimilation, incorporated into politics the sentiments which beautify and soften private society, are to be dissolved by this new conquering empire of light and reason. All the decent drapery of life is to be rudely torn off. All the super-added ideas, furnished from the wardrobe of a moral imagination, which the heart owns, and the understanding ratifies, as necessary to cover the defects of our naked shivering nature, and to raise it to dignity in our own estimation, are to be exploded as a ridiculous, absurd, and antiquated fashion. (*Reflections*, p. 171 [128])

In his famous lament for the passing of the 'age of chivalry' at the heart of the *Reflections* Burke refers his reader in Swiftian terms to the 'superadded ideas' furnished from 'the wardrobe of a moral imagination'. In this strategic deployment of elegy Burke confirms the moral imagination's central place in the formation of civilization. All the benefits of culture, convention, and custom operate through the workings of this faculty which seems to offer to the subject a comforting self-consciousness. A naked nature is raised 'to dignity in our own estimation'. In comparison, the false metaphysics of the 'rights of man' only exposes the stark reality of his own first nature. And, as the Swiftian clothes analogies make only too clear,[7] that aboriginal nature is distinctly shameful. The subject position offered here by Burke is characteristically complex. He reminds his reader of the dangers of returning to a state of nature and of the ennobling qualities of civilised, civil society without, at least at this point in his text, quite announcing the renunciation which must take place between the subject and state in order that the former benefit from all those super-added ideas. The subject nature of the individual in civil society, his contractual liberty, is enacted and projected through the imagination. As such, imagination's role in Burke's ideology of constitutional freedom is as agent and as consolation. The aesthetic politics of Burke's 'second nature'[8] use the threat of a violent return to the aboriginal chaos and the naked shame of a bare-forked animal alongside the distracting ornament of the pleasing forms of society because the other threat they have to address is the power relation informing the contract with society. And, as he confronts the formation of a false constitution in revolutionary France, Burke must make evident the nature of the citizen or subject's position in relation to the pleasing 'authority' of the British kingdom. Authority stripped of its aestheticisation is real power which might have to manifest itself as sovereign will and naked force if circumstances make it necessary. With this in mind, the sense of beauty, elegance, and glory which permeates Burke's account of the British constitution seems to offer a form of recompense for the threat of state violence which lurks behind it.[9]

This underlying sense of necessity and the potential threat of punitive state power is even evident in Burke's *Enquiry into the Origin of Our Ideas of the Sublime and Beautiful*. As is so often the case, the examples and metaphors chosen in a work of philosophical enquiry are revealing. In Burke's case it is as if punishment of a particularly heavy state kind has at some point to work its way into his text. It cannot remain absolutely hidden. A number of his examples seem to suggest that punishment is never far away from his descriptions of pain, pleasure, and power.

For instance, when he describes the tremendous effect tragedy can have on an audience, Burke suddenly undermines the power of art by reference to the most exemplary, authoritative, and final kind of catastrophe that the state can muster:

Chuse a day on which to represent the most sublime and affecting tragedy we have; appoint the most favourite actors; spare no cost upon the scenes and decorations; unite the greatest efforts of poetry, painting and music; and when you have collected your audience, just at the moment when their minds are erect with expectation, let it be reported that a state criminal of high rank is on the point of being executed in the adjoining square; in a moment the emptiness of the theatre would demonstrate the comparative weakness of the imitative arts, and proclaim the triumph of real sympathy. (*Enquiry*, p. 47)

As well as interrupting his assessment of tragedy with this awareness of the popular 'reality' of execution (thought to be based on that of Lord Lovat) Burke also refers, in anticipation of Foucault, to the spectacular death performed on the body of Robert Frances Damien, would-be assassin of Louis xv. He also refers his reader to the extraordinary mental and facial capacity of the philosopher Tomasso Campanella who could apparently enter the minds of his subjects by mimicking their facial and bodily states, thereby confirming Burke's thesis about the close connection between body and mind and the power of sympathetic feeling which runs throughout the *Enquiry*. As Burke informs us, the ultimate test of such skill for the unfortunate Campanella came on the rack in a Naples prison.

More significantly, both the sublime and the beautiful are defined in Burke's *Enquiry* as states of subjection and domination. To claim that Burke's treatise on the sublime deals in passive states of mind is hardly surprising. After all, the most famous passages in the book articulate most forcefully the prepossessing and dominating power of sublimity. '[A]stonishment,' Burke writes, 'is that state of the soul, in which all its motions are suspended, with some degree of horror. In this case the mind is so entirely filled with its object, that it cannot entertain any other.'[10] Similarly: 'There is something so over-ruling in whatever inspires us with awe, in all things which belong ever so remotely to terror, that nothing else can stand in their presence.'[11] That the effect of beauty is also 'prepossessing' tells us something more about this text's general level – that its domain is human nature, not social custom. More interesting, I think, than the by now familiar redefinitions of Burke's binary distinction between the sublime and the beautiful, however they are formulated – masculinity/femininity; individual/social; heroic/domestic; war/peace – is the recognition that both terms in each case involve a disabling passivity.

When Burke defines beauty in Part One of the *Enquiry*, in the section on 'Power', the comparison with sublimity forces out an expected opposition which would encourage a gendered reading of the text's basic distinction: sublimity is about being dominated, beauty is about dominating:

Again, we know by experience, that for the enjoyment of pleasure, no great efforts of power are at all necessary; nay we know, that such efforts would go a great way towards destroying our satisfaction: for pleasure must be stolen, and not forced upon us; pleasure follows the will; and therefore we are generally affected with it by many things of a force greatly inferior to our own. But pain is always inflicted by a power in some way superior, because we never submit to pain willingly. (*Enquiry*, p. 65)

In Part Three, where the attention is focused more directly on the definition of beauty, Burke is determined to place the effect of the beautiful at a pre-rational level so that its effect is immediate and 'natural' even to the extent of bypassing the will: 'It is not by the force of long attention and enquiry that we find any object to be beautiful; beauty demands no assistance from our reasoning; even the will is unconcerned.'[12] And later in the *Enquiry*, when he wishes to dislocate beauty from utility or 'fitness', Burke goes further, claiming a divine power in the objects which generate a sense of the beautiful: a power which puts us, as rational beings, directly at the mercy of such objects. Static materialism is given the ultimate divine sanction:

Whenever the wisdom of our Creator intended that we should be affected with any thing, he did not confide the execution of his design to the languid and precarious operation of our reason; but he endued it with powers and properties that prevent the understanding, and even the will, which seizing upon the sense and imagination, captivate the soul before the understanding is ready either to join with them or to oppose them. (*Enquiry*, p. 107)

Such immediate responses short-circuit or preempt 'judgement' – that rationalistic, discriminating comparison and choice between effects which is to be expected from Burke's man of liberal and extensive views in a civilised society. In comparison with such a social view of 'taste', Burke argues that in the realm of the beautiful: 'Here to be affected, there is no need of the concurrence of our will.'[13]

If there is some contradiction in the *Enquiry* as to the degree to which 'will' is involved in the response to beauty it is small in comparison to that which is generated in the *Reflections* by the crisis of the French Revolution. Here the conflict between freedom of response and absolute power is much more apparent and frequently has the effect of destroying the distinction between 'man in a state of nature' and 'man in civilised society'. Paradoxically, in order to support his own vision of a proper revolution Burke is in danger of breaking down his idea of social compact. While he attacks the revolutionaries in France for being savages and barbarians who tear away the 'decent drapery' of life, his own history of the age of chivalry depends on rather dubious outside forces. Under pressure to justify the Glorious Revolution of 1688 Burke has to defer to 'necessity' and cannot for a moment afford to credit such momentous events to any individual will. The acceptance of William as king was not, according to Burke, 'properly a *choice*', but 'an act of *necessity*, in the strictest moral sense in which necessity can be taken'.[14] Similarly, 'a grave and overruling necessity obliged [the glorious revolutionary fathers] to take the step they took'.[15] '*Justa bella quibus necessaria*',[16] he quotes approvingly from Livy.

It might be expected that Burke should defer to the unknown higher authority of 'necessity' in desperate defence of the Glorious Revolution. But the role of necessity and will in his definition of what he calls 'the eternal compact of society' or the body politic is similarly fraught. In his best epigrammatic vein Burke can proclaim: 'Justice is grave and decorous, and in its punishments rather seems to submit to a necessity, than to make a choice.'[17] The elegance of that 'seems' is loaded. Having argued that 'Men cannot enjoy the rights of an uncivil and of a civil state together',[18] Burke proceeds in the *Reflections* to a definition of government. His concern is to counter what he sees in the 'rights of men' as the worst kind of anarchistic individualism which provides an excuse for 'choice' – the free exercise of individual will. What he offers is his characteristic paradox of liberty with restraint. His articulation of it here might be construed as dangerously explicit:

Government is a contrivance of human wisdom to provide for human *wants*. Men have a right that these wants should be provided for by this wisdom. Among these wants is to be reckoned the want, out of civil society, of a sufficient restraint upon their passions. Society requires not only that the passions of individuals should be subjected, but that even in the mass and body as well as in the individuals, the inclinations of men should frequently be thwarted, their will controlled, and their passions brought into subjection. This can only be done *by a power out of themselves*; and not, in the exercise of its function, subject to that will and to those passions which it is its office to bridle and subdue. In this sense the restraints on men, as well as their liberties, are to be reckoned among their rights. But as the liberties and the restrictions vary with times and circumstances, and admit of infinite modifications, they cannot be settled upon any abstract rule; and nothing is so foolish as to discuss them upon that principle. (*Reflections*, p. 151 [110–11])

The central conflict here is between the idea that government is 'a contrivance of human wisdom' and the claim that it depends on a 'power out of itself'. Human contrivance alone is clearly not enough.

For this reason Burke is able to claim that the abstract rules of his revolutionary enemies are insufficient. Characteristically, Burke's geographical specificity – the idea that governments are determined by local circumstances – depends on a metaphysical support. The worldly – such as the British constitution in his terms – is allowed to be 'various' and 'mixed' precisely because it is under divine jurisdiction. As long as 'subjection' extends right through from individual to 'mass' and 'body' – to use Burke's terms – moral issues can be described as 'complex' and can be made the subject of relative opinions.

Similarly, when Burke proceeds in the *Reflections* to define his binding contract of 'society' in the face of those whom he considers to be parricide primitives, the revolutionaries who would 'hack that aged parent in pieces',[19] he reveals the extent to which this binding contract cuts against will, whether it belong to the individual, the 'mass', or the 'body'. Burke's contract of society makes choice anathema and its polite guise of 'restraint' can, if necessary, be backed by a terrible 'force':

Each contract of each particular state is but a clause in the great primaeval contract of eternal society, linking the lower with the higher natures, connecting the visible and invisible world, according to a fixed compact sanctioned by the inviolable oath which holds all physical and all moral natures, each in their appointed place. This law is not subject to the will of those, who by an obligation above them, and infinitely superior, are bound to submit their will to that law. The municipal corporations of that universal kingdom are not morally at liberty at their pleasure, and on their speculations of a contingent improvement, wholly to separate and tear asunder the bands of their subordinate community, and to dissolve it into an unsocial, uncivil, unconnected chaos of elementary principles. It is the first and supreme necessity only, a necessity that is not chosen but chooses, a necessity paramount to deliberation, that admits no discussion, and demands no evidence, which alone can justify a resort to anarchy. This necessity is no exception to the rule; because this necessity itself is a part too of that moral and physical disposition of things to which man must be obedient by consent or force; but if that which is only submission to necessity should be made the object of choice, the law is broken, nature is disobeyed, and the rebellious are outlawed, cast forth, and exiled, from this world of reason, and order, and peace, and virtue, and fruitful penitence, into the antagonist world of madness, discord, vice, confusion, and unavailing sorrow. (*Reflections*, p. 195 [147])

Just as the end of this passage reads like a description of the expulsion from Eden so, ultimately, Burke goes on to argue: 'He willed therefore the state – He willed its connexion with the source and original archetype of all perfection.'[20] With such an original archetype in place politics can only be 'contingent'. The threat provided by the French revolutionaries, on the other hand, is in overturning the archetype itself with their impious inversion of things. Their energy is clearly degenerative: it turns a beautiful creation back into an aboriginal chaos. In order to point up the threat of revolution, Burke actually creates a stronger link between this revolutionary energy and original authority, even if it is attacked as negative.[21]

From this point of view – that citizenship is a form of subjection backed by force – the fusion of aesthetics and politics in Burke's texts is far from complete. There is a disjunction in them between consent and force, elegance and power, politics and authority. It is as if the aesthetic, even in the negative form of 'delight', only provides a covering for starker, more punitive, and more heroic possibilities. The Swiftian clothes analogies in the *Reflections* operate in this way. They offer up a primitive 'other' as a threat to the supposedly civilised and fully clothed reader. If the aesthetics don't make you happy, then the ultimate deterrent of terror surely will. In this way Burke can play off the aesthetics with his binary oppositions of civilised/barbarous sane/mad. There is threat as well as troubled, covert pleasure lurking in these oppositions.

However, there is also a more integrated version of this apparent dualism lurking in both the *Enquiry* and the *Reflections*. Rather than moments of crisis bringing in a self-justifying necessity as in the case of the Glorious Revolution, there is a dynamic of long-term suffering or, in Burke's terms, 'difficulty' at work to set against the epiphanies of spectacular justice.

When in Part Four of the *Enquiry* Burke comes to answer the question 'How pain can be a cause of delight' he goes one better than his earlier claim for a natural state of indifference. Here it is apparent that such a state of indifference would be intolerable to him. It would be tantamount to that dangerous aristocratic disease of indolence which he targets in his periodic attacks on luxury. He begins the passage in typical fashion – 'Providence has so ordered it' – and manages to maintain his concentration on the physical aspect of such effects to an extraordinary degree. According to Burke's discourse in the *Enquiry*, muscle fibre and moral fibre come pretty close together.

In attempting to describe the basic aesthetic response here Burke could be said to be articulating the coercive power which provides a dynamic for each member of the body politic. That dynamic straddles the extreme poles of Burke's thinking: it is God-driven and muscle-bound. Disorder here is individualism, and individualism is a kind of self-destruction:

Providence has so ordered it, that a state of rest and inaction, however it may flatter our indolence, should be productive of many inconveniences; that it should generate such disorders, as may force us to have recourse to some labour, as a thing absolutely requisite to make us pass our lives with tolerable satisfaction; for the nature of rest is to suffer all the parts of our bodies to fall into a relaxation, that not only disables the members from performing their functions, but takes away the vigorous tone of fibre which is requisite for carrying on the natural and necessary secretions . . . Melancholy, dejection, despair, and often self-murder, is the consequence of the gloomy view we take of things in this relaxed state of body. The best remedy for all these evils is exercise or *labour*, and labour is a surmounting of *difficulties*, an exertion of the contracting power of the muscles; and as such resembles pain, which consists in tension or contraction, in every thing but degree. Labour is not only requisite to preserve the coarser organs in a state fit for their functions, but it is equally necessary to these finer and more delicate organs, on which, and by which, the imagination, and perhaps the other mental powers act. (*Enquiry*, pp. 134–35)

It is precisely this 'difficulty' which Burke finds lacking in the plans of the French revolutionaries and which disqualifies them, in his view, from a moral legislature. They might be men of ability, but without this fundamental relationship of struggle to support their idea of government, they must inhabit a moral vacuum – that world of exile, madness, and confusion which he has already given us a glimpse of:

Their purpose every where seems to have been to evade and slip aside from *difficulty*. This it has been the glory of the great masters in all the arts to confront, and to overcome; and when they had overcome the first difficulty, to turn it into an instrument for new conquests over new difficulties; thus to enable them to extend the empire of their science; and even to push forward beyond the reach of their original thoughts, the land marks of the human understanding itself. Difficulty is a severe instructor, set over us by the supreme ordinance of a parental guardian and legislator, who knows us better than we know ourselves, as he loves us better too. *Pater ipse colendi haud facilem esse viam voluit.* He that wrestles with us strengthens our nerves, and sharpens our skill. (*Reflections*, p. 278 [215])

In the realm of the French revolutionaries, 'at the end of every visto, you see nothing but the gallows'.[22] There is no pleasing aesthetic illusion of power in the form of grace or glory. They have made explicit what should have remained hidden and they have done away with any mitigating aesthetic recompense. Difficulty – a kind of moral muscle-toning – provides the underlying tension necessary for human progress.[23] Characteristically, that progress is seen imperialistically as a constant process of civilisation. Severe instruction has replaced severe punishment in this celebration of difficulty.

III

Against this threatening background of necessity and the punitive potential of state power Burke's aestheticisation of the constitution thus operates as a powerful means of apprehending the idea of one's relation to the state and enjoying one's country as itself a beautiful object. This is most famously and powerfully articulated in the text at the crescendo of Burke's lament for chivalry. After quoting Horace, '*Non satis est pulchra esse poemata, dulcia sunto*' ('It is not enough for poems to be beautiful; they must also be sweet, and divert the mind of the listener'), and after equating the construction of poems with the construction of states, the paragraph culminates with: 'To make us love our country, our country ought to be lovely.'[24] The comforting reciprocation enacted in Burke's pleasingly disposed rhetorical figure precisely captures this circularity of relationship which reconstitutes the fear of power as the authority of beauty. Burke's sentence uses repetition to stress the positive side of the relationship; the potentially coercive power relations reside in the verbs. Referring to the constitution as a beautiful object makes it seem ornamental, even distracting, especially since Burke invokes a metaphysical and religious dimension to the subject's apprehension of the state. At the very least, the aesthetic dimension to the perception of the body politic allows Burke to see it, in keeping with the Swiftian sartorial images, as separable and therefore capable of posing a threat if withdrawn, and a comforting pleasure if maintained.

Throughout his *Reflections* Burke does his best to make the British constitution and its consequent British liberty appear beautiful and, more particularly, glorious. The complexity which arises from the nature of man's contract with society, what Burke refers to as the 'artificial limitation upon rights', provides him with the explanation for this aestheticisation of politics. Because of the tension between nature and artifice, man's first and second nature, 'the constitution of a state and the distribution of its powers' become 'a matter of the most delicate and complicated skill'.[25] Given that the 'nature of man is intricate',[26] would-be legislators need to possess 'a comprehensive connected view of the various complicated external and internal interests which go to the formation of that multifarious thing called a state'.[27] In stark contrast to his French revolutionary opponents, Burke thus sees simplicity as either impossible or inadequate. Burke's self-professedly humane and liberal perspective on human affairs in the *Reflections* is given the distinguishing characteristics of aesthetics.[28] The perception of political complexity, the inter-involved combination of factors, leads on to a discourse of taste evident in his reference to 'distinguishing colour, and discriminating effect':

> I cannot stand forward, and give praise or blame to any thing which relates to human actions, and human concerns, on a simple view of the object, as it stands stripped of every relation, in all the nakedness and solitude of metaphysical abstraction. Circumstances (which with some gentlemen pass for nothing) give in reality to every political principle its distinguishing colour, and discriminating effect. (*Reflections*, pp. 89–90 [58])

By ascribing aesthetic qualities to the very structure of political life Burke at the same time invokes the appropriate affect through which it can be appreciated. If our country is lovely, the only appropriate response is to love it. This captivated and at times almost religious response is supported by an equally powerful aestheticising aspect of Burke's text which stresses the complex nature of the British constitution and, consequently, the complex minds who created it and who can perceive its complexity.[29] This is typical of the *Reflections*: the way in which the text seems able to deploy both sides of an argument. According to Burke's own tactics, the constitution can readily be internalised and reified as natural at the same time as being referred to as a deliberate contrivance, a convention, a construction and as an art-work.

The circumstantial and human complexity of political affairs and interests is thus transposed into a reified object which will reveal its meaning and working principles only to the most sophisticated of interpreters. By the same analogy, the production of a constitution becomes a question of authorship and genius. At the same time as he refers to the 'beautiful parts of our constitution'[30] as if he were invoking a revered passage from *The Book of Common Prayer*, Burke alludes to the want of genius in the authors of the current French experiment. The necessary complexity which comes from the difficulty of mixing first and second natures, of reconciling 'artificial institutions' and 'powerful instincts'[31] turns into an aesthetic of a reified wholeness based upon a principle of dynamic combination.

The 'comprehensive connected view' now becomes, in the manner of English landscape aesthetics, a case of 'see[ing] the whole together'[32] or 'a view of the whole';[33] and this is precisely what Burke finds lacking in the newly conceived French constitution. Burke cannot find in the French model of government anything which reveals 'the work of a comprehensive and disposing mind',[34] that is to say 'a variety of objects, reconciled in one consistent whole'.[35]

Once again there is a strong sense of reciprocation in which the reification of a structure or object is mitigated or softened by the presence of 'mind', the mark of humanity. As Burke puts it at the end of the *Reflections*: 'to temper together these opposite elements of liberty and restraint in one consistent work, requires much thought, deep reflection, a sagacious, powerful, and combining mind'.[36] The imprint of this mind in the act of perception is, one feels, at least as important as the structure itself.

This celebration of the whole which is susceptible to perception only by the most powerful of minds can make Burke appear like a proto-Romantic hovering on the brink of the idea of organic unity of the kind most famously celebrated by Coleridge, especially when Burke seems to take the idea of dynamic combination to its limit.[37] With historical hindsight the following passage looks dangerously like a Coleridgean precursor right down to its appropriation of the scientific neologism 'plastic':

We see, that the parts of the system do not clash . . . We compensate, we reconcile, we balance. We are enabled to unite into a consistent whole the various anomalies and contending principles that are found in the minds and affairs of men. From hence arises, not an excellence in simplicity, but one far superior, an excellence in composition . . . It is from this view of things that the best legislators have been often satisfied with the establishment of some sure, solid, and ruling principle in government; a power like that which some of the philosophers have called a plastic nature; and having fixed the principle, they have left it afterwards to its own operation. (*Reflections*, pp. 281–2 [217–18])

I would suggest that Burke's difference from a Romantic aesthetics is confirmed by his belief in reform rather than absolute change or innovation. His subscription to gradual modification rather than wholesale creative transformation suggests that Burke's aesthetic is really one of dynamic combination rather than one of either organic unity or the symbolic. This is also the case with his celebration of 'principles'. Consistency to principles was, as critics such as David Simpson have pointed out, the very thing which Coleridge praised and identified with in Burke's political philosophy and career. In his attempt at a theory of method in *The Friend* Coleridge struggles to systematize the idea of

Burkean principle into a methodological bulwark against the threat of utilitarianism.[38]

In Terry Eagleton's account of the law of the heart in *The Ideology of the Aesthetic* Burke is described as an aestheticiser rather than an aesthete.[39] Eagleton is characteristically alert to Burke's capacity to use aesthetics not simply as an alternative to the epistemic dominance of reason but also in the service of hegemony. This ideological capacity of Burke's aestheticising confirms the strategic nature of his texts. And at the same it highlights the extent to which this process both exploits and celebrates the aesthetic as that which is unrepresentable, that which is not susceptible to philosophical reason. From this point of view, to see the continuity between Burke and Coleridge in terms of the latter's rigorous philosophising of the former's idea of 'principles' is perhaps to miss an important difference and discontinuity between the two writers. This difference is perhaps central in any consideration of Burke in relation to Romanticism and in particular of this more precise claim of his being a pre- or proto-Romantic. The importance Burke attaches to 'prudence' as opposed to philosophical definition is important in assessing his approximation to Coleridgean ideas of the organic when defining the nature of the British constitution in various texts from the 1790s. In his *An Appeal from the New to the Old Whigs* (1791), for example, Burke makes the following declaration against the very idea of a mathematical, philosophical, or systematic theory of principle[40] when defining the need for prudence in matters of morality and state:

Nothing universal can be rationally affirmed on any moral or any political subject. Pure metaphysical abstraction does not belong to these matters. The lines of morality are not like the ideal lines of mathematics. They are broad and deep as well as long. They admit of exceptions; they demand modifications. These exceptions and modifications are not made by the process of logic, but by the rules of prudence. Prudence is not only the first in rank of the virtues political and moral, but she is the director, the regulator, the standard of them all. Metaphysics cannot live without definition; but Prudence is cautious how she defines.[41]

Classic descriptions of the interconnectedness, the wholeness, the complexly combined and spirit-suffused nature of this unwritten constitution stress the act of faith the political subject might be supposed to have in its existence rather than offering to the reader a means of understanding or rendering accessible to some form of apprehension the structure or entity under discussion.

Burke comes very close to articulating a Coleridgean concept of the organically unified nature of the state in the following statement from his *Speech on Moving the Resolutions for Conciliation with the Colonies* (1775) where his concern is 'freedom' in relation to the American colonies:

> This is the commodity of price, of which you have the monopoly. This is the true act of navigation, which binds to you the commerce of the Colonies, and through them secures to you the wealth of the world. Deny them this participation of freedom, and you break that sole bond, which originally made, and must still preserve, the unity of the empire. Do not entertain so weak an imagination, as that your registers and your bonds, your affidavits and your sufferances, your cockets and your clearances, are what form the great securities of your commerce. Do not dream that your letters of office, and your instructions, and your suspending clauses, are the things that hold together the great contexture of this mysterious whole. These things do not make your government. Dead instruments, passive tools as they are, it is the spirit of English communion that gives all their life and efficacy to them. It is the spirit of the English constitution, which, infused through the mighty mass, pervades, feeds, unites, invigorates, vivifies, every part of the empire, even down to the minutest member.[42]

This passage is characteristic of Burke's tactic in its projection of a constitutional identity which resists critique. The point in many other similar instances is to leave the mystery intact precisely because the constitution is not susceptible to reason or to the apprehension of the subject. Attempting to explain its workings or its nature by reference to a philosophical notion of the organic in the manner of Coleridge would be an anathema.

The pragmatic and compromised deployment of principles in conjunction with 'circumstances' is evident in the following extract from Burke's 1792 speech on religious opinions. One might even go so far as to suggest that it is the complex, infinite, potentially sublime nature of 'circumstances' which surprisingly possesses a more dynamic and originating power in this passage:

> I never govern myself, no rational man ever did govern himself, by abstractions and universals. I do not put abstract ideas wholly out of any question; because I well know that under that name I should dismiss principles, and that, without the guide and light of sound, well-understood principles, all reasonings in politics, as in everything else, would be only a confused jumble of particular facts and details, without the means of drawing out any sort of theoretical or practical conclusion. A statesman differs from a professor in an university: the latter has only the general view of society; the former, the statesman, has a number of circumstances to combine with those general ideas, and to take into his consideration. Circumstances are infinite, are infinitely combined; are variable and transient: he who does not take them into consideration, is not erroneous, but stark mad; *dat operam ut cum ratione insaniat*; he is metaphysically

mad. A statesman, never losing sight of principles, is to be guided by circumstances; and judging contrary to the exigencies of the moment, he may ruin his country for ever.[43]

Burke's idea of composition produced from combination and resulting in 'equipoise' stops short of the creative category shift implied in Coleridge's deployment of primary and secondary imaginations. And because the same kind of creative transformation is projected here it assigns a place for the aesthetic which is also correspondingly different. This is apparent in Burke's famous claim for 'a marked distinction between change and reformation'. According to Burke,

The former alters the substance of the objects themselves; and gets rid of all their essential good, as well as of all the accidental evil annexed to them. Change is novelty; and whether it is to operate any one of the effects of reformation at all, or whether it may not contradict the very principle upon which reformation is desired, cannot be certainly known beforehand. Reform is not a change in the substance, or in the primary modification of the object, but a direct application of a remedy to the grievance complained of . . .

It cannot at this time be too often repeated; line upon line; precept upon precept; until it comes into the currency of a proverb, *To innovate is not to reform.*[44]

IV

There remains in Burke's aesthetic apprehension of the object of the constitution, and of our second nature more generally, a sense of the aesthetic as ornament, supplement, and surplus. We are still working with the notion of the super-added rather than a high Romantic indissoluble union of spirit, Burkean necessity rather than the Coleridgean organic. And outside of the privileged minds deemed capable of enlarged and liberal understandings and ex-tended views, of course, there remains a strong sense of the aesthetic's capacity to operate as ideological distraction and political recompense. The afterlife of the plastic principle of the constitution also, it seems, has the capacity to generate its own culture, its own self-conscious exhibition. In Burke's description, what Hazlitt would later refer to as the gew-gaws of imagination operate as a museum of legitimacy:

our liberty becomes a noble freedom. It carries an imposing and majestic aspect. It has a pedigree and illustrating ancestors. It has its bearings and its ensigns armorial. It has its gallery of portraits; its monumental inscriptions; its records, evidences, and titles. (*Reflections*, p. 121 [85])

This graphically aesthetic sense of legitimacy's 'glory' is also borne out in Burke's otherwise strange reference to the English revolutionaries of the seventeenth century as 'the ornament of their age'.[45] The 'rising' of these 'great bad men of the old stamp' served, according to Burke, 'to illuminate and beautify the world'[46] in the same way that he argues statesmen should 'diffuse lustre and glory around a state'.[47]

In addition to the intrinsically beautiful articulation of the constitution and the concomitant glory of the working principles of the state and the achievements of its statesmen, Burke considers the historically accumulated culture produced within the state. There is thus a powerful reciprocity between the beauty of liberty and the beauty which has been produced in a state of liberty. In both cases this beauty serves to consolidate and retain the status quo by being susceptible to the visualisation of an appropriately subservient imagination. According to Burke, such beauty produces an awed and reverential response which serves as a check to change or political critique. From this perspective, members of Dr Price's Revolution Society and the French revolutionaries across the Channel have both been seen to have travestied the very idea of 'beauty' and are, as a result, only capable of indulging in a perverted form of burlesque.

For example, when Burke comes to the surplus 'expenditure of a great landed property' he has in mind something more palpable than the mere aspect of majestic liberty or the lustre of statesmen or monarchs. In his catalogue of the glorious cultural edifices of aristocratic culture, 'the accumulation of libraries', the 'great collections of antient records, medals, and coins', 'paintings and statues', and 'collections of the specimens of nature',[48] Burke offers a cultural history to rival the festivals and rituals of the new French Republic. The historical nature of this culture is used to attack the selfish and voluptuous individualism of its French counterpart. Burke stresses not only the revered, majestic, and sacred nature of the edifices, but also the work – the 'sweat' of the artisans and peasants who are differently involved in their construction and maintenance. As he plays off the religious identity of British cultural edifices against the upstart and secular nature of French festivals Burke finds a dignity in work, a dignity produced by 'the fictions of a pious imagination'.[49] At the same time as offering aristocratic culture as a sign of historical self-consciousness he is only able to guarantee social cohesion by reference to the mere fictions of a 'pious imagination' rather than the true nature of glory. This capacity to see certain forms of imagination as the psychological tool of class hegemony at the same time as celebrating the civilisation of aristocratic culture is entirely characteristic of Burke's strategy. He is not worried by this powerful combination of ornamental and transcendent glory and ideological weapon:

> [the great critics] have taught us one essential rule. I think the excellent and philosophic artist, a true judge, as well as a perfect follower of Nature, Sir Joshua Reynolds, has somewhere applied it, or something like it, in his own profession. It is this: that, if ever we should find ourselves disposed not to admire those writers or artists (Livy and Virgil for instance, Raphael or Michael Angelo) whom all the learned had admired, not to follow our own fancies, but to study them, until we know how and what we ought to admire; and if we cannot arrive at this combination of admiration with knowledge, rather to believe that we are dull than that the rest of the world has been imposed on. It is as good a rule, at least, with regard to this admired Constitution. We ought to understand it according to our measure, and to venerate where we are not able presently to comprehend.[50]

When Burke considers the glory that was *ancien regime* France he deploys a similarly complex position as he mixes reverential awe with an engagingly explicit account of the way in which such a response to the culture of second nature operates as an anti-revolutionary psychological mechanism:

> when I survey the state of all the arts that beautify and polish life; when I reckon the men she has bred for extending her fame in war, her able statesmen, the multitude of her profound lawyers and theologians, her philosophers, her critics, her historians and antiquaries, her poets, and her orators sacred and profane, I behold in all this something which awes and commands the imagination, which checks the mind on the brink of precipitate and indiscriminate censure ... (*Reflections*, p. 236 [180])

This depiction of the imagination as checked and checking the very possibility of revolutionary critique also, of course, suggests the latent dangers of the faculty. In order that it serve the appropriate ideological function, it must be commanded and overawed; it must be made moral or pious. The French revolutionaries, in comparison, are depicted by Burke as indulging in the opposite form of imaginative speculation. Rather than operating a check upon the mind, here the mind's idle curiosity and demand for novelty lead to a desire for artificially stimulated excitement, a 'magnificent stage effect' or 'grand spectacle to rouze the imagination, grown torpid with the lazy enjoyment of sixty years security'.[51]

Within his own constitutionally supported and constitutionally bolstering version of the imagination, however, the dangers of individual caprice and collective ennui are both avoided. In Burke's version of the moral and reverent imagination, its creative and transcendent capacity working under 'a pious predilection' for ancestors is capable of 'realiz[ing] . . . a standard of virtue and wisdom, beyond the vulgar practice of the hour'.[52]

Burke provides ample illustration of the powerful ways in which the imagination in conjunction with beauty can serve to secure the fabric of society by offering the pleasing aspect of aesthetic experience at the same time as displacing possible critique. Nevertheless, it might seem strange to see him at the end of the *Reflections* championing one of the more extravagant fictions of the economic imagination: the South Sea Bubble.

Just as the French revolutionaries have turned the social compact into an act of terror represented by the ubiquitous prospect of the scaffold, so, too, their financial representation is a manifestation of force. For Burke, the *assignat* is a sign of tyranny, an imposition which flies in the face of reality and the choice involved in the act of exchange:

When so little within or without is now found but paper, the representative not of opulence but of want, the creature not of credit but of power, they imagine that our flourishing state in England is owing to that bank-paper, and not the bank-paper to the flourishing condition of our commerce, to the solidity of our credit, and to the total exclusion of all idea of power from any part of the transaction. They forget that, in England, not one shilling of paper-money of any description is received but of choice; that the whole has had its origin in cash actually deposited; and that it is convertible, at pleasure, in an instant, and without the smallest loss, into cash again. Our paper is of value in commerce, because in law it is of none. It is powerful on the Change, because in Westminster-hall it is impotent. (*Reflections*, p. 357 [278–79])

In comparison with the contemporary spectacle of the financial speculators of France and the introduction of *assignats*, according to Burke, the projectors and investors in Law's doomed plan – what Burke refers to as 'Mr Law's fraudulent exhibitions' – guarantee in the very fanciful extravagance of their project an assumption and an appeal to the liberty of the subject:

A grand imagination found in this flight of commerce something to captivate. It was wherewithal to dazzle the eye of an eagle. It was not made to entice the smell of a mole, nuzzling and burying himself in his mother earth, as yours is. Men were not then quite shrunk from their natural dimensions by a degrading and sordid philosophy, and fitted for low and vulgar deceptions. Above all remember, that in imposing on the imagination, the then managers of the system made a compliment to the freedom of men. In their fraud there was no mixture of force. (*Reflections*, p. 369 [287])

Even such a delusive and disastrously speculative manifestation of the imagination has some recompense for Burke when compared to the narrowly rationalistic and atomistic abstractions of the French revolutionaries who carve up the face of the country into geometric slices. Once again, however, as in his lament for chivalry with which I began, Burke returns to the threat of force accompanied by disgust at the prospect of man's first nature. Extravagant fraud is preferable to demeaning force; a fiction, if noble, contains a possibility of dignity. For all its qualified status as a strategic example within Burke's carefully chosen critique of the French economists, this passage confirms the centrality of the faculty of imagination to Burke's conception of the workings of the state. It is nevertheless startling to find his cherished idea of freedom illustrated in the form of an extravagant fraud imposing itself on the faculty of imagination. But this example does serve to demonstrate the characteristic combination of Burke's political position in the *Reflections*. The imagination figures here as both a sign of his idea of 'freedom' and as a form of 'captivation' or subjection.

The negative revolutionary potential of the compliment to liberty to be found in the limitlessness of imaginative speculation is the subject of Burke's concern in his *Appeal from the New to the Old Whigs*. Here there is a powerful awareness of the danger of imagination cut loose from the community of feeling:

It must always have been discoverable to persons of reflection, but it is now obvious to the world, that a theory concerning government may become as much a cause of fanaticism as a dogma in religion. There is a boundary to men's passions when they act from feeling; none when they are under the influence of imagination . . . When a man is from system furious against monarchy or episcopacy, the good conduct of the monarch or the bishop has no other effect than further to irritate the adversary. He is provoked at it as furnishing a plea for preserving the thing which he wishes to destroy. His mind will be heated as much by the sight of a sceptre, a mace, or a verge, as if he had been daily bruised and wounded by these symbols of authority. Mere spectacles, mere names, will become sufficient causes to stimulate the people to war and tumult.[53]

In comparison, Burke's recourse to imagination in his *Reflections* is in the service of a common cultural identity. He produces it in order to fend off the Revolutionary Society's challenge of natural rights and, as he sees it, the false metaphysics of French philosophe thinking. In both cases Burke perceives the threat to come from a combination of abstraction and individualism. This is encapsulated in the politics of natural rights and in the workings of a too narrowly defined, Enlightenment form of reason. Burke's deployment of imagination – the faculty of apprehending specific images – thus operates in support of a specific national identity and against what he critiques as an atomistic individualism. In this respect Burke's version of the faculty represents an interesting comparison to those constructions of the imagination which were produced in the face of the rising ideology of utility in the 1820s and 1830s. In the second half of this book, those versions (and particularly those articulated by Hazlitt and Coleridge) structure this cultural and methodological crisis on an opposition between the abstract and the particular. As a precursor of those debates Burke offers a particularly potent critique of the connection between individual and abstract in revolutionary culture and, in support of his own ideological and political position, a fascinating account of the role of imagination in the formation of a national identity as cultural identity.

Indeed, the particular power of Burke's sophisticated rhetoric might be said to reside in its ability to short-circuit any crude binary opposition between the particular and abstract. His use of the aesthetic as integral to the formation and apprehension of one's civic identity does not stop him retaining a sense of the aesthetic as ornament. His strategic and, at times, inconsistent reference to first and second natures allows him to make use of both possibilities. The hegemonic potential of Burke's rhetoric depends upon a representational doubling which allows for a literal presentation at the same time as a figurative one. It is precisely the possibility of moving from an empirical to an idealist position, from a literal to a symbolic mode, from the particular to the general, that provides the enclosing circularity necessary to enforce a dominant ideological position. In this way a moral imperative can be linked with commonsense, the largest idea of the state with the 'smallest platoon' of our social life. It is characteristic of such an ideology of commonsense that it operates upon such oscillations. The fluctuation between different modes of representation allows for the presentation of pragmatics as morality. In Burke's case, as we shall see, there is a disjunction between metaphysical power and the realm of worldly concerns. The doubleness that I have identified as belonging to a symbolic mode can be found in the split between power and the political. Precisely because there is this enforcing power already at work, society and government can be legitimately plural or 'liberal', but by the same authority they must always remain contingent, mixed, and complex. Politics is thus not for theorists, speculators, or projectors, but for practical ability. Burke's desperate defences of the English system of government and the European code of chivalry can, by turns, appeal to a cohesive spirit of unity on the one hand, liberal choice and geographical specificity on the other. From this perspective it might be said that, precisely because he always falls short of a Romantic aesthetics of the organic or the symbolic and retains a sense of difference, Burke is able to avoid the alienation produced by an ideology of the aesthetic and is able to afford both imagination and beauty a central role in the formation of a dominant ideology.

V

The reactionary nature of Burke's mode of representation as it relates to the sublime and the organic has, I think, been well documented. The essentially duplicitous nature of an aesthetic experience which stages radical encounters for the purposes of self-empowerment and self-aggrandisement, and a model of representation which uses the natural as a means of short-circuiting critique, have become familiar stories underpinning the historiography of Romantic period aesthetics. By concentrating instead on Burke's idea of imagination, other more positive stories are available. It is still possible to see the appeal to freedom evident in Burke's imaginative response to the South Sea Bubble as a sign of privileged luxury: only those enfranchised few, who might also be the elite audience of Burke's own *Reflections*, can enjoy the appeal. They, at least, have a measure of liberty to enjoy. It is also possible to see such an appeal as a disarming act of chivalry whose effect is to out-face or dissolve critique. Having one's liberty appealed to maintains the fiction that one is in possession of liberty in the first place. Acknowledging these caveats, I would prefer to maintain some belief in the efficacy and power of Burke's texts. There is some appeal in his dynamic engagement with the problematical and spectral capacity of the faculty of imagination and in his idea that the workings of power need to be legitimised and given assent by self-consciousness. Self-consciousness need not inevitably be a subscription to false-consciousness; there is a possibility here for dissent and at least a strong sense of active participation which, as Burke would be the first to agree, needs intelligence and vigilance if it is to survive.

Burke's depiction of an imagination which is capable of offering an appeal or even a compliment to one's individual freedom, albeit concessionary and limited, turns out to be important for the way in which literary culture uses another version of imagination as its touchstone in the war against utilitarianism in the 1820s and 1830s. Even the compromised liberty offered as a sop by a dying aristocratic culture turns out to have its uses. For Hazlitt, literary culture is peculiarly fraught for this reason. It is always likely to side with legitimacy, but contains a well articulated discourse of individual choice which originates from a problematically constituted freedom. This capacity to register individual choice and to articulate individual experience provides the means by which his brand of dissenting humanism can offer at least some kind of counter to the ideology of utilitarianism which is seen to have ruled out choice from its ethics, soul from its metaphysics, and individual experience from its demography. This is also why the imagination is of such concern for Coleridge. It is the faculty of individual perception on which he attempts to build an epistemology and an ethics based on hope and faith. At the heart of his enterprise is the notion of choice. Even within his deployment of the organic analogy, which can undoubtedly act to occlude and more obviously naturalise (and thereby legitimate) the workings of reactionary or established power, he persistently seeks to locate a point of access for the workings of individual will.

It is my contention that Burke's deployment of imagination in response to the French revolution in his *Reflections* is a politicisation of the faculty which has as many opportunities as disadvantages. I would choose to focus on Burke's creation of a political imagination rather than on his ideological masking of the workings of hegemony evident in his subscription to a pre-Coleridgean notion of organic form – the collusive naturalising of the organic model as a way of mystifying or occluding the real forces at work in the body politic. Imagination, in contrast, offers a more unstable subject position which actually foregrounds self-consciousness, indeed, highlights the subject's self-consciousness as a prerequisite for social order. The mediatory and mediating agent of imagination performs an unsettling double-act which lies at the heart of Burke's ideology. Burke's articulation of the imagination in his *Reflections* provides a means of accessing what James Chandler has recently referred to as the essentially miscible nature of Burke's thinking.[54] Imagination not only inhabits that miscibility, it articulates it as a subject position which can be dynamically inhabited by the enfranchised citizen. That Burke's deployment of imagination as the very agent of civic self-consciousness is accompanied by an awareness of its polymorphous, even suspect nature – its capability of offering too much liberty, of, in short, offering a fantasy of freedom to the ego – makes it even more fascinating and fraught.

As Burke is reviewed and revalued in the wake of the bicentenary of his death, the instabilities of such a subject position are beginning to be appreciated and understood, and in ways which rightly complicate the assessment of the aesthetic's ideology as being one which is simply serviceable to the dominant: a history of the aesthetic which renders it marginal, even depoliticises it. Only by appreciating this other story within Burke's politicisation of the aesthetic and the imagination's particular role within it can we begin to properly rewrite the history of imagination in the Romantic period and its response to the burgeoning ideology of utilitarianism. The force of Burke's imagination was taken up by Coleridge. Hazlitt also recognised in Burke's example imagination's ideological character, its inscription of power within culture, and even its resurgent capacity within a dying aristocratic culture.

The response of Burke's most famous liberal and radical opponents in the 1790s to his deployment and defence of aristocratic culture is to consign it to the oblivion of history, to make it look like the swan-song of its age.[55] Aristocratic culture in the guise of chivalry is made to look belated, even gothic in nature. And even this, of course, can be attributed in part at least to Burke's own rhetoric: his defence of aristocratic culture sometimes appears to lack conviction, as we have seen; and the rhetorical strategy of the *Reflections* is in some large measure to offer the threat of a new age which shall sweep away all vestiges of European civilisation. It is not surprising, therefore, that both Wollstonecraft and Paine direct their attacks on Burke towards his deployment of an aristocratic aestheticising culture which their own rhetoric dismisses as belatedly historical. In some ways they could be said to turn Burke into a romanticist of the previous generation.[56] While Wollstonecraft struggles to revitalise the radical potential which sensibility had contained within the 1780s by combining it with a moral version of imagination and a progressivist rationality, Paine attempts to bypass the aesthetic of literary culture altogether and by so doing escape the need for a mediatory faculty of imagination.

CHAPTER 2

Paine's attack on artifice

I

Tom Paine's subscription to a plain style, commonsense, and a literal form of reason enables him to mount a considerable assault not only on the forms and abuses of monarchical and aristocratic power, but also on their attendant aesthetic culture and even on the category of imagination itself. Paine's attack on virtually all forms of artifice pushes aesthetics to the very brink. His literalism is posed against the divided world of imagination – that mediating and most mediated of faculties. In Paine's utopian and Rousseauvian realm of transparent truth there would be no need of such a faculty. It is almost as if aesthetics are subsumed entirely under the guise of ridding the world of political and metaphysical errors. The muted version of the rational sublime which operates in Paine's writings is contained within the singleness and transparency of his very own version of happiness in the glad day of revolution. And in this attack on artifice Paine reserves a special place for Burke's *Reflections* as the text which most powerfully uses the leisured and refined aesthetic of aristocratic culture as the tool of counter-revolutionary propaganda. In his own contributions to the revolutionary debates of the 1790s Paine must engage promiscuously with his adversary's text and risk embroiling himself in it. Burke sought to make a civic virtue and a consolidated civic identity out of a moral imagination. Where he sought to exploit this faculty's compliment to men's freedom, Paine's purpose is ruthlessly iconoclastic. Imagination, as the sign of an erroneous and divisive political system, must be exposed as false and absurd. Burke's *Reflections* must be scoured not for the workings of a moral imagination, but for evidence of imagination's intrinsic immorality. In turn, the intensity of Paine's engagement with Burke's book generates its own kind of textual anxiety which illuminates the values which lurk by implication within his own disarming plainness. In his attack on Burke, Paine reveals the repressive logic which lurks within his own literalism and the threat which comes, in the end, from not being able to avoid contamination from the realm of aesthetics. Paine's literalism – his fundamentalist belief in a single, contained, and transparent epistemology – recognises its own dependence on the various, delusive, and plural play of meaning which it has sought so consistently to avoid.

II

Exploration of the full range of Paine's writings reveals a deep-rooted suspicion of imagination. Imagination figures prominently in his work, though usually only in the form of brief adjectival constructions which distinguish it, mostly unfavourably, from reason. Apart from the poems and the use of Aesopian fable in his early political journalism, there is an expected absence of any literary use of the imagination. According to Paine's own confession, the exclusion is deliberate: '[t]he natural bent of my mind was to science. I had some turn, and I believe some talent for poetry; but this I rather repressed than encouraged, as leading too much into the field of imagination'.[1] His late pamphlet 'On Dream' provides a rare extended consideration of the imagination in relation to other mental faculties. And imagination figures as a disruptive force in the economy of the mind which this essay maps out. Paine begins his investigation of the relationship between 'the three great faculties' of 'IMAGINATION', 'JUDGMENT', and 'MEMORY' with a familiar mechanical comparison:

Comparing invisible by visible things, as metaphysical can sometimes be compared to physical things, the operations of these distinct and several faculties have some resemblance to a watch. The main spring which puts all in motion corresponds to the imagination; the pendulum which corrects and regulates that motion, corresponds to the judgment; and the hand and dial, like the memory, record the operation. (*PW*, IV, p. 361)

Imagination is the principle of motion which underlies the whole procedure or mechanism of the mind. As Paine's analogy develops, however, the idea of regulation begins to take over. As he describes the relative states of order which prevail under the respective faculties, imagination begins to look like a problem:

Now in proportion as these several faculties sleep, slumber, or keep awake, during the continuance of a dream, in that proportion the dream will be reasonable or frantic, remembered or forgotten.
If there is any faculty in mental man that never sleeps, it is that volatile thing

the imagination. The case is different with the judgment and memory. The sedate and sober constitution of the judgment disposes it to rest; and as to the memory, it records in silence and is active only when it is called upon. (*PW*, IV, p. 362)

Although primary in this scheme of things, it is clear that imagination, as well as being volatile, is also worryingly involuntary. As the essay continues, the disorder associated with it becomes more prominent:

In like manner if the judgment sleeps whilst the imagination keeps awake, the dream will be a riotous assemblage of misshapen images and ranting ideas, and the more active the imagination is the wilder the dream will be. The most inconsistent and the most impossible things will appear right; because that faculty whose province it is to keep order is in a state of absence. The master of the school is gone out and the boys are in an uproar. (*PW*, IV, p. 362)

Although it is important to recognise that this description is governed by the context of an account of the nature of dreaming, Paine's description of the anarchic action of imagination is soon supported by confirmation of its ability to deceive and be out of joint with reality. In the realm of imagination, he warns us, 'the most inconsistent and the most impossible things will appear right'.

The most animated and fascinating section of Paine's essay concerns itself even further with this dubious fictionality of imagination, but he is careful to maintain perspective, and puts his reader in no doubt as to the negative force of his subject. Even so, the renegade energy of imagination's ability to multiply levels of reality provides his prose with unexpected gusto:

But though the imagination cannot supply the place of real memory, it has the wild faculty of counterfeiting memory. It dreams of persons it never knew, and talks to them as if it remembered them as old aquaintance. It relates circumstances that never happened, and tells them as if they had happened. It goes to places that never existed, and knows where all the streets and houses are, as if we had been there before. The scenes it creates are often as scenes remembered. It will sometimes act a dream within a dream, and, in the delusion of dreaming, tell a dream it never dreamed, and tell it as if it was from memory. It may also be remarked, that the imagination in a dream has no idea of time, *as time*. It counts only circumstances; and if a succession of circumstances pass in a dream that would require a great length of time to accomplish them, it will appear to the dreamer that a length of time equal thereto has passed also.

As this is the state of the mind in a dream, it may rationally be said that every person is mad once in twenty-four hours, for were he to act in the day as he dreams in the night, he would be confined for a lunatic. (*PW*, IV, pp. 363–64)

Because it has this capacity to upset the desired harmony of the mental faculties, imagination must be kept in check, even repressed. And for

Paine, imagination's most disruptive and unsettling quality is its capacity for counterfeiting reality. For him, fictional status is not seen as an alternative to, but as a distortion of rational reality. Imaginative fantasy or projection, rather than being validated as a higher order of knowledge, cannot be dissociated from the idea of deception. Although imagination might be the main spring of Paine's watch, judgement and memory are more closely in touch with rational, commonsensical reality.

Paine's writing recognises the antagonism between the constant energy of imagination and the external criterion of truth by which it must be directed and tested. Not surprisingly, therefore, Paine has little time for the obscure kind of sublimity. When in *Age of Reason* he contemplates the phrase 'Let there be light', his attack on the authenticity of the Biblical text broadens to include a brief aside on eighteenth-century aesthetics:

Longinus calls this expression the sublime; and by the same rule the conjuror is sublime too; for the manner of speaking is expressively and grammatically the same. When authors and critics talk of the sublime, they see not how nearly it borders on the ridiculous. The sublime of the critics, like some parts of Edmund Burke's sublime and beautiful, is like a windmill just visible in a fog, which imagination might distort into a flying mountain, or an archangel, or a flock of wild geese. (*Age of Reason, PW*, IV, pp. 192–93n.)

Once again, imagination is accused of both unreality and distortion. Paine's demystification of it is intent on making it look absurd. In his 'Letter to the Abbé Raynal' he again considers the disastrous effects of imagination (and in this instance the 'warm passions') usurping its place and roving free of the constraints of judgement. On this occasion, the suggestion is that with such loss of seriousness the mind can become a travesty of itself. When the 'judgement [is] jostled from its seat', he argues, 'the whole matter, however important in itself, will diminish into a pantomime of the mind, in which we create images that promote no other purpose than amusement'.[2]

Paine's rationalism includes a recognition of the power of imagination as the source of intellectual and creative achievement. Precisely because of its power, emphasis is placed on its containment by judgement. There is a clash of source and direction. Imagination is original, but reason is directional. This basic difference is evident in Paine's two favourite metaphors. In 'The Magazine in America' (1775) he performs a similar kind of analysis on polite writing to that which we have just seen him carry out on psychology: 'The two capital supports of a magazine are Utility and Entertainment: The first is a boundless path, the other an endless spring.'[3] Because his theme here is the 'inexhaustible' nature of the arts and sciences, the two sides look closer than they really are. Imagination as infinite source, and reason as linear narrative, are in some ways radically opposed to each other. The 'endless' nature of the spring is threatening, while the 'boundless' nature of the path is not; for the latter can be accommodated to an optimistic belief in human progress and achievement.

In an essay of the same year Paine sees no problem in a harmonious coincidence of interests between utility and entertainment, when he considers the collecting of minerals and fossils. The enthusiastic pleasure of scientific knowledge can take place simultaneously with industry and commerce; nature and invention can exist side by side, if not actually join forces:

The same materials which delight the Fossilist, enrich the manufacturer and the merchant. While the one is scientifically examining their structure and composition, the others, by industry and commerce, are transmuting them to gold. Possessed of the power of pleasing, they gratify on both sides; the one contemplates their *natural* beauties in the cabinet, the others, their *re-created* ones in the coffer. (*PW*, I, p. 20)

It is precisely these two categories which are at odds with each other where the imagination is concerned. When 'entertainment' separates itself from ingenuity and knowledge the harmony disappears. Even worse, the disorder turns to depravity. What had been improvement because of ingenious discovery now degenerates into imaginative immorality:

The British magazines, at their commencement, were the repositories of ingenuity: They are now the retailers of tale and nonsense. From elegance they sunk to simplicity, from simplicity to folly, and from folly to voluptuousness. The Gentleman's, the London, and the Universal, Magazines, bear yet some marks of their originality; but the Town and Country, the Covent-Garden, and the Westminster, are no better than incentives to profligacy and dissipation. They have added to the dissolution of manners, and supported Venus against the Muses. (*PW*, I, p. 15)

In 'The Magazine in America' Paine combines this idea of moral degeneration with his belief in the importance of geographical position, with the Holbachian idea that perfectibility of human government and the state of a nation can be determined by factors of climate and abundance of natural resources. Admittedly, the subject here is wit not imagination, so there is greater potential for a derogatory statement. The way Paine characterises wit's similarity to the passions, its exuberance, and its lack of moral awareness, makes the link with imagination more compelling:

'Tis a qualification which, like the passions, has a natural wildness that requires governing. Left to itself, it soon overflows its banks, mixes with common filth, and brings disrepute on the fountain. We have many valuable springs of it in America, which at present run purer streams, than the generality of it in other countries. In France and Italy, 'tis froth highly fomented: In England it has much of the same spirit, but rather a browner complexion. European wit is one of the worst articles we can import. It has an intoxicating power with it, which debauches the very vitals of chastity, and gives a false colouring to every thing it censures or defends. We soon grow fatigued with the excess, and withdraw like gluttons sickened with intemperance. On the contrary, how happily are the sallies of innocent humour calculated to sweeten the vacancy of business! (*PW*, I, p. 18)

Perhaps the strangest thing about Paine's attack on wit here, despite all his concern, is its subordinate position. Like entertainment particularly, and art more generally, wit serves no greater purpose than that of filling in the gaps of the real world of commerce. Even in describing its negative effects, Paine categorises it with his characteristic language of economic exchange. He is particularly alert to imagination's wildness – that dangerous energy which can take it out of 'the vacancy of business' and into the realm of social and political realities. Imagination's dangerous and inappropriate entry into politics is, as far as Paine is concerned, epitomised by Burke's *Reflections*.

III

To judge from two separate comments on the subject, Paine saw the obligation to respond to Burke's *Reflections* as a mixed blessing. On the one hand, it clearly gave him the platform on which to formulate his own principles of revolution: 'Mr. Burke's attack on the french revolution, served me as a back-ground to bring forward other subjects upon, with more advantage than if the back-ground was not there.'[4] If this was the positive side, the negative was not entirely forgotten. That background might embroil his own response rather than providing a convenient spring-board. His own work, Paine remembered, 'had to combat with a strange mixture of prejudice and indifference; it stood exposed to every species of newspaper abuse; and besides this, it had to remove the obstructions which Mr. Burke's rude and outrageous attack on the French Revolution had artfully raised'.[5] This recalls the opening strategy of *Rights of Man*: that Burke's artistry and his integrity are connected. It is then consolidated as Paine links this strategy with his use of the clichéd comparison of drama with politics. The aim is to make Burke look dangerously imaginative in the realm of political debate.

The sense that Burke has flouted decorum is apparent from the very first paragraph of *Rights of Man* where Paine draws attention to his 'incivilities' and a 'conduct that cannot be pardoned on the score of manners'.[6] This is very soon supported by the claim that 'there is scarcely an epithet of abuse to be found in the English language, with which Mr Burke has not loaded the French nation and the National Assembly'.[7] Later on, Paine suggests that Burke has used the 'grossest style of the most vulgar abuse'.[8] At the same time, it is apparent that the imaginative extravagance and allusiveness of Burke's style make him anything but a populist: his aesthetics can only be deemed vulgar from the equally lofty position of Enlightenment rationalism. By castigating Burke as refined or vulgar, Paine also defines his own position as levelling philosopher. Not surprisingly, posterity remains unconvinced of his pretensions to be a philosopher or historian. While he might simultaneously point up Burke's artistry and vulgarity, recent estimates of his work see him as a populariser who thought he was writing history.[9] This double appeal in his work is most clearly evident in *Rights of Man*, but it is present in equal force in *The Age of Reason* where the effect is to demystify the revered forms of Christianity by substituting the expected veneration with the scurrilous language of the street. It is a feature of the work which did not pass unnoticed. The threat posed by *The Age of Reason* lay as much in the reflection of readership in this tactic as in its attack upon religion.[10]

One of the most powerful and complex ways in which *Rights of Man* seeks to contain and rebut Burke's *Reflections on the Revolution in France* is by engaging in what might be termed a war of genres.[11] Paine's deployment of the propriety of genres against Burke's text certainly gives him an opportunity to make his opponent look absurd and disordered, but it also betrays his own repressed anxiety. Propriety becomes the shield with which Paine fends off the promiscuous energy of Burke's *Reflections*.

By reference to generic distinctions, Paine aims to make Burke look immoral, inconsequential, and ridiculous. His initial mode of attack is double-edged: Burke is peculiarly outrageous, even vulgar, in his appeal and, at the same time, he has either wilfully or foolishly crossed the border into the realm of art. Implicit in Paine's attack is the severe criticism that Burke is not writing history. Ranged against this misuse or abuse of genre – a choice which Paine puts before his audience from time to time – is his own text which claims for itself the prestige of both philosophy and history. By categorising Burke, Paine invokes a hierarchy in which his own kind of text, and the literary persona to match it, are superior. For the issue of personality, or, more strictly, faculties of mind, is related to that of genre. As Paine attempts to swallow up Burke's text by claiming that it is not only less disciplined, but narrower and more specific than his own philosophic work, the hierarchy of forms is matched by a hierarchy of faculties. He suggests that because Burke's work is more various and prolific than his own it must be less controlled. It is indicative of an impassioned and disordered mind. By contrast, the serene emotional state of the philosopher enables him to be more expansive and universal in his sentiment as well as in his argument. His generosity and philanthropy are in accord with the strict rationality of his argument. In contrast, Burke's emotionalism is made to look partisan and unrefined; it appeals not to the understanding, but to the imagination. This peculiar double-edged kind of attack is typical of Paine: he uses both sides of the argument over vulgar and refined knowledge.[12]

In the early sections of *Rights of Man* Paine concentrates on what he sees as misuse of genre in the *Reflections* by referring to 'Mr Burke's drama'.[13] This provides ample opportunity for an attack and Paine claims that Burke manipulates history for effect. By dealing with dramatis personae his texts can only deal in inauthentic events. Paine then pushes his claim of a switch from history to drama one step further by introducing the idea of drama's degenerate emotionalism:

As to the tragic paintings by which Mr Burke has outraged his own imagination, and seeks to work upon that of his readers, they are very well calculated for theatrical representation, where facts are manufactured for the sake of show, and accommodated to produce, through the weakness of sympathy, a weeping effect. But Mr Burke should recollect that he is writing History, and not *plays*; and that his readers will expect truth, and not the spouting rant of high-toned exclamation. (*Rights of Man*, pp. 71–72 [*PW*, II, pp. 286–87])

The popular and entertaining quality of drama is to be equated not with truth, but with the deception of eye-dazzling display; it is an illustration of the claim that 'genius must be hired to impose upon ignorance, and show and parade to fascinate the vulgar'.[14] Burke, Paine claims, offers fiction for fact, distraction instead of concentration on the main issue; he has 'endeavoured to lead his reader from the point by a wild unsystematical display of paradoxical rhapsodies'.[15]

One of Paine's most famous criticisms of Burke's method clearly indicates that his lapse into theatrical presentation entails more than exaggeration. Here the contempt for weak sympathy is reinforced and explained. In 'pity[ing] the plumage, but forget[ting] the dying bird',[16] Paine suggests that Burke not only offers falsity for truth, but also engages in a spurious release of emotion. His 'degenerat[ion] into a composition of art'[17] is therefore as much a statement about the morality of emotion as it is of generic propriety; by misdirecting it he is travestying it: 'He is not affected by the reality of distress touching his heart, but by the showy resemblance of it striking his imagination . . . His hero or his heroine must be a tragedy-victim expiring in show, and not in the real prisons of misery.'[18] The immorality of this kind of display is, according to Paine, intrinsic to drama:

It suits his purpose to exhibit the consequences without their causes. It is one of the arts of the drama to do so. If the crimes of men were exhibited with their sufferings, stage effect would sometimes be lost, and the audience would be inclined to approve where it was intended they should commiserate. (*Rights of Man*, p. 82 [*PW*, II, p. 297])

The spurious nature of this emotional reaction to mere effects is, of course, but a small part of the larger argument in *Rights of Man* about going back to the first causes of government. Paine concentrates on the visual (whether pictorial or theatrical) element of Burke's text in order to encourage the impression of its discontinuous nature. Each image is made to look discrete: 'he raises his scenes by contrast instead of connection'.[19] The riotous prodigality of the *Reflections*, Paine would have us believe, means that it is both multiple and fractured: 'Mr. Burke's Book is *all* Miscellany . . . instead of proceeding with an orderly arrangement, he has stormed it with a mob of ideas tumbling over and destroying one another.'[20] As well as returning the language of politics in a mocking manner, Paine's language here also points to a self-destructive element in Burke's artistic genius. While Burke might be seen as wilfully manipulating his 'history painting', there is too a more profound sense of the inadvertency of his paradoxical rhapsodies. Burke's 'parody' turns in on itself. The sense of ridiculousness which Paine invokes in relation to Burke's misappropriation of genre turns out to be self-consuming, self-mocking. Interestingly, Paine's own text can only accommodate this sense of travesty with a certain unease. His own work becomes paradoxical as a result of this contagious spread of imaginative energy. In a strange sense, Paine advocates a repression of Burke's revolutionary aesthetics.

Paine's generic tussle with Burke's *Reflections* goes to the heart of the debate on the issues of heredity, property, and origins. This attention to a travesty of genres does not stand isolated: it reflects and reinforces Paine's main line of attack on Burke's belief in a mixed mode of government, a form of government which by implication can be seen as imaginary, ridiculous and paradoxical – against the laws of nature. According to his various metaphors, it is a mock species, a cuckoo offspring, and an infertile cross-breeding producing a mule. Burke's constitution, like his text, is made out to be an illegitimate and monstrous birth.[21]

In reviewing the Abbé Raynal's work on the French Revolution Paine once again encounters an unfortunate example of the creative faculty of imagination breaking out of the straitjacket of judgement. Like Burke, the Abbé has been tempted out of the proper province of history:

> It is undoubtedly both an ornament and a useful addition to history, to accompany it with maxims and reflections. They afford likewise an agreeable change to the style, and a more diversified manner of expression; but it is absolutely necessary that the root from whence they spring, or the foundation on which they are raised, should be well attended to, which in this work is not. The abbé hastens through his narrations as if he was glad to get from them, that he may enter the more copious field of eloquence and imagination. (*PW*, II, p. 79)

As in Burke's case, the charge against imagination is made in respect of its dangerously distracting power. Its typical characteristics are variety, diversity, and copiousness. If it is left unchecked and released from the constraints of truth, it is assumed that it will sport with numerous impossibilities: 'the more powerful and creative the imagination is, the wilder it runs in that state of unrestrained invention'. As we have seen, the necessary check upon this sportive fancy, that which keeps it in touch with reason, is provided by a 'serene mind' and a 'happy philosophical temperament'. Here the strength of the sound mind means that it can afford to play with thought, calmly dictate to it, rather than allow it to amuse itself and thereby fall foul of its own riotous inclination. In Paine's thought, the happiness of the philosopher is often seen to be the result of temperament, not just a result of rational control. The inference is very strong that not only does the imagination's playfulness dislocate it from truth, but that its chaotic anarchy of rival fictions is the product of an unhappy mind. In this respect Burke's *Reflections* can be seen not only as inconsistent and illogical, but as the inevitably disordered product of a mind feeding on the divisiveness of fear instead of relying on the harmonious force of benevolence.

In this way, Paine's attack on imagination exposes the nature of rational individualism, its subscription to a repressive model of the mind, and its quest for a sublime purity. This is apparent in his deism, and, in particular, in his wide-ranging attack on invention and in his undermining of scriptural authority in *The Age of Reason*. The attack on invention here goes well beyond the province of genre distinctions and the debate about refinement of taste. Paine's adherence to deism forces him into a much more fundamentalist position. The logic and direction of his counter-readings of texts here are much more overtly in touch with the articles of his faith. The procedure immediately seems less provisional because less practical than those encountered in *Rights of Man*.

IV

In *The Age of Reason*, invention and variety, like imagination, are seen as self-evidently flawed. In his role as a deist Paine exposes his dismissive attitude to language as he challenges the authenticity of scripture.[22] One of his basic arguments is that revelation cannot be mediated through language. All attempts to give scriptural identity to such experiences of revelation produce mere 'hearsay'. This basic idea is developed through a monotony of examples and leads to the conviction that language is itself unfit for transmitting either mediation or revelation. It is essentially corrupt. Because of its tendency to change and multiply meaning it cannot be relied upon to transmit vision in a direct and accurate manner. Its very mutability means that it cannot provide an adequate account of origins: it is continually shifting and inventing so that its histories become more and more remote from original authenticity. The history of a religious event in language is thus, for Paine, a history of its degradation and obscurity. Through this effect of progressive travesty it begins to look more and more like fiction. Religious history becomes mere fable instead of parable.

In this respect, Paine is at one with Volney's attitude to language in *Les Ruines*. Reviewing accounts of miracles or, in his terms, the 'monsters' of history, Volney writes:

The only difficulty is to ascertain how and for what purpose the imagination invented them. If we examine with attention the subjects that are exhibited by them, if we analyse the ideas which they combine and associate, and weigh the accuracy of all their concomitant circumstances we shall find a solution perfectly conformable to the laws of nature. Those fabulous stories have a figurative sense different from the apparent one; they are founded on simple and physical facts: but these facts being ill-conceived and erroneously represented, have been disfigured and changed from their original nature of accidental causes dependent on the human mind, by the confusion of signs made use of in the representation of objects, by the equivocation of words, the defect of language and the imperfection of writing.[23]

A similar belief in the flawed because figurative nature of language is to be found in the writings of Paine's associate and friend Condorcet. He too argued for the creation of a new scientific language based on the principles of physics. In his utopian vision language would thus be brought back into relation with the sensuous and rational apprehension of objects, a relationship that had been successively lost as a result of the primitive because figurative nature of early languages.[24]

Paine too laments the lack of a universal language which would purify words of their imprecision and changeability. 'Language cannot convey either the idea or the word of God' because of 'the want of an universal language'; it is subject to 'the mutability of language; the errors to which translators are subject; the possibility of totally suppressing such a word; the possibility of altering it, or of fabricating the whole, and imposing it upon the world'.[25] His response to what we (but certainly not he) might call the fallen nature of language is to displace it altogether. He switches from text to Nature and makes the latter a language. Rather than continuing in the spirit of practical rationalism like Condorcet, Paine, by what seems like a metaphorical sleight of hand, short-circuits the problem of representation. Both the terms and the method of this procedure are characteristic of his work: the idealistic drive and the polemical success of many of his arguments depend on this kind of out-facing tactic. It is equivalent to moving behind the enemy lines. Anteriority is the key position in this war of origins.

Having attacked the authenticity of Biblical testimonies in *The Age of Reason* Paine soon follows this line of thinking. Once the suitability of language as a vehicle for conveying evidence or ideas of God has been questioned, there is immediate recourse to the idea that there must be some alternative medium:

If we permit ourselves to conceive right ideas of things, we must necessarily affix the idea, not only of unchangeableness, but of the utter impossibility of any change taking place, by any means or accident whatever, in that which we would honour with the name of the Word of God; and therefore the Word of God cannot exist in any written or human language.

The continually progressive change to which the meaning of words is subject, the want of an universal language which renders translation necessary, the errors to which translations are subject, the mistakes of copyists and printers, together with the possibility of wilful alteration, are of themselves evidences that human language, whether in speech or in print, cannot be the vehicle of the Word of God. – The Word of God exists in something else. (*Age of Reason, PW*, IV, p. 38)

In Paine's text, that something else turns out to be the whole of visible creation. It stands as concrete evidence of the existence of the Creator himself. Simply by regarding the objects of creation, the perceiver is immediately and directly in touch with God. Obviously, in this scheme of things there is still a residual element of mediation: reason itself has to perform the translation to take the mind from creation to creator. Sensory knowledge and rational comprehension thus form the staple of Paine's deism. As a result of this belief, all those books which claim the status of revelation look like feeble hoaxes: 'And is not the evidence that this creation holds out to our senses infinitely stronger than any thing we can read in a book, that any imposter might make and call the word of God?'[26] Direct apprehension of the Creator through his works successfully avoids this threat of being imposed upon. All forms of human invention and contrivance fall under this suspicion. Paine's aim is to avoid any possibility of being deceived by human contrivance. And the most common medium for such deception, of course, is language. That which proclaims itself to be scripture or revelation should not have to be contrived. It should be already written:

Search not written or printed books, but the Scripture called the *Creation* . . . Man cannot make or invent, or contrive principles: he can only discover them; and he ought to look through the discovery to the author. (*Age of Reason, PW*, IV, p. 239)

Stepping behind the uncertain and impure world of human production, Paine's deist encounters the original and authentic world of objects. By securing this position, all the dangers of plurality can be avoided: in this Edenic representation truth is decidedly single and universal. More importantly, perhaps, precisely because of its aboriginal purity this 'scripture' cannot be appropriated or travestied or in any way used by the political enemy:

It is only in the CREATION that all our ideas and conceptions of a *word of God* can unite. The Creation speaketh an universal language, independently of human speech or human language, multiplied and various as they be. It is an ever existing original, which every man can read. It cannot be forged; it cannot be counterfeited; it cannot be lost; it cannot be altered; it cannot be suppressed. It does not depend upon the will of man whether it shall be published, or not, it publishes itself from one end of the earth to the other. It preaches to all nations and to all worlds: and this *word of God* reveals to man all that is necessary for man to know of God. (*The Age of Reason, PW*, IV, p. 46)

This creation is not only resistant to the counterfeitings of artifice, it also pre-dates worldly and political issues. From this fundamentalist position come the self-evident truths of commonsense. It allows those other characteristics of Paine's writing to take place. In the rationalist confidence of this position the progress of history looks like a terrible mistake. It is the force of this argument which generates Paine's texts; it provides them (to use one of his own most telling analogies) with the grammar of their existence.[27] Paine's tactical ploy of going back to origins, especially when, as we have seen, those origins are generated by something approaching a religious idealism, enables him to dismiss with suspect ease the arguments of his adversaries.

The deistical belief that God in his creation is perceived through the senses, apprehended by the reason, and that this knowledge is immediate and unchanging according to the laws of nature, makes invention look unnecessary. Such an idea cannot be included in a prospective vision of improvement. It can only be accommodated to a retrospective narrative which translates 'invention' into a process of demystification, purification, or discovery. It might be revolutionary in its impetus, but that impetus is derived from an already existing truth.

Even at his most idealistic in seeking the improvement of the human race, Paine is really looking back towards this origin. When, in *The Age of Reason*, he contemplates the possibility of a universal language, the enterprise, he tells us, 'will not be believing any thing new, but [will consist] in getting rid of redundancies, and believing as man believed at first'.[28] Even Condorcet, in *The Progress of The Human Mind*, harks back to an idyllic past where language was in a strictly rational relationship to objects and was therefore pure in the sense of being free from ambiguity and inaccuracy of expression.[29]

V

This belief in origins is important in Paine's battle with Burke. When, in the course of replying to Burke in *Rights of Man*, the squabble over precedents hots up, Paine goes straight for Burke's philosophical affiliations and turns the argument to the question of origins. At one point he focuses on a fragment which derives from Burke's aesthetics in order to discredit it. In doing so he immediately short-circuits the whole of history by making it look like a rather inadequate and forlorn product of human invention. Challenging Burke on the so-called revolution of 1688 he makes the image of the chasm rebound on its author: 'It was government dethroning government; and the old one, by attempting to make a new one, made a chasm.'[30] He does so in typical fashion, pointing up the paradoxical nature of his adversary's argument. That which is paradoxical is also impossible or fictional, it is assumed. Similarly, in the aptly titled 'Prospects on the Rubicon', Paine refers his reader to the chaos in pre-revolutionary French society; though in this instance the chaos to which he refers is real and necessary, unlike the contrived chasm which derives from Burke's aesthetics of the sublime. As a result, it is given the sanction of original authority, despite being a form of disorder:

While this change is working, there will appear a kind of chaos in the nation; but the creation we enjoy arose out of chaos, and our greatest blessings appear to have a confused beginning. (*PW*, II, p. 206)

By attempting to account positively for a form of disorder, Paine is, for once, betrayed into a penchant for obscurity, the very thing for which he castigates Burke and which clashes with his own belief in the clear and sublime light of reason. His more usual tactic is to expose the intellectual chasm in Burke's politics of the obscure sublime. According to Paine:

It is not among the least of the evils of the present existing governments in all parts of Europe, that man, considered as man, is thrown back to a vast distance from his Maker, and the artificial chasm filled up by a succession of barriers, or sort of turnpike gates, through which he has to pass. I will quote Mr. Burke's catalogue of barriers that he has set up between man and his Maker. Putting himself in the character of a herald, he says: 'We fear God – we look with awe to kings – with affection to Parliaments – with duty to magistrates – with reverence to priests, and with respect to nobility.' Mr. Burke has forgotten to put in 'chivalry.' He has also forgotten to put in Peter.

The duty of man is not a wilderness of turnpike gates, through which he is to pass by tickets from one to the other. It is plain and simple, and consists but of two points. His duty to God, which every man must feel; and with respect to his neighbour, to do as he would be done by. (*Rights of Man*, p. 89 [*PW*, II, pp. 305–6])

To regain the blissful seat of unmediated knowledge is the object of Paine's levelling rationalism. The laying low of the barriers of superstition – whether in the realms of religion or politics – prepares the ground for a new beginning, but only in the sense of restoring an original order. Paine's claim of a 'regeneration' in *Rights of Man* thus figures as an appropriately religious term.[31] Paradoxically, the moral imperative which enables a revolutionary new start can never entirely escape its metaphysical origins, and allow a clean break for the new world of free trade and commerce for which Paine has such high hopes.

The conflict in Paine's writing between progression and a reverence, both philosophical and religious, for a lost origin, derives in part from the presence of context. Certainly, the clash between these two is something of a commonplace in eighteenth-century thought. It figures prominently, for example, in the case of Rousseau where it takes the form of a contest between the noble savage and the alienating sophistication of society. Even here, however, the conflict is not simply between past and present. That lost Eden might figure prominently, but it is lost and figures now as a trope which defines the perception of the present. In Paine's case, we are reminded that the search for origins comes about under pressure from the peculiar power of Burke's text or the chaos of the present political turmoil of American independence or the French Revolution. Faced with the chaos of text or event in these instances, Paine's appeal to origins is both a philosophical ploy in keeping with his persona and an attempt at re-orientation. Confronted with the bewildering variety of the Bible in *The Age of Reason* (a variety we have already seen to be characteristic of imagination) Paine makes the following plea: 'Search not written or printed books, but the Scripture called the *Creation* . . . Man cannot make, or invent, or contrive principles: he can only discover them.'[32]

That this kind of appeal is a peculiar and necessary response to crisis is made apparent in the following extract from 'The Forester's Letters' (1775):

Whoever will take the trouble of attending to the progress and changeability of times and things, and the conduct of mankind thereon, will find, that *extraordinary circumstances* do sometimes arise before us, of a species, either so purely natural or so perfectly original, that none but the man of nature can understand them. When precedents fail to spirit us, we must return to the first principles of things for information; and *think*, as if we were the *first men* that *thought*. And this is the true reason that, in the present state of affairs, the wise are become foolish, and the foolish wise. (*PW*, I, pp. 154–55)

Even as he claims the status of an unprecedented event, Paine is, of course, politically committed. The case of the French Revolution makes it perfectly clear that one of the attempts of the forces of reaction was to trap the revolution in an already existing paradigm: to tame it by making it conform to a preexisting category. In this particular instance, Paine gives a good indication of the way in which his appeal to origins is capable of reversing categories, of turning everything upside-down. It contains within itself the ability to make things appear paradoxical and therefore as ridiculously aesthetic as the workings of a febrile imagination. Much of the power of his own writing comes from precisely this aim of making a persuasive argument look contradictory or paradoxical: it is certainly the basis of his strategy in dealing with Burke and the Bible.

By way of explaining the method of his attack on Burke in *Rights of Man*, Paine anecdotally offers the reader the following specific geographical analogy. As he points to the vacuity of Burke's work he is led to contemplate the nature of paradox. The irony is that he cannot simply dismiss it as an empty hoax: instead, he has to read through it, and thereby allow it to make its imprint on his own text. What he describes as a delusory walk upon the shore turns out to be the very thing which dictates the crab-like nature of his own attack:

> I know a place in America called Point-no-Point; because as you proceed along the shore, gay and flowery as Mr Burke's language, it continually recedes and presents itself at a distance before you; but when you have got as far as you can go, there is no point at all. Just thus it is with Mr Burke's three hundred and fifty-six pages. It is therefore difficult to reply to him. But as the points he wishes to establish, may be inferred from what he abuses, it is in his paradoxes that we must look for his arguments. (*Rights of Man*, p. 71 [*PW*, II, p. 286])

It is not fortuitous that Paine focuses here on what he sees as the disorientating effect of Burke's language: it is a frequently deployed tactic supported by metaphors and analogies which stress Burke's waywardness and, of course, his own sure direction. As we have already seen, he considers the Abbé Raynal's work on the French Revolution to be possessed of the same unfortunate imaginative luxuriance as Burke's. As a result, the abbé's writings are also capable of leading the reader astray and of masking the fact with an intoxicating pleasure: they are 'uncentral and burdened with variety. They represent a beautiful wilderness without paths; in which the eye is diverted by every thing without being particularly directed to any thing; and in which it is agreeable to be lost, and difficult to find the way out.'[33] Clearly, the censure is not without a puritanical foundation: a fear of temptation assailing through the senses, and taking place in a convenient wilderness. For the most part, however, the analogy is removed from a religious significance. As Paine proceeds to 'follow Mr Burke through a pathless wilderness of rhapsodies'[34] the effect of the exposé is to generate ridicule from the superior vantage-point of rationality rather than exude moral condemnation from an indignant sense of self-righteousness. The convenient thing as far as Paine is concerned is that the arrogant superiority of his position can easily be easily combined with popularity. That is its real power. As he argues in 'Letters to American Citizens': 'The right will always become the popular, if it has courage to show itself, and the shortest way is always a straight line.'[35]

Confronted with the chaos of political crisis or the variety of the artistic text, Paine deploys this analogy of the straight line. It can be conveniently used to connect his belief in geometry with his belief in individualism; it can be made to fit with the universal laws of nature and with the individual's intervention on behalf of social enlightenment. This is particularly apparent in the *Crisis Papers* where the analogy is frequently ushered in to support the overall attempt to stabilise and mobilise opinion on behalf of American independence. The straight line thus figures as natural law and individual experience. As we have already seen, in the case of Burke's *Reflections*, where, it is claimed, turnpikes have been placed in the way of nature, Paine's straight lines frequently take the form of metaphors of the road. The obstructions of Burke's artifice represent a degradation of nature and a distancing of the individual from God or from the world of 'His' creation. On a more practical level, of course, such barriers cut the individual off from his/her rights; or more practically still, as the analogy itself suggests, from the benefits of free trade. Where the contrast needs to be more extreme, Paine switches the metaphor slightly and contrasts the journey by road with the uncertainty of a voyage by sea: the singleness of a journey by land is compared with the alarming prospect of a plural ocean. The Bible itself receives a similar treatment at the hands of Paine's critique: 'Is it not more safe that we stop ourselves at the plain, pure, and unmixed belief of one God, which is deism, than that we commit ourselves on an ocean of improbable, irrational, indecent, and contradictory tales?'[36]

When Paine's attack on the variety of imagination is connected with this device – metaphors which contain a latent narrative – it can be seen that the attack is a response to the threat which such variety offers to the reader. Instead of being idly amused with the multiplicity of objects that go to make up a refined aesthetic experience, the spectator or reader, according to Paine's way of thinking, should be disconcerted, ill-at-ease, or, at the least, confused. His strategy is to undermine the leisured position guaranteed by the authority of good taste. By applying reason to make it look chaotic and inconsistent, Paine also makes it look frantic and disordered.

The more one considers Paine's metaphors which promise a narrative, the more they seem to function only on a spatial level. Thematically, it is as if Paine's texts are struck between two loyalties: a belief in progress and an adherence to origins. The system of metaphors we have been looking at seems to serve merely as a pivot between the two. The resultant indeterminacy is particularly disconcerting since the liberating potential of these straight lines is so compelling; as for instance, in the following statement: 'The genuine mind of man, thirsting for its native home, society, condemns the gewgaws that separate him from it. Titles are like circles drawn by the magician's wand, to contract the sphere of man's felicity. He lives immured in the Bastille of a word, and surveys at a distance the envied life of man.'[37] When the nature of principles is explained, it becomes apparent that these potentially liberating lines are really severed from time and history. These lines turn out to be either manifestations of, or the quickest routes through to, invisible 'principles'.

In 'First Principles of Government' Paine seems to suggest that the straight line as opposed to the imprisoning circle is in accord with origins: 'It is by tracing things to their origin that we learn to understand them: and it is by keeping that line and that origin always in view that we never forget them.'[38] The problem here, of course, is in deciding the extent to which the two are separate: is Paine suggesting that we keep both the origin and the access to it clear in our minds? For the extent to which they are separate is important in determining whether a scheme of history is involved in the evolution of such principles. Two further statements from the same work would suggest that there is some conflict on this issue. When Paine challenges the idea of heredity becoming a right through usage, he is prepared to dismiss time (in the sense of custom) as a valid criterion by which to judge of right:

This would be supposing an absurdity; for either it is putting time in the place of principle, or making it superior to principle; whereas time has no more connection with, or influence upon principle, than principle has upon time. The wrong which began a thousand years ago, is as much wrong as if it began today; and the right which originates today, is as much a right as if it had the sanction of a thousand years. Time with respect to principles is an eternal NOW: it has no operation upon them: it changes nothing of their nature and qualities. But what have we to do with a thousand years? Our life-time is but a short portion of that period, and if we find the wrong in existence as soon as we begin to live, that is the point of time at which it begins to us; and our right to resist it is the same as if it never existed before. (*PW*, III, p. 260)

From this it is clear that the insurrectionary force of his writings derives not only from the attack on precedents, but also from a much more inclusive assault on the category of time itself. With each new generation time begins anew; history is forgotten, but the eternal principles are forever kept in view by the straight lines of reason. But in contrast to this clear-cut statement for the political activist, Paine later makes greater concessions to the force of custom and usage. The gradualist approach evident in the following passage is at least aware of the recalcitrance of the popular consciousness to revolutionary change. For once, commonsense is not immediate and transparent:

There never yet was any truth or any principle so irresistibly obvious, that all men believed it at once. Time and reason must co-operate with each other to the final establishment of any principle; and therefore those who may happen to be first convinced have not a right to persecute others, on whom conviction operates more slowly. The moral principle of revolutions is to instruct, not to destroy. (*PW*, III, p. 277)

Although the process of his own true principles is still seen as inevitable (just slower) in this statement, there is at least a grudging awareness of the slavish power of opinion. For it is an 'opinion' that is supported by all the resources of imagination, despite the use of the demeaning term 'gewgaws'. Paine shares with Hazlitt a perception of the extent to which imagination can reinforce mere customary usage and thereby act on behalf of the forces of reaction.

So here we have two conflicting, though not strictly contradictory, ideas of time as it affects Paine's eternal principles. The latter are separate from considerations of time and place; yet for them to take effect duration and practical application are required. (One assumes in the foregoing quotation that establishment is not synonymous with formation.) If this concern with time and its relationship with principle is considered more particularly with regard to Paine's idea of each generation legislating for itself, the same conflict emerges. Paine again invokes this idea of a single straight line leading back to the originating principles which guarantee universal rights when he asserts that: 'The rights of men in society, are neither devisable, nor tranferable, nor annihilable, but are descendable only; and it is not in the power of any generation to intercept finally, and cut off the descent.'[39] He might well be doing for the rights of man exactly what he denies to the property and heredity rights of Burke's patriarchal system; but in advocating a line of continuity at all, he puts in motion an idea which clashes with the right of each generation to 'begin the world over again'.[40]

If, in the main, the principles to which Paine refers are eternal and universal, the time scheme they suggest is an eternal now. It is not surprising, therefore, that history should look inadequate or ridiculous: according to these principles history can only be the telling of stories; and, as a result, all narrative structures begin to look redundant. At least, this is so until we consider another aspect of Paine's writings: one which leads to entrances onto the stage of politics. This is Paine's awareness of man as a physical, decaying body. As in many a case of eighteenth-century rationalism, the idealisms of an unageing intellect are matched by a particularly acute awareness of the dying animal.

VI

Hereditary kingship is attacked throughout Paine's political writings, and is responsible for generating two strands of thought in his work: the investigation of the relationship between generations, and the exploration of the individual. In the case of the latter, Paine's egalitarianism leads to the articulation of a new form of individualism, and a new way of looking at the body. Both strands are, despite the extremes of the debate, controlled by the prevailing economic mode of thought; yet they share the same paradigms. They are determined by the same issues. In order to combat Burke's idea of hereditary succession to entailed property, Paine puts the body in the place of property. According to his self-proclaimed egalitarianism, the mature free agent replaces the entailed child. From the very beginning of his career, in an anti-slavery essay, Paine reacts strongly against the right of property invading the person: 'The base idea of man having property in man.'[41] That his interest in the body is at least partly inspired by economics is immediately apparent in the following declaration from 'First Principles of Government'. Having described the person as 'sacred', his attention is very soon turned to a different sort of value:

> The protection of a man's person is more sacred than the protection of property; and besides this, the faculty of performing any kind of work or services by which he acquires a livelihood, or maintaining his family, is of the nature of property. It is property to him; he has acquired it; and it is as much the object of his protection as exterior property, possessed without that faculty, can be the object of protection in another person. (*PW*, III, p. 269)

Clearly, Paine is not so much interested in arguing for the inviolable rights of the private individual as in extending the way in which the individual – even his/her body and its labour – is situated in relation to production – an aspect of political economy which was to interest Cobbett as well as Marx and Engels. (In this he is at least as thoroughgoing as Burke.) Similarly, when he comes to consider the origin and the right of representative government in the same work, it is a case of transferring the language of property to the body: 'Man is himself the origin and the evidence of the right. It appertains to him in right of his existence, and his person is the title deed.'[42] Man has not property in man, but each man has the rights of property in himself as long as he shall live.

On the same principle, Paine argues, must each generation function. It has the rights of its existence, but when that lapses so do the rights: 'The vanity and presumption of governing beyond the grave is the most ridiculous and insolent of all tyrannies. Man has no property in man, neither has one generation a property in the generations that are to follow.'[43] According to this idea, properly disinterested legislation has no hold beyond the limits of natural life. In 'The Eighteenth Fructidor' Paine comments: 'The Constitution, in this respect, is as impartially constructed as if those who framed it were to die as soon as they had finished their work.'[44] From what we have already seen of eternal principles, those other respects not referred to are clearly important. Paine is equally aware of the dangers. He is alert to the absurdity and difficulty of a system in which, as he puts it: 'Every new election would be a new revolution, or it would suppose the public of the former year dead and a new public in its place.'[45]

Even so, his depiction of the nation in 'First Principles of Government' focuses on the difficulty of finding a still point from which legislation can be legitimate. (He resolves the same problem in his prose by addressing it to the mature reader.)[46] The problem in characterising the nation is that it is forever on the move – at different stages between birth and death:

A nation, though continually existing, is continually in a state of renewal and succession. It is never stationary. Every day produces new births, carries minors forward to maturity, and old persons from the stage. In this ever running flood of generations there is no point superior in authority to another. Could we conceive an idea of superiority in any, at what point of time, or in what century of the world, are we to fix it? To what cause are we to ascribe it? By what evidence are we to prove it? By what criterion are we to know it? A single reflection will teach us that our ancestors, like ourselves, were but tenants for life in the great freehold of rights. (*PW*, III, pp. 261–62)

At the very point where it seems that his sense of urgency makes it impossible to act provisionally, along comes the familiar revelation of truth; a truth expressed once more in the language of property.

It is this strong sense of the mortal nature of man which clashes so strongly with Burke's ideas of heredity. According to Paine, Burke offends against religious nature of man's existence. Strangely, the logic of Paine's argument is that in denying the inevitability of death, Burke denies the fact of life: in going against 'the nature of man' he has effected an 'annihilation'. He has set up his own creation in defiance of the creator:

It is the nature of man to die, and he will continue to die as long as he continues to be born. But Mr Burke has set up a sort of political Adam, in whom all posterity are bound forever, he must therefore prove that his Adam possessed such a power, or such a right. (*Rights of Man*, p. 66 [*PW*, II, p. 280])

Burke has made an unnatural monster out of Adam, an Adam whose work is a divinely sanctioned imprisonment. The force of Paine's deism makes Burke's idea of the authority of kingship look like a grotesque parody of the Fall.

In his relentless opposition to kingship, Paine attempts to set up a form of government which overcomes the inconsistencies and caprices of the individual and even those of single generations. Gradually it becomes apparent that it is government which is able to uphold the rights of man, overcome the tyranny of the body, and transcend man's mortal state. Representative government, Paine argues,

places government in a state of constant maturity. It is, as has been already stated, never young, never old. It is subject neither to nonage, nor dotage. It is never in the cradle, nor on crutches. It admits not of a separation between knowledge and power, and is superior, as government always ought to be, to all the accidents of individual man, and is therefore superior to what is called monarchy. (*Rights of Man*, p. 203 [*PW*, II, p. 424])

At this point, Paine makes explicit the difference between his ideal system and the body; and, more particularly, he highlights the inappropriateness of the analogy. The body is supplanted by geometry:

A nation is not a body, the figure of which is to be represented by the human body; but is like a body contained within a circle, having a common centre, in which every radius meets; and that centre is formed by representation. To connect representation with what is called monarchy, is eccentric government. Representation is of itself the delegated monarchy of a nation, and cannot debase itself by dividing it with another. (*Rights of Man*, p. 203 [*PW*, II, p. 425])

This might appear very similar to Burke's strategy – a way of maintaining continuity by overcoming death. It looks like an attempt to put the idealisms of man beyond nature.

When Bishop Watson responds to Paine's *Age of Reason*, in his *Apology for the Bible*, he argues vehemently on behalf of hereditary succession and describes it rather luridly in terms of the body politic. According to Watson, it is precisely the civilised virtues and their maintenance through inheritance which stand opposed to the unseemly fact of death. Clearly, there is a different kind of religious transposition going on here: relations of property are made sacred; by inheritance death is conquered. Even if one doesn't make a link between 'common stock' and the 'fetid mass of corruption', Watson's allegiances are fairly clear, his values threatened:

One of the principal rights of man, in a state either of nature or of society, is a right of property in the fruits of his industry, ingenuity, or good fortune. Does government hold any man in ignorance of this right? So much the contrary, that the chief care of government is to declare, ascertain, modify, and defend this right; nay, it gives the right, where nature gives none; it protects the goods of an intestate; and it allows a man, at his death, to dispose of that property which the law of nature would cause to revert into the common stock. Sincerely as I am attached to the liberties of mankind, I cannot but profess myself an utter enemy to that spurious philosophy, that democratic insanity which would equalise all property, and level all distinctions in civil society. Personal distinctions, arising from superior probity, learning, eloquence, skill, courage, and from every other excellency of talents, are the very blood and nerves of the body politic; they animate the whole, and invigorate every part; without them, it's bones would become reeds, and it's marrow water; it would presently sink into a fetid senseless mass of corruption.[47]

As one might expect, Rousseau is closer to Paine on this issue. In the 'Discourse on Political Economy' he too had been sceptical about using the body metaphor to describe the system of government: 'I shall take the liberty of making use of a very common, and in some respects inaccurate comparison.'[48] Significantly, when he addresses the issue again, in *Du Contrat Social*, it is under the chapter heading 'The Death of the Body Politic'. Here there is that same sense of mortality; and the impulse to see government as a means of overcoming it, which we have seen in Paine. At this point he too has to contend with the conflict between nature and artifice:

> The body politic, as well as the human body, begins to die as soon as it is born, and carries in itself the causes of its destruction. But both may have a constitution that is more or less robust and suited to preserve them a longer or a shorter time. The constitution of man is the work of nature; that of the state the work of art. It is not in men's power to prolong their own lives; but it is for them to prolong as much as possible the life of the State, by giving it the best possible constitution.[49]

As we have just seen, Paine avoids having to make this sharp distinction between art and nature when he describes his idea of representative government. For him, the assumption governing his unchanging geometric model is that it is not a human invention at all, but a discovery of the immutable laws of creation. For him, the body becomes sacred; but only representative government can overcome the transitory body or even those dying generations.[50] In this rather extreme way, Paine is both beneath and beyond the thinking of his Burkean contemporaries. Instead of allowing for the possibility of a symbolic image which is capable of being individual and general at the same time in a mystery of representation, Paine moves extremely from material object to invisible principle. In his thinking, there is no accounting for the transference which takes place, and certainly no obscure aesthetic exchange of the kind Coleridge might argue for as 'transubstantiation'. And there is no subscription to the expansive mediating culture of 'second nature' which Burke envisages.

In propounding an idea of imagination as part of a divisive world of human contrivance and muddled, inconsistent plurality, Paine's philosophy grounds itself in two ideas which represent a unity which makes any aesthetic category look redundant: in one, the system of representation is idyllic in that it contains no sense of difference; in the other, we have a typical response to that which is supposed to stand resolutely outside it – the body. It figures as natural object. As a solution that, too, is fraught with problems. For it raises perhaps the most fundamental issue of Paine's period in the political sphere and the one which most closely bears on popular notions of imagination in the literature of the period – whether, in the form of sympathy or projection, it constitutes an act of knowledge which is capable of judging social realities. The tyranny of the individual represented by monarchy is to be replaced by the confinement of the body: in terms of representation the symbolic individual is to be replaced by one which is supposed to stand outside the signifying chain altogether. When he develops his description of the representative form of government in *Rights of Man* it inevitably leads to a language which is no language at all:

Like the nation itself, it possesses a perpetual stamina, as well of body as of mind; and presents itself on the open theatre of the world in a fair and manly manner. Whatever are its excellences or its defects, they are visible to all. It exists not in fraud and mystery; it deals not in cant and sophistry, but inspires a language, that, passing from heart to heart, is felt and understood. (*Rights of Man*, p. 204 [*PW*, II, p. 426])

Ultimately, Paine's literalist mistrust of language and artifice, like many others, turns out to be grounded in a kind of fundamentalism. The apparently egalitarian openness of this passage is coupled with an organic vision of the body politic and an accession to commonsense ideology. Paine's radical literalism offers rational demystification alongside intuitive, affective truth.

As such, it is as likely to be appropriated by the 'born-again' Right as it is by the rationalist Left. In his acceptance speech for the Republican nomination in 1980 Ronald Reagan invoked the figure of Tom Paine writing 'in the darkest days of the American Revolution'. *Common Sense* provided him with the rhetoric with which to launch the revolution of 'Reaganomics': 'We have it in our power to begin the world over again.'[51] The words echoed eerily in the nuclear arms negotiations and 'star wars' debates that followed. That Reagan's appropriation of Paine might seem surprising to some on the Left suggests that as much attention should be given to analysing the ideological grounds of Paine's texts as to chronicling his role in the successes of Enlightenment rationalism. Paine has been subject to a variety of appropriations: revolutionary, seditious pamphleteer, popular philosopher, free-trader, champion of liberalism, and father of American independence. Without an awareness of the specific identity of Paine's mode of representation, such powerful appropriations as Reagan's will always come as a disabling shock.

CHAPTER 3

Wollstonecraft, imagination, and futurity

I

Wollstonecraft's response to revolution consists of a radical attempt to redefine subjectivity in line with a perfectibilist optimism in the progress of history. Her writing engages in a thorough-going reconstruction of the psychic economy of the individual which renegotiates the relationship between enlightened reason and refined sensibility. Within its proclaimed rationalism it re-imagines the value of emotions. Imagination lies at the heart of this ambitious project and is subject to all the consequent pressures as Wollstonecraft attempts to articulate this new relationship between heart and head for both men and women. And, as we shall see, the cultural reverberations of this economy are far-reaching. Wollstonecraft's work raises the question as to whether aesthetic issues are important at all in the larger context of historical improvement and an increasingly technical political economy.

Imagination, for Wollstonecraft, functions as an agent of moral improvement. It supports the present moment of revolutionary critique with the reassuring speculative capacity of seeing into the future, of sustaining an act of faith that the project to reform the present really is part of a larger moral, even metaphysical, narrative of improvement. For Wollstonecraft, imagination plays a key role in keeping hope alive. It sustains her optimism in the narrative of the moral and civilising progress of history and it acts as a bolster to individuals like herself, who are engaged in a dominantly self-abnegating process of social change.[1] As we shall see, there are many instances when Wollstonecraft finds it difficult to sustain an optimistic vision of the progress of humanity. There are moments when the connection between the larger historical process and the individual seems to have broken down altogether, and times when history and nature even appear purposeless. At these times, Wollstonecraft's imaginative speculations seem to operate in reverse. Instead of hope, and the heavenly prospect of an exalted happiness, there is only doubt, death, and a vision of entropy. This manifests itself most prominently in what is perhaps her most daring text: *Letters Written During A Short Residence in Sweden, Norway, and Denmark*. But this counter-narrative of degeneration underscores many of Wollstonecraft's other works. The dynamic of most of her writing is double-edged: it depends upon the prospect of improvement and the threat of degeneration. Her versions of imagination inhabit this fraught dynamic.

This threat of degeneration informs Wollstonecraft's complicated engagement with Rousseau in *A Vindication of the Rights of Woman* and her vitriolic attack upon Burke in *A Vindication of the Rights of Men*. In the case of Rousseau the battle takes place over sensibility and the temptations of a brutish desire; in the case of Burke it focuses on what she sees as his degrading appeal to instinctive feelings. In Rousseau she sees the potential for an exalted imagination degraded into a libertine fantasy, while in Burke she sees the aesthetic of an aristocratic culture mobilised to promote a slavishly dependent mentality. Wollstonecraft's attack on two of the most prominent men of her age on the grounds of their debased sensibility also draws attention to the power of such false forms of refinement. This aristocratic and libertine culture has the capacity to degrade its victims. In this respect, it carries the same degenerative threat as the luxury of wealth provided by the new possibilities of trade. Wollstonecraft's vision of moral improvement supported by an exalted imagination must also encounter the new methodologies designed to measure happiness in accordance with the benefits of trade.

Wollstonecraft is quick to make comparison between entrepreneurial free-trade and libertinism, most tellingly (not surprisingly perhaps) in a letter to Imlay in which she comes close to articulating her own version of genius and its connection with imagination. She even upbraids him for not paying this faculty sufficient respect:

Believe me, sage sir . . . I could prove to you in a trice that it is the mother of sentiment, the great distinction of our nature, the only purifier of the passions . . . the imagination is the true fire, stolen from heaven, to animate this cold creature of clay, producing all those fine sympathies that lead to rapture, rendering men social by expanding their hearts, instead of leaving them leisure to calculate how many comforts society affords.

If you call these observations romantic I shall be apt to retort, that you are embruted by trade and the vulgar enjoyments of life.[2]

This is the positive manifestation of Wollstonecraft's imagination: divine in origin, social and practical in its manifestation. Sympathy, not abstracted social theory, is its means of circulation. Happiness is not produced by the speculations of a leisured aesthetic, but by the activity of social interaction.

Across the range of her writings Wollstonecraft sees imagination not only as a passive faculty operated on for good or ill by outside forces – so that a false refinement of taste can make it libidinous, or a healthy respect for religion can exalt it above an appetite of the sense. She can also refer to it as a dynamic force in its own right: a faculty which has its own transforming power.

But even as she confidently, even aggressively, announces its power in this letter, Wollstonecraft betrays the insecurity of an imagination which must contend with 'trade and the vulgar enjoyments of life' and which can so easily be dismissed as merely 'romantic'. Imagination articulates itself as part of the larger historical process of improvement in line with a religious vision of the rapture of happiness, but even as it does so it must register the threat to its existence from an aristocratic aesthetic of false refinement and a degrading consumption of luxury.[3]

II

This dynamic interface between idealism and degradation lies at the heart of *Rights of Woman* in Wollstonecraft's critique of Rousseau.[4] Here she confronts the duality of imagination: its capacity for future happiness and its susceptibility to an indolent and degrading consumption of the present. Although Wollstonecraft's project is clearly to point up the inequality and illogicality of *Émile*, in many respects Rousseau is also a powerful ally. Both writers contend with similar problems; both attempt to imagine happiness; both see imaginative desire as a powerful element in the individual which must be appreciated and curbed; and both realise the extent to which their approach to happiness is likely to be compromised by the prevailing structure of society and its system of government.

In *Émile* Rousseau isolates imagination as a major cause of our unhappiness. Imagination enlarges the bounds of human possibility, but at the same time it stimulates a desire which always exceeds possessed happiness.[5] The motive force of human behaviour is thus structured on an impossibility. For Rousseau, 'man' the rational (and most passionate) animal suffers the fate of Tantalus because of the fundamental asymmetries and paradoxes which bear down on his experience in the form of the well-known, and often over-simplified, split between nature and society, and another perhaps equally important division between *'homme'* and *'citoyen'*. For these reasons, the precariousness of social position plays a major part in the plan of education outlined in *Émile*.[6] As well as addressing the social constraints which stop the individual realising his or her full potential, Rousseau addresses the internal contradiction of 'man's' nature. Faced with the loss of innocence produced by the enervating effect of civilisation, however, Rousseau's tactics appear to be retrograde. In Wollstonecraft's view, he attacks the wrong side of the equation: instead of remedying the weakness produced by an effete and corrupt civilisation, he tinkers with desire and pulls his whole enterprise back into the confines of a spurious and contradictory ideology.

Ironically, it is focusing his attack so exclusively on imagination rather than its wider social context which draws Rousseau irredeemably apart from Wollstonecraft's line of thinking. Instead of purifying this dangerously powerful faculty, as she argues, he simply curbs it and puts an artificial restraint upon it. Painfully aware that: 'The world of reality has its bounds, the world of imagination is boundless', Rousseau offers a liberation based on compromise: 'as we cannot enlarge the one, let us restrict the other; for all the sufferings which really make us miserable arise from the difference between the real and the imaginary'.[7] This ironised dualism is seen by Wollstonecraft to be a false form of contradictoriness which only serves to perpetuate the inequality and exploitation of gender difference.

In so far as Rousseau's idea of imagination contains an essentialist logic, it represents a curb on human nature. Though offered in the spirit of a practical liberation of the body, Rousseau's restrictions on the power of imaginative desire in *Émile* are seen to compromise the optimistic idealism of his philosophy. Basing his educational plans on a form of restraint raises serious doubts about his view of human nature and makes him look remote from Wollstonecraft's hopes of perfectibility.

Throughout *Émile* it is difficult to determine whether imagination is origin or symptom of the problem of the unattainability of the object of desire. At times it seems as though the problem can actually be overcome, that a realignment of emotions can clearly be brought about. There is, for example, an engaging confidence in the following declaration: 'That man is truly free who desires what he is able to perform, and does what he desires. This is my fundamental maxim'; and at another point, as if to justify such confidence, Rousseau can claim that 'it is the imagination which stirs the senses. Desire is not a physical need; it is not true that it is a need at all' which implies that desire is actually the product of imagination.[8] Other statements in the same work point to the latent possibilities of imagination, its potentialities, as he refers us to its infinite scope, its agency as social sympathy, and its antipathy to habitual experience. One of the peculiarities of Rousseau's perception of imagination, however, is the extent to which it is inescapably linked with unhappiness. Even at its most socially constructive, imagination leans towards misery and is associated with a melancholic form of sentimentalism.[9]

Wollstonecraft parts company with Rousseau at this point where he is seen to suggest that there is something innately wrong with the structure of human feelings. In keeping with the religious aspect of her thought, she remains optimistic about re-aligning feeling.[10] Rousseau's suggestion that 'man's' nature is out of joint might well be read by her as blasphemous.

Wollstonecraft's reaction to Rousseau is obviously dominated by the inequality of the different kinds of education he recommends for the sexes in *Émile*. Her trenchant investigation of his work exposes its illogicality and her attack looks like an indictment of an emergent Romantic sensibility ruined by a pathological susceptibility to powerful feelings and a suggestive imagination. This complicated interchange between Wollstonecraft and Rousseau on the possibility of a realignment of affective values and the related question as to the innate morality of powerful feelings belies any suggestion of a simple, antagonistic relationship between the two. And an understanding of the entangled nature of Wollstonecraft's disagreement with Rousseau over the structure of feelings actually makes it easier to see how she herself imagines the possibility of psychological reform.

Rousseau's posthumous and notorious *Confessions* (1782 and 1789) are as influential in Wollstonecraft's appreciation of Rousseau as are his life and his educational and philosophical writing. She sees the misery and libertinism of his life at one with the problems he addresses in his work. Her appreciation is, then, as much a critique of his sensibility as it is of his theory of education.[11] As in her attack on Burke in *Rights of Men* there is much to be gained by casting her eminent male adversaries as victims of a rakish sensibility. She is also painfully aware of the sham responses of literary fashion and the close proximity of the genius to the voluptuary. 'Men of wit and fancy', she instructs her reader in *Rights of Woman*, 'are often rakes; and fancy is the food of love.' Similarly, 'men of genius', she claims, 'have commonly weak, or to use a more fashionable phrase, delicate constitutions'.[12]

Wollstonecraft's claim is that Rousseau's work represents a lamentable and pernicious set of half-measures which, if carried out, would lead to the immorality and misery of his own life. Above all, his work is a tragic and blasphemous compromise. In order to save half the human race from its libidinous desires the other half must be denied any spiritual status. That their souls might be refined, women must be confined to the material world. The results of this compromise are even worse on a practical level. Far from promoting chastity, the curtailed and moderated behaviour of women which is advocated actually encourages and arouses sexual passion. Not only does his theory rest on a false spiritual premise, therefore, it also sponsors and initiates desire in the form of false refinement or 'coquettishness'. The exquisite thrill to be found in Rousseau's depiction of half-reluctant female sexual desire is a prime target of Wollstonecraft's invective. And her biographical reading of Rousseau's philosophy has him directly suffering the paradoxes and compromises of his thought. He is subject to the agonies of desire and all the voluptuousness of restraint. Instead of concurring with his view of the nature of desire, Wollstonecraft argues that the unattainability he bemoans is itself a product of his self-denial. His attempt to extricate himself from the problem is its cause, she suggests in a statement which reveals her own complex response to be a mixture of sympathy and critique:

But all Rousseau's errors in reasoning arose from sensibility, and sensibility to their charms women are very ready to forgive! When he should have reasoned he became impassioned, and reflection inflamed his imagination instead of enlightening his understanding. Even his virtues also led him farther astray; for, born with a warm constitution and lively fancy, nature carried him toward the other sex with such eager fondness, that he soon became lascivious. Had he given way to these desires, the fire would have extinguished itself in a natural manner; but virtue, and a romantic kind of delicacy, made him practise self-denial; yet, when fear, delicacy, or virtue, restrained him, he debauched his imagination, and reflecting on the sensations to which fancy gave force, he traced them in the most glowing colours, and sunk them deep into his soul. (*Rights of Woman*, *WW*, v, p. 160)

In identifying imagination as a major source of Rousseau's problem Wollstonecraft is not offering a simple diagnosis which has the benefit of hindsight – Rousseau himself sees the problem in the same light. What Wollstonecraft reacts against, in this respect, is the solution offered. To her, it clearly appears that Rousseau falls foul of one of his own paradoxes: arguing that one must compromise in order to attain happiness, Rousseau compromises his own idealism. Instead of achieving transparency he creates mystery. Exactly how Wollstonecraft differentiates herself from Rousseau in this respect is most significant for an understanding of her own work. Her weighing of future happiness against present 'content' involves a difficult renegotiation of sensibility and imagination in relation to a moral view.

Wollstonecraft would have found an interesting account of the relationship between sensibility, imagination, and religious sentiment in Jacques Necker's *De l'Importance des Opinions Religieuses*, a corrective to materialist scepticism which she translated for Joseph Johnson to publish in 1788. Even though its political implications may have been far from appealing (its opening section argues for a pervasive religious attitude to be adopted on the grounds that it makes people less critical of government) its moral scheme may have attracted Wollstonecraft. Addressing those who 'have sensibility' and therefore suffer from that 'painful inquietude' which is 'perpetually tormenting . . . and troubling those soft, tender affections which constitute your happiness', Necker provides the solution: thinking of God. He is optimistic in his enterprise, claiming that: 'Religious instructions have the peculiar advantage of seizing the imagination, and of interesting our sensibility'.[13] In particular, Necker can rely on the peculiar suitability of imagination to religious belief. Unlike 'the discoveries of [our] reason', imagination, he argues, 'excites us continually to action, by presenting to our eyes a great space, and by keeping us always at a certain distance from the object we have in view'.[14] Imagination is here the energetic force which allows for the possibility of belief. Its vagueness, the very fact that it is characterised by the quest for an object rather than the possession of an object, makes it the faculty most suited to thoughts of futurity. Whereas Rousseau links imagination with roving desire, Necker links it with an unspecific religious object. His claim is that this leads to ultimate bliss and makes for social stability. For Necker, it is important that imagination is a spur to moral action and that it is never self-satisfied by gratification in the present moment. When it has a sublime religious object it can lead to bliss instead of the misery of shifting desire: 'It is then, because that there is nothing limited in the ideas of happiness and duration, with which religious sentiments impress us, that our imagination is not forced to recoil on itself, when it is insensibly lost in the immensity of futurity.'[15] Unlike the materialist view, happiness is here not a thing of the present; it is a promise in the hereafter. Necker turns imagination's dangerous unspecificity to moral account and makes a virtue out of sensibility's 'painful inquietude'. Wollstonecraft would have recognised the common ground in this, even if she might be suspicious of its collusiveness with the forces of reaction. And her own engagement with sensibility finds it more difficult to escape the anguish of sensibility.

Wollstonecraft recognises in sensibility the potential to highlight the social capacity of feeling; or, more accurately, to draw attention to the social feelings rather than the private ones. In its penchant for sympathy and compassion, sensibility offers a possibility of harmonising society, of making emotion look like a positive bond between the classes. Susceptibility to feeling can thus be joined with active virtue; empathy can lead on to philanthropy.[16]

But sensibility can only perform a useful social service for Wollstonecraft if it is combined with intellectual forces. If it is only a limited materialism it can provide no escape from the dangers of egoism, and if it lacks an intellectual act of mind it is repugnant to her. True sensibility, as well as being virtuous, must also be original: part of the creative and genial spirits of individuality. It must also be an act of choice, a product of intellectual free-thinking. This explains the vehemence of her attack on Burke's sensibility in his *Reflections*. She sees his version of sensibility as a demeaning, slavish mentality. In *Rights of Men*, for example, she makes the following equation between commonsense and sensibility. For her, these two represent an arbitrary authority equivalent to the superstition of the *ancien regime*:

A kind of mysterious instinct is *supposed* to reside in the soul, that instantaneously discerns truth, without the tedious labour of ratiocination. This instinct, for I know not what other name to give it, has been termed *common sense*, and more frequently *sensibility*; and, by a kind of *indefeasible* right, it has been *supposed*, for rights of this kind are not easily proved, to reign paramount over the other faculties of the mind, and to be an authority from which there is no appeal. (*Rights of Men*, *WW*, v, p. 30)

This is sensibility in the service of arbitrary power, sensibility as a craven, unthinking adherence to things as they are.

Earlier in her career Wollstonecraft had reached different conclusions on the subject of natural and innate feelings and their connection with morality. In *Thoughts on the Education of Daughters* (1787), Wollstonecraft, like many others before her, defers to Locke's treatise on this subject. One of the first steps that parents must take, 'To be able to follow Mr Locke's system', she argues, is that they 'must have subdued their own passions'; and she is fully aware of the power such natural passions have. '[R]eason and duty together', she observes, 'have not so powerful an influence over human conduct, as instinct has in the brute creation.'[17] In other words, the selfish, natural feelings must be played down to make way for social and moral ones. This commonsensical strategic advice is soon followed by a fairly dogmatic assertion:

> It is, in my opinion, a well-proved fact, that principles of truth are innate. Without reasoning we assent to many truths; we feel their force, and artful sophistry can only blunt those feelings which nature has implanted in us as instinctive guards to virtue. (*Education of Daughters*, WW, IV, p. 9)

Here instinct is far from degrading; it is part of the moral scheme of things. However, when Wollstonecraft again suggests a relationship between instinct and sensibility later in the same work, she is careful to discriminate between the different areas over which such instinctive reaction and 'common humanity' have jurisdiction. By 'common humanity' she presumably means social identity, as opposed to the atomistic, biological individualism of other forms of sensibility: 'Common humanity points out the important duties of our station; but sensibility (a kind of instinct, strengthened by reflection) can only teach the numberless minute things which give pain or pleasure.'[18]

Instinct has no rightful authority as far as Wollstonecraft is concerned. As a measure of human action it is demeaning by comparison with reason. Reason is a divine attribute; instinct is a reminder of 'man's' brutish nature.

As *Thoughts on the Education of Daughters* suggests, Wollstonecraft's response to sensibility is complex because she is unwilling to dismiss its virtuous side. She realises the potential in joining feeling usefully with 'mind', and instead of single-mindedly opting for hard-headed rationality she characteristically draws a distinction between true and false versions of sensibility.[19] By arguing for a true delicacy of mind and a susceptibility to real feeling, Wollstonecraft immediately sets herself up as an exponent of natural reason. False sensibility is the product of society; it is artificial and characterised by hypocrisy. Her own positive version of sensibility is pushed out of the realm of social convention and construction into the realm of natural, unmediated truth and sincerity – the guise in which she sometimes comes forward in *Rights of Woman*. By removing herself from a false form of fashion she has to associate (like Paine) with a literal form of reason.

Sensibility provides a particularly difficult test case for Wollstonecraft's ideas of innate or cultivated knowledge. Not only does it raise the possibility or otherwise of the social usefulness and virtuousness of feeling, it also raises the issue of how much of human behaviour can be opened to improvement and be susceptible to rational awareness.

In *Rights of Men*, Wollstonecraft responds to Burke's *Reflections* with a dual attack on arbitrary authority and sensibility.[20] Burke's text reveals the pampered sensibility of its author which makes him subject to the prevailing political system. Wollstonecraft launches an assault on his notion of '*inbred* sentiments' which reveals her own priorities: 'The appetites are the only perfect inbred powers that I can discern; and they like instincts have a certain aim, they can be satisfied – but improveable reason has not yet discovered the perfection it may arrive at – God forbid!'.[21] The fixed and circumscribed nature of instincts and appetites, it would seem, is easily distinguished from the sublime infinity of 'improveable reason'. (One can also see the connection here between Wollstonecraft's reason and Rousseau's desire.) Her radical challenge to Burke's inbred sentiments – his psychological version of heredity – produces the same distinction between those aspects of the mind which are susceptible to moral improvement and those which are not:

Children are born ignorant, consequently innocent; the passions, are neither good nor evil dispositions, till they receive a direction, and either bound over the feeble barrier raised by a faint glimmering of unexercised reason, called conscience, or strengthen her wavering dictates till sound principles are deeply rooted, and able to cope with headstrong passions that often assume her awful form. What moral purpose can be answered by extolling good dispositions, as they are called, when these good dispositions are described as instincts: for instinct moves in a direct line to its ultimate end, and asks not for guide or support. But if virtue is to be acquired by experience, or taught by example, reason, perfected by reflection, must be the dictator of the whole host of passions, which produce a fructifying heat, but no light, that you would exalt into her place. (*Rights of Men*, *WW*, v, pp. 31–2)

The suggestion here – that instinctive passions are amoral and only become subject to moral judgement after their combination with reason – explains some of Wollstonecraft's hostility to fashionable sensibility. In arguing against Burke she commits herself to the view that virtue is absolutely a product of 'experience' and 'example'. There is no mention here of the innate morality of feeling broached in *Thoughts on the Education of Daughters*.

Wollstonecraft's seemingly modern concern for the socially constructed nature of gendered identity is produced by this historical distinction between divine reason and brutish instinct. This is a central concern of her political morality: the question of the individual's moral improvement or degradation. We have already seen how Wollstonecraft uses the verb 'embrutes' in a private context when she upbraids Imlay for not perceiving the important purifying force of imagination – a blindness she puts down to his being 'embruted by trade'.[22] Such a statement reminds us that, for all its radicalism, Wollstonecraft's culture is one of refinement, and it suggests a difficulty in accommodating economic forces – at least an emergent free-market commercialism – into her social and cultural ideal. Her highly charged use of the word 'embrute' is indicative: it emerges precisely at those points in her work where her ideal cultural vision is most under threat.

The metaphysical or religious force of Wollstonecraft's investment in the idea of brutishness can also be gauged by her response to Burke:

The power of exercising our understanding raises us above the brutes; and this exercise produces that 'primary morality,' which you term 'untaught feelings.'
If virtue be an instinct, I renounce all hope of immortality; and with it all the sublime reveries and dignified sentiments that have smoothed the rugged path of life: it is all a cheat, a lying vision. (*Rights of Men*, *WW*, v, p. 33)

While she polarises reason and feelings in this attack on Burkean custom, Wollstonecraft is equally alert to the dangers of a complacent rationality. She is unwilling to rule out altogether the experiential knowledge which comes from tumultuous feeling. This double castigation – of brutish instinct and cold rationality – is nicely captured in her measured reading of the Fourth Voyage of *Gulliver's Travels*:

ambition, love, hope, and fear, exert their wonted power, though we be convinced by reason that their present and most attractive promises are only lying dreams; but had the cold hand of circumspection damped each generous feeling before it had left any permanent character, or fixed some habit, what could be expected, but selfish prudence and reason just rising above instinct? Who that has read Dean Swift's disgusting description of the Yahoos, and insipid one of Houyhnhnm with a philosophical eye, can avoid seeing the futility of degrading passions, or making man rest in contentment? (*Rights of Woman*, *WW*, v, p. 181)

True to her philosophical reading of Swift's text, Wollstonecraft does not fall into the familiar trap of idealising the Houyhnhnms: the act of 'degrading' pertains to both Houyhnhnm and Yahoo. Her reading is clearly supported by religious belief: 'resting in contentment' denies her cherished prospect of advancing towards future immortality and promised bliss.

Wollstonecraft's belief in an exalted state rising above 'contentment' or subsistence is clearly evident in the following passage from *Letters Written in Sweden, Norway, and Denmark*. A life which deals with no more than the bare necessities is brutish. For a real 'social life' to take place people must be removed from the physical cares of the moment – they must have that 'imagination' which leads them to refinement and which enables them to fulfil their potential as God's accountable creatures:

> I did not immediately recollect that men who remain so near the brute creation, as only to exert themselves to find the food necessary to sustain life, have little or no imagination to call forth the curiosity necessary to fructify the faint glimmerings of mind which entitles them to rank as lords of the creation . . . their very curiosity appeared to me a proof of the progress they had made in refinement. Yes; in the art of living – in the art of escaping from the cares which embarrass the first steps towards the attainment of the pleasures of social life. (*Letters Written in Sweden, Norway, and Denmark*, WW, VI, p. 245)

In such a passage Wollstonecraft articulates precisely how her refined aesthetic is be linked to religious morality with the aid of imagination. Having attacked the limited definition of refinement within a Burkean notion of aristocratic culture, Wollstonecraft creates her own more expansive moral version of it. Her much more metaphysical version of refinement also expands the definition of the aesthetic into 'the art of living' and 'the pleasures of social life'.

'Refinement' for Wollstonecraft involves moral purification. The fact that she writes of a refinement of feelings in terms of 'true' and 'false', weakness and strength, might obscure this. In *Rights of Woman* she frequently draws attention to the enfeebling power of false refinement and sensibility, an insistent tactic which seems to suit her rationalist persona. 'Gentlewomen', she argues at one point, 'are too indolent to be actively virtuous, and are softened rather than refined by civilisation';[23] the distinction reminds us that her brand of refinement claims to result in moral strength. This is straightforward enough – one can see how avoidance of effete and debilitating passions will lead to fortitude and self-discipline. Once again, if understanding and feeling are separated, the position is clear: false refinement gives free rein to dangerous emotions; true refinement keeps them in check. From this point of view, Wollstonecraft consistently argues for a sense of refinement in which sentiment prevails over passion and in which delicacy is not fragile, but powerful. She rails against the chaos of strong feelings not simply as a rationalist who wishes to dismiss them altogether, but as a moralist who wishes to appropriate their affective power for her own concerns.

The difficulty involved in this act of appropriation can be gauged from her struggle with Rousseau over the definition of love in *Rights of Woman*. It is a definition which has very specific implications for her version of imagination. She begins with a claim of love's unearthly status: 'Love, such as the glowing pen of genius has traced, exists not on earth, or only resides in those exalted, fervid imaginations that have sketched such dangerous pictures.' She then makes a characteristic distinction between pleasure and virtue, arguing that: 'Virtue and pleasure are not . . . so nearly allied in this life as some eloquent writers have laboured to prove' which leads her into an attack on the visionary, delusory promise of love provided by the literary imagination. Though this is most certainly an attack, Wollstonecraft concentrates on the idealising power of imagination to such an extent that, at times, her attitude might be mistaken for one of celebration:

An imagination of this vigorous cast can give existence to insubstantial forms, and stability to the shadowy reveries which the mind naturally falls into when realities are found vapid. It can then depict love with celestial charms, and dote on the grand ideal object – it can imagine a degree of mutual affection that shall refine the soul, and not expire when it has served as a 'scale to heavenly'; and, like devotion, make it absorb every meaner affection and desire. (*Rights of Woman*, WW, v, pp. 142–43)

Though we are constantly reminded of a controlling fantasy/reality antithesis (evident here in the word 'dote'), the very nature of imagination – its propensity towards immateriality and idealisation – makes it attractive. As the passage develops, the overriding distinction between virtue and pleasure takes second place to that between powerful and feeble feelings. The paragraph concludes with a rejoinder to those who would decry such 'reveries': 'they, therefore, who complain of the delusions of passion, do not recollect that they are exclaiming against a strong proof of the immortality of the soul'. By this point the fantasy/reality antithesis is by no means as sure as we may have thought. Realising that these most ideal delusions are not to be the main object of her attack, Wollstonecraft adds a corrective. Her targets are not 'strong, persevering passions', but 'romantic wavering feelings'. She wishes to guard against those 'paradisiacal reveries' which are the 'effects of idleness', not those which are the products of a 'lively fancy'.

To judge by her handling of imagination here one might think that her concern was exclusively pragmatic, firmly based on the reality of the present, but, as is already apparent, the separation of idealism from realistic practicalities is indicative of a problem. So, too, is the valuation of the two kinds of imaginative vision: one the product of powerful minds, the other the vain amusement of the feeble-minded. Wollstonecraft's work contains problematic conceptions of the specially gifted individual – prototypes of the suffering Romantic artist.

Nowhere is Wollstonecraft's admission of her belief in powerful feelings, including the passions, so evident as in her comments on creative genius. The genial spirits of the artist provide her with a particularly strong justification of such affective power, even when it cannot be controlled and adequately accounted for. A Romantic conception of creativity lets in an ambivalent force of feelings. In *Letters from Sweden, Norway, and Denmark*, for example, she makes a distinction which might surprise a reader of *Rights of Woman*. Here powerful feeling is above rectitude. It is of mysterious origin and cannot be precisely defined:

He is a man with a great portion of common sense, and heart, – yes, a warm heart. This is not the first time I have remarked heart without sentiment: they are distinct. The former depends on the rectitude of the feelings, on truth of sympathy: these characters have more tenderness than passion; the latter has a higher source; call it imagination, genius, or what you will, it is something very different. (*Letters Written in Sweden, Norway, and Denmark*, WW, VI, pp. 293–94)

In her writings on creative genius Wollstonecraft sees feeling as primary and certain. Its truthfulness seems self-evident from its power and its naturalness. And not surprisingly, she is eager to distinguish it from the artifice and hypocrisy which she associates with the tag 'romantic'. She is always alert to this word, realising its potential to drain her work of its hard-won intellectual status. Her estimate of the contemporary literary scene in the following passage is thus coloured as much by the vitriol of self-defence as it is by a passionate belief in the simple force of genial passions:

From observing several cold romantic characters I have been led to confine the term romantic to one definition – false, or rather artificial, feelings. Works of genius are read with a prepossession in their favour, and sentiments imitated, because they were fashionable and pretty, and not because they were forcibly felt.

In modern poetry the understanding and memory often fabricate the pretended effusions of the heart, and romance destroys all simplicity; which, in works of taste, is but a synonymous word for truth. This romantic spirit has extended to our prose, and scattered artificial flowers over the barren heath; or a mixture of verse and prose producing the strangest incongruities. (*Rights of Men*, WW, V, p. 29)

Typically, the heat of passion is reserved for the poet and the painter whom she invests with her own Promethean metaphors. Working with 'natural affections and unsophisticated feelings' these artists have the power of 'vibrating with each emotion' which enables them to paint with 'a pencil of fire'.[24]

These analogies of fire illuminate Wollstonecraft's complex mixture of enlightened rationalism and emotion. As in the case of Paine, a natural rationalism has little problem accommodating powerful emotion. There is more difficulty in Wollstonecraft's case however, because she goes beyond claims of truthfulness, naturalness, and simplicity towards a mystification of individualistic temperament and sensibility. The artist who suffers the shocks and agitations of emotion also has an affinity with solitude and has somehow managed to rise above base materiality. An idea of the artist as mystical visionary is not very far away: 'The generality of people cannot see or feel poetically, they want fancy, and therefore fly from solitude in search of sensible objects; but when an author lends them his eyes they can see as he saw, and be amused by images they could not select, though lying before them.' With a peculiar concentration on affective response, Wollstonecraft claims that 'Shakespeare never grasped the airy dagger into a nerveless hand, nor did Milton tremble when he led Satan forth from the confines of his dreary prison'. The reason for such control is not emotional detachment – far from it. The explanation is that 'they must have had iron frames'.[25] Despite the obvious instability of genial feelings – their oscillation between agony and joy – Wollstonecraft has no doubts about attesting to their reality. Though such feelings are individualistic, experienced in solitude, unstable, immaterial, and momentary, she is convinced of their reality. As the heroine of *Mary* claims in a 'rhapsody', sensibility provides ineffable moments of spiritual expansion tinged with exquisite sadness:

Sensibility is the most exquisite feeling of which the human soul is susceptible: when it pervades us we feel happy; and could it last unmixed, we might form some conjecture of the bliss of those paradisiacal days when the obedient passions were under the domain of reason . . . It is this quickness, this delicacy of feeling, which enables us to relish the sublime touches of the poet, and the painter; it is this, which expands the soul . . . (*Mary*, *WW*, I, p. 59)

Such moments support a belief in the hereafter; they provide intimations of immortality. As is often the case with these moments, their ineffable quality – 'it is only to be felt; it escapes discussion' – is not solely a result of the primacy given to feeling: language is considered to be inadequate for other reasons as well. So, too, their sadness, and indeed their transitoriness, provide an awareness of the limitations of mortality, a resigned acceptance of material shackles: resignation because the melancholy of such moments is assuaged by their promise. 'Sensibility is indeed the foundation of all our happiness,'[26] Mary says, leaving unspoken the fact that happiness is elsewhere and hereafter. Sensibility's delicious melancholy is triggered by the difference between temporal and eternal.

Much of Wollstonecraft's supposed puritanical suppression of pleasure and her correctives of contemporary libertinism are underscored by the logic to be found in such intimations. Though her polemic is addressed to the malpractices of the present – to conduct, manners, taste, as well as revolution – it is not simply pragmatic and materialist. In the case of *Rights of Woman* this is difficult to see if one assumes that Wollstonecraft is engaged in an act of ventriloquism; that she is adopting the macho language of the Enlightenment rationalist and suppressing her feelings. But the assumption that reason is completely antithetical to emotion is too stark to do justice to the particular historical moment and the configuration of discourses in which Wollstonecraft's texts are situated.

For all her awareness of the revolutionary moment in which she wrote, Wollstonecraft's texts consistently bear witness to a Christian futurity. Much of her writing on women is concerned to reveal how they are confined in the present moment. This has much potential for a radical polemic which would argue that the present must be demolished to make way for a new order. But it is also part of her wide-ranging argument about the way in which women are continually distracted from issues of real importance. False modesty is a poor substitute for the ultimate goal of virtue which is eternal, not present, happiness. It can seem that Wollstonecraft engages only in a tactical ploy with her enemies when she accuses them of reducing women to worldly beings, of denying them the status of 'accountable creatures'. To judge of the rest of her writings, though, one would have to accept that, far from toying with religious arguments, she is seriously attached to them. For example, when she reveals her investment in the future it is clearly prefaced by a statement of strong religious faith:

A curse it might be reckoned, if the whole of our existence were bounded by our continuance in this world; for why should the gracious fountain of life give us passions, and the power of reflecting, only to imbitter our days and inspire us with mistaken notions of dignity? Why should he lead us from love of ourselves to the sublime emotions which the discovery of his wisdom and goodness excites, if these feelings were not set in motion to improve our nature, of which they make a part, and render us capable of enjoying a more godlike portion of happiness? . . . I build my belief on the perfection of God.

Rousseau exerts himself to prove that all *was* right originally: a crowd of authors that all *is* now right: and I, that all will *be* right. (*Rights of Woman*, WW, v, p. 84)

For Wollstonecraft, then, the present is at worst seriously flawed, at best provisional. 'Life', she claims in *Rights of Woman*, 'is merely an education, a state of infancy' in which women should be 'preparing . . . [their] affections for a more exalted state'.[27] One might improve one's lot, but the pursuit of happiness should be qualified by an awareness of what is possible. Women 'ought never to forget', she argues 'that life yields not the felicity which can satisfy an immortal soul'. This might sound as if desire specifically, and passions more generally (happiness more philosophically), are to be repressed and deferred by making them prospective pleasures under a strict religious control. But Wollstonecraft's strategy is by no means as simple or as clear as this. She is well aware of the dangers of opting out of the present, of putting off action by hoping for eternal ecstasy. False forms of hope are familiar to her.

As we have already seen, Wollstonecraft is much concerned with the way modish behaviour has supplanted morality. According to the false fashions of her age, the manners and conduct, especially of women, are now to be dictated by the pleasures of the moment. As a result of false refinement 'the rational hopes of futurity are all to be sacrificed to render women an object of desire for a *short* time'. The corrosive and self-defeating power of women's emotions originates from the same insistence on the moment: 'Most of the evils of life arise from a desire of present enjoyment which outruns itself' – a statement which recalls forcibly Rousseau's agony of the unattainability of desire. The prevailing system of manners dissipates women's power. Women may be 'degraded by the same propensity to enjoy the present moment' as men, but they may also be deflected by the familiar psychological deferral by which they are able to live only vicariously through their children: 'Her children have her love, and her brightest hopes are beyond the grave, where her imagination often strays.' And in *Rights of Woman* Wollstonecraft swaps one peep into futurity for another when she severely questions the morality of another pastime of women: fortune-telling. 'Do you acknowledge', she demands of her reader,'that the power of looking into futurity and seeing things that are not as if they were, is an attribute of the Creator?'[28]

Significantly, Wollstonecraft's awareness of false hopes extends beyond crystal-ball gazing. She also makes it clear at one point in *Rights of Woman* that her attack on the present and her investment in the future are a redressing of the balance. The present is not to be given up. Her argument is philosophically precise. This search for happiness leads to futurity, but the road to improvement is here and now. Morality partakes of reality:

Men will not become moral when they only build airy castles in a future world to compensate for the disappointments which they meet with in this; if they turn their thoughts from relative duties to religious reveries . . . (*Rights of Woman*, *WW*, v, p. 184)

In support of such engaged morality, and in her most exultant and militant vein, Wollstonecraft can come forward in the same work with a revolutionary clarion-call worthy of any of her contemporaries: 'Whilst reason raises man above the brutal herd, and death is big with promises, they alone are subject to blind authority who have no reliance on their own strength! They are free – who will be free!'[29] Rather than a religious put-down, this is characteristic in its keeping the three elements in the equation together: reason, religion, and liberation.

Typically, at the point where religious hope manifests itself in Wollstonecraft's writing, Enlightenment reason is shown to be inadequate and sublimity enters. Such hope even defines itself precisely in terms of reason's incapacity. Far from being denigrated for its incapacity, reason in this relationship is still celebrated for the role it plays in a reciprocal act of knowledge. Starting with a word which resonates oddly with the gender base of her argument Wollstonecraft, in *Rights of Woman*, offers another justification for her belief in the hereafter:

The stamen of immortality, if I may be allowed the phrase, is the perfectibility of human reason; for, were man created perfect, or did a flood of knowledge break in upon him, when he arrived at maturity, that precluded error, I should doubt whether his existence would be continued after the dissolution of the body. But in the present state of things, every difficulty in morals that escapes from human discussion, and equally baffles the investigation of profound thinking, and the lightning glance of genius, is an argument on which I build my belief of the immortality of the soul. Reason is, consequently, the simple power of improvement, or, more properly speaking, of discerning truth . . . the nature of reason must be the same in all, if it be an emanation of divinity, the tie that connects the creation with the Creator ... (*Rights of Woman*, *WW*, v, p. 122)

Despite maintaining that reason is simply and straightforwardly a measure of the connection between creature and creator, Wollstonecraft regards it as an inferior, if worthy, form of knowledge. It is hardly a spark of divinity. It cannot compare with the sublimity of divine power.

Wollstonecraft's much reiterated belief that reason alone among the human faculties is sacred, is seriously challenged by the way religion figures as a sublime object. So, too, the religious aspect of her project is pressurised by her belief in refinement:

That civilisation, that the cultivation of the understanding, and refinement of the affections, naturally make a man religious, I am proud to acknowledge. – What else can fill the aching void in the heart, that human pleasures, human friendships can never fill? (*Rights of Men*, *WW*, v, p. 39)

This is typical of Wollstonecraft's predicament. The common-place belief in rationalistic control of the mind to be found in *Thoughts on the Education of Daughters* – 'our passions will not contribute much to our bliss, till they are under the dominion of reason, and till that reason is enlightened and improved' – is accompanied by its solution that: 'The sighing will cease, and all tears will be imped away by that Being in whose presence there is fullness of joy.'[30] The gap between worldly improvement and the religious attainment of perfection is typically elided.

Improvement is a moral scheme in which the individual is geared up to a self-conscious and shared process. Reason is both individually located and universally shared. Despite being allied to an intransigent form of individualism, the sentiments of trembling sensibility must be weighed against social conformity. Not only are the visions of genius fitful, they are also original. They are authentic as suffering and as vision. Imagination is thus both delusion and insight. It might stand outside the gradualist programme of enlightenment, but it is integral to the moral quest for future happiness.

III

The promises of futurity glimpsed by the isolated individual consciousness are complemented by Wollstonecraft's explicit commentaries on the progress of history. Her extensive considerations on the connection between government and civilisation are to be found in her significantly titled *An Historical and Moral View of the Origin and the Progress of the French Revolution*. And her most interesting observations here come by way of reflection aside from her detailed narrative. Like Burke and many other commentators on the French Revolution and its sources in the structure of French society, Wollstonecraft points out the isolation of the nobility. Unlike England, France possesses no correcting mixture of monied and landed interest:

> In Italy and France, for example, where the mind dared to exercise itself only to form the taste, the nobility were, in the strictest sense of the word, a cast, keeping aloof from the people; whilst in England they inter-mingled with the commercial . . . This monied interest, from which political improvement first emanates, was not yet formed in France . . . (*French Revolution*, WW, VI, p. 70)

Such 'taste' is repugnant to Wollstonecraft for it is not only limited to a narrow social group; it is also a self-centred and degenerating form of egotism. 'The french', she argues, 'were arrived . . . at that degree of false refinement, which makes every man, in his own eyes, the centre of the world.'[31] On the grounds of removing such 'gross selfishness' and 'complete depravity' she feels confident in recommending radical social change.

Somewhat surprisingly, when Wollstonecraft refers to the French ennui that gives rise to this insulated taste she does not dismiss it, but sees it as a harbinger of 'improvement'. In this respect, taste is part of a cultural progression. It remains a mark of civilisation despite its immoral and degenerate tendencies. From the potentially decadent impulse for variety (in order to stave off ennui, itself a product of idleness and depravity) comes a contact with that refined culture which has something to offer. And, typically, the figure of the literary genius rises again:

> Still in the same degree as the refinement of sentiment, and the improvement of taste advance, the company of celebrated literary characters is sought after with avidity; and from the prevalence of fashion, the empire of wit succeeds the reign of formal insipidity, after the squeamish palate has been rendered delicate even by the nauseous banquets of voluptuousness. (*French Revolution*, WW, VI, p. 225)

Out of a false delicacy comes forth a true one. Similarly, she writes of the ennui of the French court replacing 'chivalrous and gothic tournaments' with 'sentiment' to leave the way open for higher things. As she puts it: 'the reign of philosophy succeeded that of the imagination'. In Wollstonecraft's moral progress of civilisation imagination is given an early and therefore primitive position. She can invoke the savage in order to score a point against false forms of refinement. This squares with her claims to a natural simplicity, of course, but it is at odds with her view of civilisation. The savage, she claims, is 'brave, hospitable, and magnanimous'. Because he has 'surrendered . . . his rights the civilised man has lost the noble qualities of the heart'. Similarly, she is willing to argue that 'a barbarian, considered as a moral being, is an angel compared with the refined villain of artificial life'. Wollstonecraft's view is that the stages in the process of civilisation are marked by perfection in the different fields of human endeavour. In her scheme of things the arts are at the bottom of the list and the achievement of the ancients is open to question, though she grants the latter a 'savage grandeur of the imagination'[32] and offers a rather disparaging assessment of the Greek tragedies in which it is easy to gauge her distance from Burke:

The sublime terrour, with which they fill the mind, may amuse, nay, delight; but whence comes the improvement? Besides, uncultivated minds are the most subject to feel astonishment, which is often only another name for sublime sensations. (*French Revolution, WW*, VI, p. 112)

The moral effect outweighs any merely aesthetic experience. In this 'youth of the world', she argues, 'the imagination alone was cultivated, and the subordinate understanding merely exercised to regulate the taste, without extending to its grand employ, the forming of principles'.[33] Her criticism is not restricted to the intrinsic limitations of taste: she is equally aware of its social elitism. 'Civilisation', she claims, 'has hitherto been only a perfection of the arts . . . tending more to embellish the superiour rank of society, than to improve the situation of all mankind.' According to her egalitarian view of government: 'it is a palpable errour to suppose, that men of every class are not equally susceptible of common improvement'.[34]

If the history of human improvement has hitherto been the history of partial cultivation of taste, Wollstonecraft clearly sees herself heralding the dawn of a new age which shall replace the arts as the forces of improvement with philosophy, morals, politics, and economics. She addresses herself particularly to these last two. Not surprisingly, the event which she credits as having made this substitution apparent is the French Revolution. When reflecting on how the Revolution has been mishandled, she characteristically argues that gradual change is necessary for any such substitution to take place:

The improvements in philosophy and morals have been extremely tardy. All sudden revolutions have been as suddenly overturned, and things thrown back below their former state. The improvements in the science of politics have been still more slow in their advancement than those of philosophy and morals, but the revolution in France has been progressive. It was a revolution in the minds of men; and not only demanded a new system of government to be adapted to that change. (*French Revolution*, *WW*, VI, p. 183)

The most urgent need of the present political upheaval and the one thing which could have stopped the degeneration of a major symbolic libertarian event into only another form of tyranny is a new science of government and economics: the emerging discipline of political economy. Wollstonecraft demands its proper development. To be included within its purview are the material, moral, and ultimately heavenly requirements of humanity:

Can it then be expected, that the science of politics and finance, the most important, and most difficult of all human improvements; a science which involves the passions, tempers and manners of men and nations, estimates their wants, maladies, comforts, happiness, and misery, and computes the sum of good or evil flowing from social institutions; will not require the same gradations, and advance by steps equally slow to that state of perfection necessary to secure the sacred rights of every human creature? (*French Revolution*, *WW*, VI, p. 183)

It is precisely because she senses the appropriateness and force of political economy that Wollstonecraft argues for such an accommodating and moral version of it. Not for her the narrow functional utilitarian discipline which some of her contemporaries were about to produce. The vehemence of her commentaries against trade and commerce must be read with this in mind.

In common with many advocates of the French Revolution Wollstonecraft confidently attacks the representation of landed hereditary property. Using one of her most negatively charged verbs, she declares in *Rights of Men* that: 'Hereditary property sophisticates the mind'[35] and in *Letters from Sweden, Norway, and Denmark* she pronounces: 'In short, under whatever point of view I consider society, it appears, to me, that an advocation of property is the root of all evil'. Whereas Burke had attempted to put forward an argument to mix the landed interest and the new monied interest so that the dangerous energy of the latter might be contained, Wollstonecraft attacks both forces, but is under no illusion as to which is the most powerful: 'England and America owe their liberty to commerce, which created a new species of power to undermine the feudal system. But let them beware of the consequence; the tyranny of wealth is still more galling and debasing than that of rank.'[36] In *French Revolution* she sees the power of wealth and commerce, especially when it functions as a mock version of the previous order, as a retrograde step in the civilising and improving process of society. Wollstonecraft could well foresee the extent to which industrialised capitalism could dictate a negative economy of the mind:

> The destructive influence of commerce... The most pernicious, perhaps, is its producing an aristocracy of wealth, which degrades mankind, by making them only exchange savageness for tame servility, instead of acquiring the urbanity of improved reason. Commerce also, overstocking a country with people, obliges the majority to become manufacturers rather than husbandmen; and then the division of labour, solely to enrich the proprietor, renders the mind entirely inactive. The time which, a celebrated writer says, is sauntered away, in going from one part of an employment to another, is the very time that preserves the man from degenerating into a brute. (*French Revolution*, *WW*, VI, pp. 233–4)

This perception of the degenerating power of wealth and its ability to swap one form of injustice for a more deeply structured one, explains her tirades against the brutalising effect of the 'low cunning of trade'.[37]

As we have already seen, Wollstonecraft launches one of her most vehement attacks on trade in a private letter to Imlay where she distinguishes its demeaning, immoral influence from the purifying power of an exalted imagination. Imagination is here the unique hallmark of the divinity of the human mind, and that which makes us accountable creatures capable of improvement. It is 'the great distinction of our nature' which produces 'all those fine sympathies that lead to rapture'. It proceeds by means of social sympathy, not by a leisured calculation of the 'many comforts society affords'.[38]

Wollstonecraft's vision of progress articulated in her history of the French Revolution implies the replacement of imagination as a sign of a particular and exclusive aristocratic culture – a narrowly defined notion of taste – by a vision of imagination as an expansive moral capacity which can control economic and technological developments and stop them degenerating into a new aristocracy of wealth. Faced with the power of a new economics, Wollstonecraft appeals to that most equivocal of faculties: the one in her view which can encourage the most debilitating and debauched forms of false refinement, and changes it into the one that can provide us with the greatest hopes and insights while we make our preparations, not our utilitarian 'calculations', for happiness.

IV

For Wollstonecraft's hopes are articulated in the shadow of the burgeoning ideology of utilitarianism. And in her moments of doubt she encounters the spectre of that ideology's materialism. Nowhere in Wollstonecraft's work is the fluctuation between perfectibilist optimism and the threat of degeneration so extreme as in her *Letters Written During a Short Residence in Sweden, Norway, and Denmark*. What makes this text even more exceptional is that it exposes how this threat actually lurks within Wollstonecraft's vision of improvement. As her letters announce the possibility of a new self which combines reason and sensibility,[39] they contemplate the biological determinism of the species and the possibility of a disinterested realm of nature divorced from any idea of creation. In this respect Wollstonecraft prefigures that crisis of the utilitarian imagination most commonly associated with John Stuart Mill and which I shall be examining in chapter six. To imagine the end of social improvement exposes the insignificance, expendibility, and even the surplus nature of the individual self.

The seventeenth of her *Letters Written in Sweden, Norway, and Denmark* has become the focus of the study of Wollstonecraft's involvement with the masculine aesthetic of the Romantic sublime and its capacity to operate at the expense of woman. Here she describes her reaction to the famous 'cascade' at Trollhatten:

Arrived at Trolhaettae, I must own that the first view of the cascade disappointed me: and the sight of the works, as they advanced, though a grand proof of human industry, was not calculated to warm the fancy. I, however, wandered about; and at last coming to the conflux of the various cataracts, rushing from different falls, struggling with the huge masses of rock, and rebounding from the profound cavities, I immediately retracted, acknowledging that it was indeed a grand object. A little island stood in the midst, covered with firs, which, by dividing the torrent, rendered it more picturesque; one half appearing to issue from a dark cavern, that fancy might easily imagine a vast fountain, throwing up its waters from the very centre of the earth.

I gazed I know not how long, stunned with the noise; and growing giddy with only looking at the never-ceasing tumultuous motion, I listened, scarcely conscious where I was, when I observed a boy, half obscured by the sparkling foam, fishing under the impending rock on the other side. How he had descended I could not perceive; nothing like human footsteps appeared; and the horrific craggs seemed to bid defiance even to the goat's activity. It looked like an abode only fit for the eagle, though in its crevices some pines darted up their spiral heads; but they only grew near the cascade; every where else sterility itself reigned with dreary grandeur; for the huge grey massy rocks which probably had been torn asunder by some dreadful convulsion of nature, had not even their first covering of a little cleaving moss. There were so many appearances to excite the idea of chaos, that, instead of admiring the canal and the works, great as they are termed, and little as they appear, I could not help regretting that such a noble scene had not been left in all its solitary sublimity. Amidst the awful roaring of the impetuous torrents, the noise of human instruments, and the bustle of workmen, even the blowing up of the rocks, when grand masses trembled in the darkened air – only resembled the insignificant sport of children. (*Letters Written in Sweden, Norway, and Denmark*, WW, VI, pp. 316–17)

As other commentators have indicated,[40] Wollstonecraft's engagement with this sublime moment is fraught with evasion, and it contains a sense of dislocation and disappointment which extends beyond the conventional reaction of sublime reverie. Even for a text which characteristically blends social critique, topography, commerce, and romance, this is a particularly mixed moment. In Wollstonecraft's terms 'nature' here is being measured against 'art'. The motive for visiting Trollhatten, as Wollstonecraft indicates in the first paragraph of the letter, is a mixture of tourist aesthetic and social improvement: 'I wished not only to see the cascade, but to observe the progress of the stupendous attempt to form a canal through the rocks.'[41]

When Wollstonecraft informs her reader that 'I could not help regretting that such a noble scene had not been left in all its solitary sublimity' one might be tempted to read this as a sentimental attachment to the sublime aesthetic's demand for purity, but the capacity of the sublime to diminish the idea of human progress is perhaps a more disquieting and compelling aspect of her text. What promises to be powerfully mysterious – the fanciful 'throwing up' of 'waters from the very centre of the earth' (which Coleridge could appropriate in 'Kubla Khan'), the mysterious, seemingly impossible, manifestation of the boy on the ledge, and the apparent disconnection between the falls – ultimately gives way at the end of Wollstonecraft's account to the threat of chaos and its capacity to put in doubt the very idea of improvement.

The unease manifest in this passage is characteristic of the *Letters Written in Sweden, Norway, and Denmark* as a whole as they oscillate between the utopian promise of social improvement and the threat of regression. The power of the sublime is here indicated not so much by its exclusive purity as by its threat to the power of progress. Rather than making itself available as a discrete aesthetic moment, Wollstonecraft's text observes nature serving a historical process of civilisation and social improvement. From this perspective (which might jar with the eco-sensitive late twentieth-century reader), the landscape is a commodity which serves the growth of population and the development of society. Equally, Wollstonecraft's text enjoys the 'solitary sublimity', the otherness of 'wastes', which lies beyond the use-value of progress and population.

The dizzy rapture characteristic of such self-threatening moments is figured as a conflict between two kinds of potentially degenerative power: the chaos of the sublime in the form of an impassive, dehumanising nature and the precariousness of economic development which imposes itself on, or uses, nature, but which itself, as the power of commerce, is capable of 'embruting' entrepreneurs like Gilbert Imlay. Throughout the text Wollstonecraft warns against 'the tyranny of trade' and, for her, 'commerce' is a mark of civilisation which is always precarious, always capable of being 'sophisticated' by luxury. As she observes Norway's merchants eroding the power of the aristocracy Wollstonecraft, with her eye on the United States, is quick to sound a cautionary note: 'the tyranny of wealth is still more galling and debasing than that of rank.'[42] As the text continues, the debasing capacity of commerce and trade colours her accounts of Copenhagen and Hamburg. And, of course, the wider moral critique of the luxury and false sophistication produced by trade is inflected throughout by Wollstonecraft's commercial engagement with Imlay. Within this critique, the body becomes a particularly charged site of meaning so that at one point the moral degeneration of trade coincides powerfully with Wollstonecraft's metaphors of death. While, as we have seen, Wollstonecraft may 'bury herself in the woods', she hopes that Imlay will 'shake off the vile dust that obscures [him].'[43]

Letters Written in Sweden, Norway, and Denmark articulates the relationship between the individuated body and the social body in a variety of ways. The body is considered, by turns, as a healthy resource, the tremulous surface of an authentic sensibility, a site of emotional vulnerability, and, ultimately, the dust of decomposition.[44] For the way in which the body is situated within this oscillatory combination of cool, abstractive observation and warm, effusive sensibility focuses the text's exploration of the construction and articulation of a self in response to political economy.

On a more general level, *Letters Written in Sweden, Norway, and Denmark* seems to subscribe, for the most part, to the widespread Enlightenment view (following David Hume and Adam Smith) that the healthy state of a nation is measured by the capacity of its population to reproduce. Healthy bodies are an indicator of a healthy state. It is a view which optimistically assumes that reproduction is itself a positive power, and not a problem.[45] 'The increasing population of the earth must necessarily tend to its improvement, as the means of existence are multiplied by invention,'[46] Wollstonecraft confidently announces in her ninth letter. Despite this, there are some disturbing passages in Wollstonecraft's text which put such optimism in doubt by posing the death of the individual body against the longer process of historical progress. Here the improvement of the individual meets the amelioration of society head on. The perfectibilist drive of Wollstonecraft's texts, the promise of continuous improvement, depends upon an act of faith that the individual will not simply be martyred to the larger cause, but that the individual's moral improvement will itself continue, thanks to the promise of eternal happiness. In these remarkable passages there is a sense of the disgusting, degrading, and even entropic capacity of the body – as well as its annihilation.[47] The unnerving and epistemologically shocking prospect of unresponsive nature is connected to the threat of the dying body as Wollstonecraft's *Letters Written in Sweden, Norway, and Denmark* dares to imagine both nature and the individual body as nothing more than mechanistic dust. Such potentially impious imaginings are testimony to the innovative nature of this text: they represent the dark entropic underside of Wollstonecraft's perfectibilist optimism and they put in doubt her vision of a providential process of history.

Perhaps the most interesting and sustained of these passages stems from Wollstonecraft's visit to the church of St Mary in the ancient Norwegian town of Tonsberg where she finds embalmed bodies in 'a little recess full of coffins' and describes them as 'the most disgusting image of death'.[48] The effect upon her is to produce a comparison between a necessary and appropriate sense of historical process (such as one might find in the Enlightenment topos of the ruin with all its associated eighteenth-century reverberations);[49] and the seemingly pointless and futile process of time registered upon the body. The best, but misguided, efforts of the embalmers of Tonsberg clearly challenge Wollstonecraft's sense of history, religion, and personal relationship. And she reacts not only as an intellectual, but as a body:

The contemplation of noble ruins produces a melancholy that exalts the mind. – We take a retrospect of the exertions of man, the fate of empires and their rulers; and marking the grand destruction of ages, it seems the necessary change of time leading to improvement. – Our very soul expands, and we forget our littleness; how painfully brought to our recollection by such vain attempts to snatch from decay what is destined so soon to perish. Life, what art thou? Where goes this breath? this *I*, so much alive? In what element will it mix, giving or receiving fresh energy? – What will break the enchantment of animation? – For worlds, I would not see a form I loved – embalmed in my heart – thus sacrilegiously handled! – Pugh! my stomach turns. – Is this all the distinction of the rich in the grave? – They had better quietly allow the scythe of equality to mow them down with the common mass, than struggle to become a monument of the instability of human greatness . . . (*Letters Written in Sweden, Norway, and Denmark*, WW, VI, p. 279)

This is the underside of 'population': the hideous prospect of the ruin of the body. Wollstonecraft's own text reciprocates in kind as her 'stomach turns'.

After a paragraph of absorbed detail which considers the quality of the mummies' teeth, nails, skin, and wrappings, the text continues with a troubled rumination on the likelihood of the day of judgement and a speculation on the form the body might take in a future life:

I feel a conviction that we have some perfectible principle in our present vestment, which will not be destroyed just as we begin to be sensible of improvement; and I care not what habit it next puts on, sure that it will be wisely formed to suit a higher state of existence. (*Letters Written in Sweden, Norway, and Denmark*, WW, VI, p. 279)

Since this last statement is prefaced with just a dash and 'a God bless you!', there is an ambiguous link between the embalmed corpses and her 'anonymous' correspondent who is finally invoked at the end of the letter with the promise of the writer's affections: 'I therefore assure you that I am your's, wishing that the temporary death of absence may not endure longer than is absolutely necessary.'[50] Characteristically, the text conflates time and space; sensibility mixes Enlightenment optimism with religious piety, humour with the agony of romance.

Wollstonecraft's reaction after seeing the soldiers at 'the residence of prince Charles of Hesse-Cassel' in Schleswig leads her to a speculation on the harsh reality of the divine force in nature which she describes as 'an old opinion of mine'. There is an insistence on the infirmity of flesh here which reinforces the strong sense of disgust at the decaying mummies of Tonsberg. Here a vision of the species, as biologically productive and successful, and consistent with Enlightenment optimism, has to be reinforced with what looks like an increasingly desperate belief in God's wider plan. Attention seems firmly focused on the casualties. However, matching the individual experience with the larger utopian or heavenly project seems to be more difficult. Here the casualties are in danger of having no meaning:

> it is the preservation of the species, not of individuals, which appears to be the design of the Deity throughout the whole of nature. Blossoms come forth only to be blighted; fish lay their spawn where it will be devoured: and what a large portion of the human race are born merely to be swept prematurely away. Does not this waste of budding life emphatically assert, that it is not men, but man, whose preservation is so necessary to the completion of the grand plan of the universe? Children peep into existence, suffer, and die; men play like moths about a candle, and sink into the flame: war, and 'the thousand ills which flesh is heir to,' mow them down in shoals, whilst the more cruel prejudices of society palsies existence, introducing not less sure, though slower decay. (*Letters Written in Sweden, Norway, and Denmark*, *WW*, VI, p. 336)

Such an intense vision of the decaying body exposes a deeper level of anxiety about believing in a beneficent nature. If nature is beneficent only in its general principles and, consequently, treats particular specimens or actual individuals as expendable, faith might be seriously challenged. Wollstonecraft's text takes on this challenge by posing a very particular sense of the decaying body against her utopian flights of philanthropy. The sense in which the physical body dies and needs feeding challenges the vision of improvement and perfectibility. This might help to explain an otherwise peculiar passage in the book where Wollstonecraft reacts to the desolate coast of Rusoer:

> The view of this wild coast, as we sailed along it, afforded me a continual subject for meditation. I anticipated the future improvement of the world, and observed how much man had still to do, to obtain of the earth all it could yield. I even carried my speculations so far as to advance a million or two of years to the moment when the earth would perhaps be so perfectly cultivated, and so completely peopled, as to render it necessary to inhabit every spot; yes; these bleak shores, Imagination went still farther, and pictured the state of man when the earth could no longer support him. Where was he to fly to from universal famine? Do not smile: I really became distressed for these fellow creatures, yet unborn. The images fastened on me, and the world appeared a vast prison. (*Letters Written in Sweden, Norway, and Denmark*, *WW*, VI, pp. 294–95)

At such a moment Wollstonecraft is caught between equally debilitating effects of sensibility: she is the victim of her own nervous susceptibility draining her body and its energies; and, even in the act of philanthropic imagination, she suffers the futuristic and hypothetical distress of the unborn. Bending reason to pity, surviving the emotional burden of sensibility, being a mother, surviving romance and maintaining a perfectibilist optimism in the future of society take a heavy toll. This is the optimistic view of population coupled with scientific advancement taken to such an extreme that it ends up being negative. Wollstonecraft's speculative flight of fancy produces the Malthusian nightmare which was to haunt the radical and the liberal imagination for the next two decades.[51]

In her deployment of imagination as a bulwark against the newly combined forces of utility and political economy, Wollstonecraft prefigures the authors whose work forms the second half of this study. She shares with Hazlitt an acute reaction to utility's perceived threat to the divine and spiritual status of human beings, even though he has more difficulty than she in subscribing to a metaphysical conception of imagination and its attendant aesthetic. And while both writers, like Paine and Cobbett, direct some of their most venomous attacks against a literary imagination whose origin lies in what they see as a morally bankrupt, libertine aristocratic culture, they share with Burke, the arch proponent of such a culture, the same successful tactic of constructing a version of imagination which can conveniently inhabit and occupy the material and the metaphysical, the political and the spiritual. Burke's harnessing of the ideological force of a civic imagination which could appeal to liberty already contains, in its depiction of the French revolutionaries as economists and speculators, a critique of utility as the province of narrow-minded theorists. This was a legacy which both Hazlitt and Coleridge sought to exploit.

PART II

Imagination and utility

When deliberating on the meaning of good and evil in the middle of his *Enquiry Concerning Political Justice*, William Godwin confidently announces that it 'is not difficult to form a scale of happiness'. His philosophy of social utility is based, as his equally confident account of the abolition of the slave trade makes clear, on the notion of a shared human nature conceived in positive, perfectibilist terms. The scale of happiness Godwin then goes on to image is thus premised on improvement, on the hope of advancing up the scale. Not for him a dangerously simplistic appeal to the 'rights of man' which can only 'reduce all to a naked and savage equality'.[1]

In a series of cameos, Godwin provides a portrait of the hierarchical structure of English society (familiar to readers of his novel *Caleb Williams*) which incorporates one of the 'labouring inhabitants of the civilized states of Europe', one of 'the men of rank, fortune, and dissipation', the 'man of taste and liberal accomplishments', and, finally, the 'man of benevolence'. For our purposes, the scale is at its most interesting when it moves to consider 'the man of taste and liberal accomplishments'. This is the point at which we are given a clear indication of the role of the arts and the aesthetic in Godwin's vision of society:

The beauties of nature are all his own. He admires the overhanging cliff, the wide-extended prospect, the vast expanse of the ocean, the foliage of the woods, the sloping lawn and the waving grass. He knows the pleasures of solitude, when man holds commerce alone with the tranquil solemnity of nature. He has traced the structure of the universe; the substances which compose the globe we inhabit, and are the materials of human industry; and the laws which hold the planets in their course amidst the trackless fields of space. He studies; and has experienced the pleasures which result from conscious perspicacity and discovered truth. He enters, with a true relish, into the sublime and the pathetic. He partakes in all the grandeur and enthusiasm of poetry. He is perhaps himself a poet. He is conscious that he has not lived in vain, and that he shall be recollected with pleasure, and extolled with ardour, by generations yet unborn. In this person, compared with the two preceding classes, we acknowledge something of the features of a man. They were only a better sort of brutes; but he has sensations and transports of which they have no conception.[2]

It quickly becomes apparent to the reader that this scale performs a trumping of the established norm. We are asked to go one better than the conventional liberal pursuits of the arts and the life of the mind represented by the humanities. The man of benevolence represents the pinnacle of happiness where happiness is to be considered from the utilitarian perspective of the social aggregate. The self-consciousness of doing good, the knowledge of one's own ethical capacity to generate social felicity, stands in for private pleasure. Benevolence completes the loop between personal and social good, or so Godwin would have us believe:

But there is a rank of man more fitted to excite our emulation than this, the man of benevolence. Study is cold, if it be not enlivened with the idea of happiness to arise to mankind from the cultivation and improvement of sciences. The sublime and the pathetic are barren, unless it be the sublime of true virtue, and the pathos of true sympathy. The pleasures of the mere man of taste and refinement, 'play round the head, but come not to the heart'. There is no true joy but in the spectacle and contemplation of happiness . . . No man so truly promotes his own interest as he that forgets it. No man reaps so copious a harvest of pleasure as he who thinks only of the pleasures of other men.[3]

An older eighteenth-century form of sensibility is here grafted onto Godwin's utilitarian philosophy in a manoeuvre which inverts the dominant and caricatured vision of popular Benthamite utilitarianism some three or four decades later. Here it is the traditional aesthetic – particularly the poetic – which is deemed cold and unfeeling. Despite its capacity for intellectual self-consciousness, it figures only as an ornamental accomplishment, not as a heart-felt attachment or passion. Bentham's opponents, as we shall see, were quick to claim as their own the feeling heart and the psychic consolations of an ethical humanism as the touchstones of the imagination.

This brief example from Godwin's *Political Justice* provides us with an insight into the difficulty of accommodating utilitarian philosophy along with aesthetics and ethics. At the same time it reminds us of the complexity and variety within the conflict between utility and imagination in this period. Godwin clearly straddles the divide between the two sides of the debate and is himself an interesting example of writer who, late in his career, came to reappraise the value of imagination in education.[4] This variety of response within the debate between imagination and utility is also evident, as we shall see, within Cobbett's writing. His often reactionary and popular form of utility provides a necessary counter to philosophical utilitarianism. His is a very different, but equally important story of the antagonism within English culture between imagination and utility which issues in a rethinking of the meaning of the aesthetic. Although involved in the same movement for radical reform as Benthamite utilitarianism, Cobbett provides an important cultural alternative to Bentham's intellectual and progressive strand of utilitarianism which would reach its apogee not simply amongst the intellectuals of the *Westminster Review*, but also, in a modified and internalised form, amongst a new and dominant middle class which had begun to develop a new morality by the 1830s.[5] Cobbett's agrarian radicalism deploys a complex mixture of old Tory values alongside those of a more populist tradition based upon ideas of the Magna Carta and a mythical vision of Old England involving Saxon Wessex. It also contains its own progressive technological mode of thinking in relation to agricultural and horticultural practices. In its own very particular way, Cobbett's attack on the refined aesthetics of the eighteenth century also contains an act of repression to match that of the Benthamite intellectual; one which illustrates on another level my more general argument about the re-formulation of the imagination: its capacity not simply to be redefined by utility, but to have the capacity to re-articulate itself in the face of it. In the two cases of Cobbett and John Stuart Mill, as we shall see in the following chapters, this re-articulation takes the form of the return of the repressed.

Bentham's detractors have often eagerly portrayed him as a cultural philistine. Even before his reputation endured Dickens's popular attack on Gradgrindism – the assertion of fact over fancy – in *Hard Times*, his infamous declaration that push-pin is as valuable as poetry and all the other fine arts became a target for his enemies. By the mid-nineteenth century Bentham's philistine utilitarianism had come to represent the defining cultural opponent to Coleridge's literary idealism. This opposition, as it has been dealt with by Mill, I. A. Richards, Raymond Williams, and others,[6] occupies a familiar and important place in British literary history. My intention in the second half of this study of imagination as a vital and integral component of cultural critique in the Romantic period is to return to the question of utility and utilitarianism in order to reassess the foundations of this opposition: to understand how imagination was, in some significant instances, produced out of this relationship with utilitarianism. Rather than just repeating the old story of castigating Bentham for his deficiency of imagination and his repression of it – the story which, as we shall see, unfolds in Mill's famous essays on Bentham and Coleridge and in the equally famous crisis in his *Autobiography* – I wish to return to the scene of Bentham's critique in order to assess his wholesale attack upon fallacies, fictions, rhetoric, language, and poetry and its implications for the creation by his rivals of the counter-fiction and ideology of imagination.

Bentham's significance to our story of the militant imagination as propounded by Hazlitt and Coleridge lies in his espousal, after 1809, of the democratic question of constitutional reform. Before that date, Bentham inhabits the scholarly seclusion which Hazlitt ridicules; after that date he becomes the philosophical leader of the movement for Reform which Hazlitt fears. According to Halévy's classic study, between 1809 and 1818 Bentham, along with Cartwright, 'the father of Reform', became the philosopher of the party, 'the Chief thinker of Radicalism'.[7] Bentham's role as radical critic in the second decade of the century posed a real threat to Hazlitt's liberal/radical politics. The 'New School of Reform' with Bentham as its theorist threatened to replace the old radical order. The new radicalism undercut both Painite radicalism and his own nostalgic reverence for the Revolution and its Napoleonic aftermath. Bentham cuts through 'the rights of man' along with the other fictions and fallacies he sees as unnecessary in this new age of reason. And by the 1830s Bentham's thinking lives on, modified by utilitarians in the previous decade, to become absorbed into the new middle-class bourgeois ideology. In this sense it is not only Bentham per se, but also Bentham's collusion with the cause of reform and his absorption by popular thinking which makes him a figure who must be countered by a powerful re-articulation and re-figuring of imagination in the writings of Hazlitt and Coleridge.

Perhaps because of Bentham's accommodation by bourgeois thinking, it is easy to elide the difference between the competing ideologies of imagination and utility in this period. For example, Terry Eagleton's otherwise comprehensive and rigorous history of aesthetics pays surprisingly little attention to Bentham.[8] In the wider argument about false consciousness this most vehement debate within bourgeois culture is occluded. Since utilitarianism is in some ways the major re-articulation of aesthetics in the period with its reassessment of happiness or felicity based on pain and pleasure this dismissal is surprising. And, even though he does offer a brief section on Bentham in his history of 'theory', David Simpson's own study of romantic nationalism is more concerned to point up the shared inexactitude of the exponents of the literary imagination and the utilitarian philosophers than to focus on their significant differences.[9]

In his first published work, *A Fragment on Government* (1776), Bentham performs a wholesale critique of Blackstone's *Commentaries* (1765), that elegant articulation of the British system of law which he had himself just been asked to revere as a law student at Oxford. His self-appointed task as 'censor' is to critique rather than statically observe this noble edifice of the legal establishment. As a 'citizen of the world' in a new 'busy age . . . in which knowledge is rapidly advancing towards perfection',[10] Bentham's role is to expose the gothic pile of Blackstone's text to the levelling gaze of Enlightenment universalism. It is a role reminiscent in a number of ways of Paine and Wollstonecraft in their critiques of Burke's *Reflections* where, as we have seen, they attempt to subvert Burke's text by making it look like an outmoded form of literary romance, the product of a gothic sensibility. Two decades earlier, Bentham attacks the legal edifice of aristocratic culture and makes it look ridiculously superannuated by exposing its fictional status and thus its epistemological absurdity. The way in which he does so is very different from the strategies employed by Paine and Wollstonecraft: Bentham defers neither to natural rights nor to the power of a moral sensibility. His claim to expose fiction is even more far-reaching than Paine's and his claim to be operating a new systematic method of critique and classification makes this a unique venture in English culture.

In this first book Bentham establishes his characteristic mode of critique and launches his attack on the fictions and rhetorical forms of address which put a barrier of 'darkness' and 'confusion' in the way of his confident advance towards the light of sterling truth, a truth based on his adoption of the key axiomatic assumption of his philosophical position that 'it is the greatest happiness of the greatest number that is the measure of right and wrong'.[11] From this foundation he proceeds to a thorough demystification of Blackstone's obscurity. Bentham begins by admitting the merits of the *Commentaries*, but it soon becomes apparent that the modernisation Blackstone has performed, his teaching 'Jurisprudence to speak the language of the Scholar and the Gentleman' and to have 'cleansed her from the dust and cobwebs of the office', lacks that sign of his own true modernity: 'precision'. In the end, its 'enchanting harmony' speaks only of a dangerous appeal to the ear. This 'correct, elegant, unembarrassed, ornamented . . . *style*' turns out to be 'vicious in point of *matter*'.[12] Thus, even though published only thirteen years earlier, Blackstone's text exemplifies in its elegant, confused, fictive and barbaric style the self-professed Gothic state of English law: '. . . he turns the Law into a Castle, for the purpose of opposing every idea of "fundamental" reparation'.[13] In Bentham's description of it, Blackstone's text approaches the status of a poem, its vaunted elegance and rhetorical energy making it more a matter of style than substance, its sensuous appeal to the ear representing the danger of poetic arts where the need is for the plain, transparent, and immediate truth of reason. Bentham's dream of perfect understanding – 'Men, let them but once clearly understand one another, will not be long ere they agree' – is based on his corresponding assumption of the inadequacy of language: the 'dangerous solecism and confusion in *discourse*'[14] which stems not only from language's lack of precision, but its infection by human passion. The merits of Blackstone's *Commentaries* 'which recommend it so powerfully to the imagination'[15] represent a threat to sound judgment. Although he initially concedes these aesthetic and ornamental merits of Blackstone's text, Bentham soon turns against it for displaying the dangerous, dazzling distractions which lead away from the path of truth. As a work of the aristocratic imagination it might be superannuated, but it is still dangerous.

The extent of the problem caused by language to Bentham's mode of critique erupts periodically in *A Fragment on Government*. 'Solecism and confusion' demand the intervention of his own 'Censor[ship]' to the extent that he has to construct strangely negative categories of meaning and representation.[16] There is a clash of interests here between Bentham's professed primary interest in utility and his accompanying epistemology of truth. While admitting to the false power generated by legal fictions, he is unwilling to admit that such fictions might have some utility or efficacy in achieving his aim of general happiness.[17] This means that his characteristic metaphors of disease used to describe the energy of fictions – as in the phrase 'the pestilential breath of fiction' – speak only of a negative form of power which must be cleansed by his own modernising and cathecting mode of reason. The combination of utility and reason is at such moments an uneasy and, to some extent, illogical alliance. It bears the pressure of excluding the aesthetic. Bentham's own transparent rationalism has to create a special category in which to place the imaginative opposition. Towards the end of *A Fragment on Government*, for example, he draws attention to the problematically embroiled nature of his own task of critique when he dismisses Blackstone's linguistic confusion:

> I now put an end to the tedious and intricate war of words that subsisted, in a more particular manner during the course of these two last chapters: a logomachy, wearisome enough, perhaps, and insipid to the reader, but beyond description laborious and irksome to the writer. What remedy? had there been sense, I should have attached myself to the sense: finding nothing but words; to the words I was to attach myself, or to nothing. Had the doctrine been but false, the task of exposing it would have been comparatively an easy one: but it was what is worse, unmeaning, and thence it came to require all these pains which I have been here bestowing on it: to what profit let the reader judge. (Bentham, *Fragment on Government*, p. 113)

Similarly, Bentham's description of the helpful role he is playing for his reader ends up being peculiarly negatively defined, especially when at the same time the opposition is said to be nonsensical. By subscribing in this way to a monologic notion of truth and meaning, Bentham is also in danger of diminishing his own role as 'censor', a role premised on a frighteningly detailed attachment to the prior text. His justification for the preceding hundred or so pages of analysis is:

> to help him [the reader] to emancipate his judgment from the shackles of authority:- to let him see that the not understanding a discourse may as well be the writer's fault as the reader's:- to teach him to distinguish between shewy language and sound sense:- to warn him not to pay himself with words:- to shew him that what may tickle the ear, or dazzle the imagination, will not always inform the judgment:- to shew him what it is our Author can do, and has done: and what it is he has not done, and cannot do . . . (Bentham, *Fragment on Government*, p. 114)

The manner in which the prior text imposes itself on Bentham's critique is as important here as his negatively defined categories. The combination of the two signals the problem of representation for Bentham and belies the confidence with which he can pronounce upon the dawn of a new age of reason. Perhaps the most famous statement of this kind within *A Fragment*, the following argument on the 'original contract' of government, assigns a distinctly worrying afterlife to fiction at the same time as pronouncing upon its extinction:

> The indestructible prerogatives of mankind have no need to be supported upon

the sandy foundation of a fiction.

With respect to this, and other fictions, there was once a time perhaps, when they had their use. With instruments of this temper, I will not deny but that some political work may have been done, and that useful work, which, under the then circumstances of things, could hardly have been done with any other. But the season of *Fiction* is now over: insomuch, that what formerly might have been tolerated and countenanced under that name, would, if now attempted to be set on foot, be censured and stigmatized under the harsher appellations of *incroachment* or *imposture*. To attempt to introduce any *new* one, would be now a crime: for which reason there is much danger, without any use, in vaunting and propagating such as have been introduced already. In point of political discernment, the universal spread of learning has raised mankind in a manner to a level with each other, in comparison of what they have been in any former time: nor is any man now so far elevated above his fellows, as that he should be indulged in the dangerous licence of cheating them for their good. (Bentham, *Fragment on Government*, pp. 52–53)

What had for Bentham been a negative category now becomes a punitive one. Not to be part of this proudly announced new age is to commit a crime against truth. The levelling gaze is based upon a coercive system of ethics, a system of rewards and punishments.

In his attack on the philosophy of natural rights and its embodiment in the new constitution of revolutionary France in his *Anarchical Fallacies* (1816), Bentham takes this attack on fiction one step further. While exposing what he sees as the bankruptcy and, more particularly, the vacuity of the language which composes the revolutionary rhetoric of rights, Bentham turns away from the French example before him to offer a particularly searing critique of English political culture. This critique centres on the nature of the English language. Here Bentham's almost Hobbesian suspicion of the equivocating nature of language leads him into a fierce attack on his own culture and the way it has been infected or intoxicated with the literary. The very richness of the English language has, it seems, made it particularly difficult for him to operate a language of truth and precision. English is a form of Quixotism which makes its users unable to distinguish between fiction and reality. And once again, for Bentham, the fictive is both negative – a non-sense – and tantamount to a dangerous irrationality signalled by his word 'magic'. At this point the universalist 'censor' seems to find himself trapped in a barbarous and monstrous form of mis-representation:

It is in England, rather than France, the discovery of the *rights of man* ought naturally to have taken its rise: it is we – we English, that have the better *right* to it . . . It is in English, and not in French, that we may change the sense without changing the word, and, like Don Quixote on the enchanted horse, travel as far as the moon, and farther, without ever getting off the saddle. One and the same word, right – right, that most enchanting of words – is sufficient for operating the fascination. The word is ours, – that magic word, which, by its single unassisted powers, completes the fascination. In its adjective shape, it is as innocent as a dove: it breathes nothing but morality and peace. It is in this shape that, passing in at the heart, it gets possession of the understanding: – it then assumes its substantive shape, and joining itself to a band of suitable associates, sets up the banner of insurrection, anarchy, and lawless violence.

. . . *Right*, the substantive *right*, is the child of law: from *real* laws come *real* rights; but from *imaginary* laws, from laws of nature, fancied and invented by poets, rhetoricians, and dealers in moral and intellectual poisons, come *imaginary* rights, a bastard brood of monsters, 'gorgon and chimaeras dire'.[18]

Bentham's proclaimed transparent rationalism thus imagines a scene of nightmarish transformation in which the dove gives birth to classical monsters. And at a stroke, Bentham joins together the Painite revolutionaries and the Burkean subscribers to a poetic, chivalrous, aristocratic culture: a manoeuvre sufficient to horrify Hazlitt, a liberal radical with a confirmed belief in the aristocracy of letters and the poetics of the Burkean imagination. In defining his position in this way, however, Bentham creates the opportunity for the language of literary culture and imagination to reassemble itself with greater vigour. As his mechanistic materialism was beginning to become popular in the guise of a confident, sometimes puritanical, middle-class morality, the proponents of the imagination were mounting their own re-articulated defence.

Nothing better illustrates Bentham's own difficulty with the aesthetic than the following passage from his *Rationale of Reward* (1825) where he categorises the 'arts and sciences of amusement'. Here his attempt to turn pleasure solely towards the goal of social utility leaves unanswered (in both experiential and theoretical terms) the nature of pleasure, and in particular the complex economy of pleasure which we might term desire. The passage is quoted at length because the analogy between poetry and push-pin has so often been taken out of context and simplified:

By arts and sciences of amusement, I mean those which are ordinarily called the *fine arts*; such as music, poetry, painting, sculpture, architecture, ornamental gardening, & c. & c. Their complete enumeration must be excused: it would lead us too far from our present subject, were we to plunge into the metaphysical discussions necessary for its accomplishment. Amusements of all sorts would be comprised under this head.

Custom has in a manner compelled us to make the distinction between the arts and sciences of amusement, and those of curiosity. It is not, however, proper to regard the former as destitute of utility: on the contrary, there is nothing, the utility of which is more incontestable. To what shall the character of utility be ascribed, if not to that which is a source of pleasure? All that can be alleged in diminution of their utility is, that it is limited to the excitement of pleasure: they cannot disperse the clouds of grief or of misfortune. They are useless to those who are not pleased with them: they are useful only to those who take pleasure in them, and only in proportion as they are pleased.

[...]

The utility of all these arts and sciences – I speak both of those of amusement and curiosity, – the value which they possess, is exactly in proportion to the pleasure they yield. Every other species of pre-eminence which may be attempted to be established among them is altogether fanciful. Prejudice apart, the game of push-pin is of equal value with the arts and sciences of music and poetry. If the game of push-pin furnish more pleasure, it is more valuable than either. Everybody can play at push-pin: poetry and music are relished only by few. The game of push-pin is always innocent: it were well could the same be always asserted of poetry. Indeed, between poetry and truth there is a natural opposition: false morals, fictitious nature. The poet always stands in need of something false. When he pretends to lay his foundations in truth, the ornaments of his superstructure are fictions; his business consists in stimulating our passions, and exciting our prejudice. Truth, exactitude of every kind, is fatal to poetry. The poet must see everything through coloured media, and strive to make every one else to do the same. It is true, there have been noble spirits, to whom poetry and philosophy have been equally indebted; but these exceptions do not counter-act the mischiefs which have resulted from this magic art. If poetry and music deserve to be preferred before a game of push-pin, it must be because they are calculated to gratify those individuals who are most difficult to be pleased.[19]

Here there is at least an awareness of a problem within the workings of pleasure. In the notion of the difficulty of being pleased, Bentham registers a further complication in the economy of desire: the possibility of recalcitrance or dissidence. Ultimately, however, this glimmer of difference is subsumed under a more characteristic manouevre of social control imposing a puritanical order on the individual psyche. The passage above is soon followed by an admission that: 'All the arts . . . possess a species of moral utility . . . They are excellent substitutes for drunkenness, slander, and the love of gaming.' One suspects that this particular species of pleasure is not high on the evolutionary ladder. The calculus of pleasure which Bentham envisages here veers between a qualitative judgment based on truth and which consigns the 'fine arts' to the realm of error, and an assessment of sheer volume which consigns the pleasures of the arts to an elitist side-show. Bentham's argument forces a link between truth and pleasure which elides the difference of different pleasures by force of the assumption that only truth can be real pleasure. It makes an interesting comparison with Godwin's scale of happiness where, as we saw, benevolence triumphs over the traditional aesthetic. For Godwin, virtuous self-consciousness is conveniently joined to self-abnegation. Here in Bentham's text the levelling gaze of truth sees pleasure as an end in itself.

Bentham would have it that exclusive pleasure is not really leisure, that its fictional foundation invalidates it as non-sense, even non-pleasure. While one might agree with Bentham's diagnosis of the elitist particularity of the fine arts, he embarks on much more problematic ground when he addresses their lack of a therapeutic capacity. Once again, a gothic ghost haunts his rationalist text. This particular ghost of melancholic despair – of grief – is one which returns with a vengeance, as we shall see, in the psyche of J. S. Mill. Bentham's swingeing Platonic attack on the fictitious, immoral, constitutional falsehood of the poet is summed up in that uncanny and aphoristic sentence: 'The poet always stands in need of something false' begs to be re-written with the last word changed to 'else'.

Aside from this explicit and to some extent infamous attack on the established literary culture, Bentham's materialist utilitarianism also offended liberals like Hazlitt because it struck more generally at the heart and soul of their metaphysics. Like Malthusian population theory, Benthamite radicalism represented a threat to the soul of man.[20] By redefining aesthetics according to a minutely graded calculus of pain and pleasure applied to the social abstract of the general good Bentham questioned some of the most sacred tenets of liberal individualism. He challenged the very possibility of altruism and philanthropy operating as adequate motives in human behaviour. The claim of his opponents that his was a philosophy of selfishness and self-interest is never quite answered in his thinking despite his best attempts to wrestle with the idea of benevolence.[21] At the same time as critiquing traditional religious belief therefore, Bentham also challenged the capacity of traditional aesthetics to occupy the hinterland of moral pleasure. He ruled out religious hope at the same time as he derided the possibility of aesthetics providing some spiritual compensation. This could be seen as a spur to those opponents of his who wished to occupy a compensatory realm of imagination. In their efforts to lay claim to a new form of metaphysical reality which preserved the possibility of self and self-transcendence, self-development and benevolence, Bentham's offence to traditional notions of spirituality could be an advantage. It might even be suggested that Bentham's philosophy pushes the proponents of the literary imagination into that powerful combination of spiritual consolation and educational psychology which becomes such a potent force in Victorian writing.

4

Hazlitt and the limits of the sympathetic imagination

I

Hazlitt's aesthetics are caught between sympathy and power, the learned and the vulgar, the body and ideas. His voluminous journalistic output in the first three decades of the nineteenth century characteristically defies system or theory, even though it contains clearly discernible preoccupations and consistent modes of thought.[1] Throughout his career Hazlitt is concerned with the capacity of sympathy to enable individuals to rise above mere selfishness and to enter a community of feeling. This is the substance of his first published and most systematic work *On the Principles of Human Action* (1805) and of one of his last articles, 'On Benevolence and Self-Love', published in the *New Monthly Magazine* in 1828. His aesthetics might thus be roughly described as celebrating the power of the sympathetic imagination.[2] But Hazlitt's writing resists such an oversimplification, not least because such an overview belies the conflicts and contradictions within his kind of oppositional writing, and also because the word 'celebration' denies the unease which haunts his sense of the aesthetic.

Hazlitt's writings represent a conscientious attempt to test the efficacy of the sympathetic imagination against the negative effects of the dominant ideology.[3] In this chapter I have chosen to represent this career-long examination by focusing on his complex responses to Burke and Coleridge and on his collections of essays from 1818 to 1826, rather than the early *Essay on the Principles of Human Action*, his famous art criticism, or his infamous *Liber Amoris* – all of which contribute significantly to this issue. In the second decade of the century leading up to Peterloo, Hazlitt experiences greater difficulty in maintaining a happy coincidence of interests between his liberal radicalism and his subscription to the fine arts and literary culture more generally. His testing of the limits of the sympathetic imagination now takes the form of a fierce and concerted assault on what he terms 'Legitimacy' which culminates in his most brilliant political performance, the two articles which form 'What is the People?' (1818). In the more famous collections of articles which follow in the 1820s – *The Plain Speaker* (1826) and *The Spirit of the Age* (1825) – Hazlitt is forced to address the rising ideology of utilitarianism; and it is this which provides the last great challenge to his ideal of imaginative sympathy and which affords an opportunity for his corresponding rhetoric of invective.

II

Hazlitt's response to Burke is extensive and complex.[4] As such it provides us with a helpful means of analysing the inter-connection between literature and politics across the whole range of his journalistic output. More particularly, precisely because it always straddles the political and literary divide Hazlitt's response to Burke offers an insight into the limits of the role of imagination in his thinking which is not so evident from a reading of his more famous literary criticism. In his career-long negotiation with Burke's rhetoric Hazlitt can be seen to question the very validity of a combination of political and aesthetic ideas and at the same time to show his characteristic awareness of the ideological nature of literary culture and its version of imagination. Burke's texts also make Hazlitt aware of the contradictory links which exist between imagination, public opinion, and abstraction. Hazlitt's response to Burke reveals a conflict between aesthetic and political power which severely tests his concept of imagination.

Burke functions as one of Hazlitt's favourite control models,[5] and Burke's prose-style is as much a touchstone for Hazlitt as is Shakespeare's genius. In terms of political consistency, too, Burke figures as the terrible example in the previous generation of apostasy to the revolutionary cause. For Hazlitt, the historical example provided by the figure of Burke functions in two categories: the literary example of his writings which is praiseworthy, and the lamentable example of the inconsistent political man of action. Two kinds of power are thus drawn together in Hazlitt's commentaries on the mixed mode of Burke's prose, a kind of writing which appeals to an overtly literary taste, but is never removed or separate from the consequences of political action.

Hazlitt consistently distinguishes Burke from other prose writers on the grounds that his work so evidently displays the presence of imagination. In the series of essays on key political figures which he published between 1806 and 1807, Burke's imagination is used as the key point of comparison. But even here it is not presented in straightforwardly positive terms. In its most luxuriant form it can be linked with sound political expertise as in this comparison: '[Pitt] had none of the profound legislative wisdom, piercing sagacity, or rich, impetuous, high-wrought imagination of Burke';[6] but then in a comparison with Fox its surfeit is seen to have the dangerous consequence of denying practicalities: 'Fox had too little imagination, Burke had too much: that is, he was careless of facts, and was led away by his passions to look at one side of a question only.'[7] It can be travestied as well as being delusive: 'Burke, who was a man of fine imagination, had the good sense . . . to defend the moral uses of the imagination, and is himself one of the grossest instances of its abuse.'[8] Imagination is clearly capable of a negative partiality divorced from the truth; though this faculty can and ideally should have a relationship with moral good, this is far from guaranteed.

Though Hazlitt praises Burke's combination of the poetical and the practical, his writing suggests that it is precarious and potentially contradictory. The extent to which Burke possesses imagination, for instance, is a measure of his lack of popularity; his refined literariness is at odds with the workings of political power:

Fox was a reasoner, Lord Chatham was an orator. Burke was both a reasoner and a poet; and was therefore still farther removed from that conformity with the vulgar notions and mechanical feelings of mankind, which will always be necessary to give a man the chief sway in a popular assembly. (*Works*, VII, p. 300)

In this instance the alignment of vulgarity and popularity suggests that the practical workings of parliamentary politics limit the efficacy of Burke's verbal power. Hazlitt seems to have been equally aware, however, of the unspoken, pervasive ideological power of Burke's writings and of the need to counter this effect.[9]

Given the fragility of this combination of poetical and practical for which Burke is consistently celebrated, it might seem surprising to find a statement such as the following in Hazlitt's essay 'On the Prose-style of Poets':

Burke's execution, like that of all good prose, savours of the texture of what he describes, and his pen slides or drags over the ground of his subject, like the painter's pencil. The most rigid fidelity and the most fanciful extravagance meet, and are reconciled in his pages. (*Works*, XII, p. 12)

Burke's prose is singled out as a place where fiction and the aesthetic, reality and the political, can be found together, but despite the claim of reconciliation attention is centred on the antagonistic extremes.

Even when celebrating such a union Hazlitt focuses on the potential conflict; a conflict generated by the difference between two types of writing. The aesthetic realm of the free play of creativity is pitted against the mechanical activity of descriptive, discursive prose. Hazlitt's simile tests the ethereal against the physical in an argument between 'fine' and applied modes of writing. More importantly, he suggests that these different modes construct different kinds of truth and that they can present us with two different notions of reality.

The tension that results from these opposites in Hazlitt's appreciation of Burke is more easily seen in a longer description of his style in the same essay from *The Plain Speaker*. This paragraph recalls through its extended landscape analogies Burke's own aesthetic distinctions in his *Enquiry on the Sublime and Beautiful*. It concentrates initially on the narrow divide between poetic prose and poetry. Less expected, perhaps, is its espousal of the idea that 'fine' writing is not simply fictional, but also empty – a conclusion to which Hazlitt is led as a direct consequence of championing Burke. Instead of imaginative creativity being seen to lead to a higher level of reality, here it is considered as a hollow imposition upon the reader. It has no substance, no foundation in reality:

It has always appeared to me that the most perfect prose-style, the most powerful, the most dazzling, the most daring, that which went the nearest to the verge of poetry, and yet never fell over, was Burke's. It has the solidity, and sparkling effect of the diamond: all other *fine writing* is like French paste or Bristol-stones in the comparison. Burke's style is airy, flighty, adventurous, but it never loses sight of the subject; nay, is always in contact with, and derives its increased or varying impulse from it. It may be said to pass yawning gulfs 'on the unstedfast footing of a spear': still it has an actual resting-place and tangible support under it – it is not suspended on nothing. (*Works*, XII, p. 10)

By this point in the passage we might think that it is 'all other *fine writing*' (with the play on the word 'fine') which bears the disparaging connotations, but the passage develops so that it is the comparison with poetry which takes over. Poetry has to carry the accusation of sham hollowness:

[Burke's style] differs from poetry, as I conceive, like the chamois from the eagle: it climbs to an almost equal height, touches upon a cloud, overlooks a precipice, is picturesque, sublime – but all the while, instead of soaring through the air, it stands upon a rocky cliff, clambers up by abrupt and intricate ways, and browses on the roughest bark, or crops the tender flower. The principle which guides his pen is truth, not beauty – not pleasure, but power. He has no choice, no selection of subject to flatter the reader's idle taste, or assist his own fancy: he must take what comes, and make the most of it. (*Works*, XII, p. 10)

Hazlitt's concentration on 'solid reality' leads to a state of affairs where taste is almost inevitably 'idle'. The literary side of the equation is suddenly made to look effete and vacuous. The effect of this concentration is to force a split between the poetic and the discursive at the very point where the two are supposed to come together in Burke. Ironically, when celebrating Burke's style as an example of writing which combines politics and art, Hazlitt is betrayed into a distinction which separates the two: 'truth' and 'power' are now nicely dissociated from 'beauty' and 'pleasure'.

Although this combined style shares with poetry the sublime prospect of a precipice, the figure is negative rather than awe-inspiring. Aesthetic power is made to look ambivalent and its relevance to power of a political kind is severely questioned. For the moment, however, Hazlitt is still preoccupied with poetry, and, as his paragraph continues, his estimate of the prose writer's position is imbued with a sense of mechanical compromise; originality comes first, ingenuity second. The richness and variety this writing produces are the effects of a difficult position:

[Burke] works the most striking effects out of the most unpromising materials, by the mere activity of his mind. He rises with the lofty, descends with the mean, luxuriates in beauty, gloats over deformity. It is all the same to him, so that he loses no particle of the exact, characteristic, extreme impression of the thing he writes about, and that he communicates this to the reader, after exhausting every possible mode of illustration, plain or abstracted, figurative or literal. Whatever stamps the original image more distinctly on the mind, is welcome. The nature of his task precludes continual beauty; but it does not preclude continual ingenuity, force, originality. (*Works*, XII, pp. 10–11)

The difficulty which produces these discontinuous artistic effects, we eventually learn, is a result of working in an area alien to the organic realm of beauty and art. The world of politics and abstract ideas reacts harshly, even violently, to combination:

He had to treat of political questions, mixed modes, abstract ideas, and his fancy (or poetry, if you will) was ingrafted on these artificially, and as it might sometimes be thought, violently, instead of growing naturally out of them, as it would spring of its own accord from individual objects and feelings. (*Works*, XII, p. 11)

Although this passage begins by classing Burke's style as perfect in its own category, by the end the stress is placed on the separation between this discursive form and its 'fine' relation, poetry. The disconcerting element in all this is that the confined and artificial activity of Burke's writing is allied to 'truth' and 'power'. That the perspective offered here on Burke is itself an artistic one could, of course, be seen as a moderating factor. Burke provides Hazlitt with an example of imaginative power in a distinctly unpromising context. He is to be praised for having transcended the usual boundaries of a limited and limiting discipline; he offers artistic refinement in an area where it is not usually encountered.

In distinguishing the delicately poised position of Burke's style, however, certain implicit problems arise as to Hazlitt's own precarious relationship to the literariness of polite culture. His celebration of Burke's originality implicitly challenges the privileged status of the poetic and literary culture more generally.

This simultaneous separation and relegation of the aesthetic realm of pure art is taken even further in Hazlitt's more overtly political assessment of Burke in other articles. Here the poetic element in Burke's prose is often treated as a dangerous intruder since it is associated with the delusive and counterfeiting faculty of fancy or imagination. As we shall see, on some occasions Hazlitt condemns the intrusion of imagination into Burke's writings explicitly on the grounds that it is not suitable for deciding issues of state. Despite this he is unwilling to dissociate it from perceptions of truth. This shifting term imagination reveals a number of different facets as it is forced to accommodate competing literary and political sympathies in Hazlitt's writings on Burke. As a consequence of this struggle, imagination is, by turns, separated from politics, equated with truth, seen as deceitful, associated with the despotic status quo, and ultimately dissociated from prevailing opinion due to a belief in refinement. But even in this last instance the problematic relationship between imaginative and political power is not really resolved: refinement has, somehow, for a partisan or committed radical, to be equated with action.

Beyond these competing ideas of literary and political truth, Burke provides Hazlitt with a particularly interesting case of imaginative power divorced from popularity. It is not simply a question of the belated Jacobin empathising with the revolutionary apostate on the grounds of isolation caused by his subscription to a literary culture. In Burke Hazlitt identifies the difficulty of turning truth into power, of making the imagination positively ideological.

In his 1807 article 'On the Character of Burke' the comparison is with Chatham's 'clear understanding' and 'strong sense', both of which are seen to guarantee political action.[10] In this context, Hazlitt is quite happy to come forward as an apologist for Burke's failure to make an impact on the popular mind:

If he did not produce the same effects on vulgar minds, as some others have done, it was not for want of power, but from the turn and direction of his mind. It was because his subjects, his ideas, his arguments, were less vulgar. The question is not whether he brought certain truths equally home to us, but how much nearer he brought them than they were before. In my opinion, he united the two extremes of refinement and strength in a higher degree than any other writer whatever. (*Works*, VII, p. 304)

Burke's speeches and writings are seen to contain a power which springs from their refinement, and which is distinct from vulgar or popular notions of power. In this instance Hazlitt reclaims that dynamism for the aesthetic which seemed to be lacking in the last example, but at a cost. Truth and power are now the products of refinement, of a polite culture; they are inscribed in an artistic aspect of language rather than being objective, transparent realities which inform and dictate to a passive descriptive language. Whereas before Hazlitt's distinctions implied that the refinement of art needed to be substantiated through contact with the tangible realities of the world, now the claim is that the complexity found in a literary refinement of style is a necessary adjunct to encountering truth:

The subtlety of his mind was undoubtedly that which rendered Burke a less popular writer and speaker than he otherwise would have been . . . But for my own part I cannot help thinking that the most important truths must be the most refined and subtle . . . (*Works*, VII, p. 304)

Hazlitt's admission of this split between important truths and popularity clearly differentiates him from other opponents of Burke's political influence from the 1790s onwards. By propounding the idea that the literariness of language is invested with truth, Hazlitt distinguishes himself from the previous generation of Painite radicals: 'It will be seen from what I have said, that I am very far from agreeing with those who think that Burke was a man without understanding, and a merely florid writer.'[11] Against the grain of many of his fellow liberal reformers, Hazlitt continues to subscribe to an idea of literary culture which desperately attempts to combine literature and politics, but at the same time remains seemingly aloof from mass communication and democracy.

Hazlitt's vehement defence of Burke's literariness is only part of the story, however. He is equally aware of the pervasive power of Burke's texts. From this opposite perspective, Hazlitt's critique of Burke's rhetoric leads him to an understanding of imagination's susceptibility to the dominant ideology: how the intrusion of imagination into the political arena can lead to a slavish submission to legitimacy.

In another essay on the 'Character of Mr Burke' in 1817, Hazlitt concentrates on what he considers to be the pernicious influence of his political writings. Instead of insisting on the complexity and subtlety of truth, here he focuses on the danger of this intrusion. Imagination is seen to be as capable of working for slavish opinion and prejudice as it is for abstracted, disinterested political principles. The long-standing dissembling propensity of the creative faculty is evident in Hazlitt's attack on Burke's consistency. The issue is typically seen in terms of personal identity as Hazlitt parades Burke's contradictory stances with regard to the French monarchy:

Mr Burke, the opponent of the American war, and Mr Burke, the opponent of the French Revolution, are not the same person, but opposite persons – not opposite persons only, but deadly enemies ... In the one, he insulted kings personally, as among the lowest and worst of mankind; in the other, he held them up to the imagination of his readers, as sacred abstractions. (*Works*, VII, pp. 226–27)

Such an antithesis between personal and abstract is a central tenet of much of Hazlitt's criticism.[12] It is evident that imagination (or the image-making faculty) can work in conjunction with abstract power: its specific illustrations can reinforce certain political or ideological positions. On another level, of course, imagination is necessary in order to move beyond particularities, which may be selfish and limiting, towards a sound political viewpoint based on a general principle.

Given the example of Burke, such a combination of imagination and political power can lead to disastrous results. Compared to the abstract concepts of right and equality which had been promoted by Painites (for all their accessible, aggressively non-literary style) such theatrical images of actual events have an impressive power to take hold of the imagination of any reader. Despite Hazlitt's claim that Burke's 'fine fancy' is divorced from 'sound and practical judgement', its results have had such a significant impact on the practical world of politics that the effects of its literary power must be vehemently attacked and repeatedly analysed. Because Burke lacks both 'practical judgement' and 'high or rigid principles' there can in his case be no mediation between particularities and abstractions. Instead of performing an act of reconciliation between the two poles, 'fine fancy' indulges in a free play of creativity and avoids the check on its activities which should be provided by a fidelity to particular facts:

Facts or consequences never stood in the way of this speculative politician. He fitted them to his preconceived theories, instead of conforming his theories to them. They were the playthings of his style, the sport of his fancy. They were the straws of which his imagination made a blaze, and were consumed, like straws, in the blaze they had served to kindle. The fine things he said about Liberty and Humanity, in his speech on the Begum's affairs, told equally well, whether Warren Hastings was a tyrant or not: nor did he care one jot who caused the famine he described, so that he described it in a way that no one else could. On the same principle, he represented the French priests and nobles under the old regime as excellent moral people, very charitable and very religious, in the teeth of notorious facts – to answer to the handsomest things he had to say in favour of priesthood and nobility in general; and, with similar views, he falsifies the records of our English Revolution, and puts an interpretation on the word *abdication* of which a school-boy would be ashamed. He constructed his whole theory of government, in short, not on rational, but on picturesque and fanciful principles; as if the king's crown were a painted gewgaw, to be looked at on gala-days; titles an empty sound to please the ear; and the whole order of society a theatrical procession . . . (*Works*, VII, p. 228)

By ignoring facts Burke's theoretical position gives free rein to imagination and produces a false vision of things. Contrary to Hazlitt's artistic appreciation of Burke's style, which claimed that his prose bore the impression of reality along with it, this political commentary confronts the frightening prospect of imagination let loose to create fictions imbued with a suspect power. Hazlitt's venomed critique has to work hard to make Burke's society look like a meretricious spectacle and to turn his symbols of monarchical power into vacuous signs.

When Hazlitt stops to consider Burke's friend and opponent Charles James Fox in the *Life of Napoleon*, he naturally turns to Burke's negative impact in determining British attitudes to revolutionary France. The problem with Burke's imagination here is not simply conceived of as a personal one. Imagination belongs to an aesthetic category which should remain separate from politics. Hazlitt rules out the possibility that it can be appropriated for both right and wrong political causes – that it is a merely neutral faculty dependent on the nature of its possessor. Rather, the problem with imagination arises when it moves beyond its limits: it has no proper place in questions of a political kind; it should remain within its artistic confines and deal only in matters of taste:

He had not been the dupe of Mr. Burke's romantic and fanciful view of the French Revolution, with his high-coloured descriptions of the Queen of France and the rest of his apparatus for theatrical effect; for Mr. Fox, with that justness of thought which is the result of goodness of heart, saw or felt that the whole drift of Mr. Burke's theory went to make politics a question or department of the imagination, and that this could never be true, because politics treat of the public weal and the imagination can only be appealed to by individual objects and personal interests, and must give a false verdict in all other cases. It would never do, he saw, to make choice of half a dozen *dramatis personae*, to adorn them with tropes and figures, and sacrifice to this paltry foreground and meretricious embellishing the welfare of millions, who because they were millions could never be brought forward by the imaginative faculty and could only be weighed in the balance of abstract truth and reason. (*Works*, XIV, p. 274)

In the interests of counteracting Burke's political influence, Hazlitt divorces speculative abstraction from imaginative particularity. At the same time, he rehearses one of the major methodological and psychological arguments of his age. As he considers the abstract 'millions' travestied in Burke's theatrical rhetoric he inadvertently moves into the territory of Malthusian population discourse and the new problems of knowledge posed more generally by utilitarian philosophy. As we shall see later in this chapter, this dichotomy between imagination and abstraction is to dominate many of his later writings.

The urgency of Hazlitt's concern to separate imagination from politics in this last instance can be understood if one considers some of the many statements in his writings which describe how this faculty can reinforce reactionary values. In this context, imagination becomes a means of silently inculcating a conservative ideology. So strong is its effect in this respect, Hazlitt believes, that even the vestigial remains of a despotic regime must be swept away. The relics of a past system are capable of familiarising the mind with its outward signs to such an extent that they are taken for granted. Should a counter-revolution take place, its ideological position will be readily assimilated and naturalised. This negative relationship with ideology is dependent upon Hazlitt's idea of the customary imagination; imagination as a habitual reflex, or even dull routine, can be easily susceptible to the powerful sway of opinion. Considered from this negative point of view, the celebrated literary or imaginative power is reduced to handling details and has a propensity to dupe the self-conscious rational mind. Ultimately, it creates an ideological position akin to prejudice and one which is assumed to be cut off from 'reality':

The very name of the Inquisition is in itself an insult to common sense and humanity, from which all good and honest minds revolt. But by keeping up the outward form, the imagination is familiarised with it, is taught to look upon it as harmless; the tendency, the pretensions of bigotry and fanaticism are still virtually acknowledged and kept in view by their adherents, and by always having the name ready, opportunity may not be wanting to restore the *thing*! Hence the tenaciousness with which its advocates uniformly adhere to every relic of arbitrary power, and hence the determination with which all such claims, grounded on their apparent insignificance, should be resisted. The whole science and study of social improvement may be reduced to watching the secret aim and rooted purpose of power, and in opposing it step by step and in exact proportion to the obstinacy of its struggle for existence. (*Works*, XIII, p. 263)

This passage offers a powerful insight into the ideological watchfulness and pertinacity of Hazlitt's oppositional writing. It also confirms his awareness of the significance of symbols and social signs in the birth and formation of political regimes.

Indeed Hazlitt's journalism frequently draws attention to the mind's willingness to create 'bug-bears [of] the imagination',[13] a tendency which the English, he argues, took to an extreme in their demonisation of Napoleon. In this respect it is evident that 'ignorance is power'[14] and that the imaginative faculty is easy game, not simply in a process of cutting people off from reality, but of infusing them with a conservative bias. Imagination works in harness with the forms of legitimacy. In this negative state of affairs Hazlitt describes the problem with imagination in terms of subjection, rather than concentrating exclusively on its essential depravity. Indeed, some of his most vituperative writing is directed against the inexplicable facility and positive willingness of the people to engage in this submission:

This strange and voluntary bias of a large proportion of a people to return to a slavery that had bowed them down for centuries, and to escape from which had cost oceans of blood and indignities unparalleled, is one of those phenomena in the history of modern times, which would be wholly unaccountable but for the fascination and despotic influence which power in the abstract (and the older and more corrupt the more it is an object of veneration) exercises over the imagination of the thoughtless, the cowardly, and the selfish, who feel pride only in having a master, ease and security, in chains! (*Works*, XIII, p. 308)

Past estimates of Hazlitt make it difficult not to read this passage as further testimony to the negative effect of abstraction, and to assume a straightforward opposition between imagination and the abstract; but the debate taking place in Hazlitt's work is at once more particular and complex than this would suggest. Here there is evidence of imagination's dangerous affinity with abstraction, as another means of diverting attention from political reality. Certainly it suggests the stultifying capacity of imaginative power, its potential passivity in the face of action. But the full force of the attack is, as one might expect, directed against a comfortable selfishness rather than either imagination or abstraction *per se*. The inclusion of 'the thoughtless' also raises the question of Hazlitt's position as a learned commentator. In attacking the hold of corrupt power on the popular consciousness (gained by its dominion over the imagination), Hazlitt points out how suspect that popular consciousness must be if unsupported by other faculties necessary to make the right kind of committed political action. At least part of the urgency generated here derives from a crisis affecting precisely those faculties which constitute his position – from a belief that 'bigotry and prejudice, unlike reason, and philosophy, never despair'. He laments in the people the 'servile subjection of their imagination to their habitual convictions'[15] because it provides one of the most resistant obstacles to the desired object of social and political change.

These cultured virtues which Hazlitt repeatedly promotes, and which define his position as a polite spokesman for the radical cause, involve a process of self-consciousness, an escape or release from the silent workings of power. When Hazlitt turns his attention to public opinion (as opposed to the 'philosophical structure of opinion') he naturally distinguishes its pervasive and secret actions from 'knowledge' and, more importantly, from the action of a rather different notion of imagination:

Public opinion is always pressing upon the mind, and, like the air we breathe, acts unseen, unfelt. It supplies the living current of our thoughts, and infects without our knowledge. It taints the blood, and is taken into the smallest pores. The most sanguine constitutions are, perhaps, the most exposed to its influence. But public opinion has its source in power, in popular prejudice, and is not always in accord with right reason, or a high and abstracted imagination. (*Works*, XVII, p. 27)

From the exalted, even aloof, position afforded by learned culture imagination becomes not only compatible but synonymous with reason and truth. In an article entitled 'Parliamentary Eloquence' Hazlitt writes that Mr Whitbread's 'enthusiasm ran away with his judgement, and was not *backed* by equal powers of reasoning or imagination'.[16] Of course, in so far as Hazlitt performs the role of disinterested polite essayist this solution is not problematic, but where his work also contains the writings of a committed radical journalist the solution appears less satisfactory. Hazlitt himself addresses the problem when considering the 'character' of a partisan. Once again there is a split between a concern for immediate objects which can easily turn to selfishness and an abstract idealism which can be divorced from reality or become self-consuming:

> I have in my time known few thorough partisans; at least on my own side of the question. I conceive, however, that the honestest and strongest-minded men have been so. In general, interest, fear, vanity, the love of contradiction, even a scrupulous regard to truth and justice, come to divert them from the popular cause. It is a character that requires very opposite and almost incompatible qualities – reason and prejudice, a passionate attachment founded on an abstract idea. He who can take up a speculative question, and pursue it with the same zeal and unshaken constancy that he does his immediate interests . . . is the true partisan. (*Works*, XVII, p. 34)

The qualifications of the first sentence are significant; for the difficulty of reconciling 'almost incompatible qualities' is particularly relevant to Hazlitt's own case. His 'partisan' characteristically errs on the side of philosophy rather than prejudice – on attention to the abstract. Intellectual debate is in opposition to 'the popular cause', its tendency being to generate internal, rarified dispute at the expense of action. The likelihood is that the philosophical absolutes of truth and justice will divert attention from the practical world of politics. Philosophy and reason are naturally at odds with popularity.

The problem of intellectual refinement for Hazlitt's particular kind of partisan can also be seen in a general statement from the *Life of Napoleon* which arises out of a consideration of Baboeuf. In this instance, reformers are very close to being reduced to 'speculative reasoners', and imagination figures not as a successfully mediating power, but as the associate of refinement, extravagance, and unreality:

> All reformers, all speculative reasoners, it is to be observed, belong to the class of those, in whom imagination or the belief and hope of *what is not* bears sway over *what is*, and are more or less tinctured with this weakness. The honestest among them are not the least so; though on the other hand it is true that men of much speculative refinement in general are not inclined to action, and for the most part confine their extravagance and credulity to words and theories . . . (*Works*, XIII, p. 303)

If the faults of both partisan and reformer are combined, failure is likely not only because of the philosophical subtlety of the enquiry, but also because the abstract ideal is seen as nothing more than a fiction – a product of imagination.

In his most urgent and politically engaged writing Hazlitt confronts this gap between theory and action, words and reality, and makes an evaluation in favour of the latter. Under the heading 'On the Spirit of Partisanship', for example, he draws attention to the typical error of 'confounding the distinction between theory and practice'. In the very next clause there is no doubt about a decision when the distinction is between 'the still-life of letters and the tug and onset of contending factions'.[17] In the same article Hazlitt considers this political debility in relation to two of the key objects of his inquiries – 'opinion' and 'imagination':

There is a natural timidity of mind, also, which can never go the whole length of any opinion, but is always interlarding its qualified assent with unmeaning *buts* and *ifs*; as there is a levity and discursiveness of imagination which cannot settle finally in any belief, and requires a succession of glancing views, topics, and opposite conclusions, to satisfy its appetite for intellectual variety. (*Works*, XVII, p. 42)

In Hazlitt's numerous commentaries on Burke we see, therefore, not simply a contradiction between radical sympathies and an 'appetite for intellectual variety', but a more fundamental definition of the connection between aesthetic and political power. Under the pressure of political argument the notion of imagination is shown to be a power creative, but not necessarily revealing. Indeed its creativity is disparaged as fictional and is considered to be unworthy of trust in matters of state. Public opinion reveals a further negative aspect which reflects the ambivalence of Hazlitt's own position. By providing an example which both illustrates and contradicts the union of aesthetic and political values, the figure of Burke reveals an important opposition within Hazlitt's writing between the radical and the essayist. The same journalist who wrote to counteract the pernicious effect of Burke's political influence could also write, in the essay on the 'Character of the Country People', that: 'They have no knowledge of literature or the fine arts; which if once banished from the city and the court, would soon "be trampled in the mire under the hoofs of a swinish multitude."'[18]

Hazlitt's critique of Burke exposes many of the fault-lines in his own ideas of the aesthetic as well as revealing his own precarious position as a cultural commentator. For our purposes, it provides us with a foundation for our investigation into the production of imagination at times of social crisis. It offers us a more explicit definition of this representational crisis than would be provided by a more traditional account of Hazlitt's descriptions of creative genius in his poetic or artistic contemporaries. In the tangled web of Hazlitt's negotiation with Burke's rhetoric we can begin to see how imagination is at the centre of Hazlitt's thinking on the subject of knowledge and the formation of ideology. Before moving on to his clash with utilitarian philosophy, however, it is first necessary to see how ruthless he can be about one of his poetic contemporaries when the crisis of reform is at stake. The poet as well as the poetic imagination is here sacrificed as a result of Hazlitt's commitment to social change.

III

Hazlitt's critique of Coleridge's prose writings in his reviews of 1817 confirms his mistrust of the abuse of the imagination.[19] And here once again there is a story of political apostasy and the seeming incompatibility of imagination and realpolitik. Given the particular moment of crisis for liberal reform and its assault on legitimacy, Hazlitt goes even further here in his suggestion of the separation of aesthetics and politics. In his responses to the *Lay Sermons* and *Biographia Literaria*, Hazlitt also confronts his own fraught belief in a liberal and enlightening print culture and the popular transmission of ideas. As in the case of Burke, Coleridge's prose works lead him to question explicitly the relationship between imagination and ideology.

Hazlitt's scathing attack on *Biographia Literaria* in 1817 presents us with a familiar portrait of the failed Coleridge. It works moralistically by drawing attention to the wreck of addiction and a self at the mercy of its own too prodigious talent, before culminating in a vision of 'our disappointed demagogue', 'indulging his maudlin egotism and his mawkish spleen in fulsome eulogies of his own virtues, and nauseous abuse of his contemporaries'.[20] But Hazlitt's review is as interesting for its dismissal of imagination as it is for any personalised attack on his former idol. In his consideration of Coleridge's famous abstract theory of imagination and fancy, Hazlitt is quite prepared to make the sacrifice: he quite happily consigns imagination to the limited realm of the aesthetic. At this particular moment he allows for the fact that imagination and power must be parted.

Hazlitt seems to be less than impressed with Coleridge's famous act of 'desynonymisation', claiming that 'chap. iv begins the formidable ascent of that mountainous and barren ridge of clouds piled on precipices and precipices on clouds, from the top of which the author deludes us with a view of the Promised Land that divides the regions of Fancy from those of the Imagination'.[21] This is a devastating image of delusive vacuity and self-referring insubstantiality, reminiscent of Hazlitt's attack on Shelley and a reminder of his championing of the groundedness of Burke which we have just considered. But Hazlitt reserves his most powerful shots for the last round of his review when he offers his own disquisition on imagination which fills in for Coleridge's (by now infamous) strategic omission. Hazlitt's withering attack begins with an interestingly measured and qualified statement which clearly reveals the pressure of the time. 'Reason and imagination', he suggests, 'are both excellent things; but perhaps their provinces ought to be kept more distinct than they have lately been.'[22]

The attack on poets which follows is clearly motivated by the threat which they might inadvertently offer to the delicate situation in which the republic of letters finds itself towards the end of the second decade of the nineteenth century. As Hazlitt puts it, the poets 'are disposed to meddle with every thing, and mar all'.[23] Careful to assure us that he is no Plato ('We would not . . . absolutely banish poets from the commonwealth; but we really think they should meddle as little with its practical administration as may be'), he then proceeds to catalogue their dangerous and excessive susceptibility to change and innovation, all of which, he argues, is based on their vain quest for novelty. Hazlitt sounds almost Burkean as he castigates the unstable vanities of these feminised men of letters. He is also aware of the peculiar licence they have as poets: 'Their inordinate vanity runs them into all sorts of extravagances; and their habitual effeminacy gets them out at any price.'[24] This riot of relativising Romantic subjectivities, which Hazlitt conveys along with a thinly veiled attack on personal morality, is seen to put at risk his vision of liberal progress:

Preposterously seeking for the stimulus of novelty in truth, and the éclat of theatrical exhibition in pure reason, it is no wonder that these persons at last become disgusted with their own pursuits, and that, in consequence of the violence of the change, the most inveterate prejudices and uncharitable sentiments have rushed in to fill up the *vacuum* produced by the previous annihilation of common sense, wisdom, and humanity. (*Works*, XVI, p. 138)

Such, according to Hazlitt, is 'the true history of our reformed Antijacobin poets; the life of one whom is here recorded'.[25] This gives the impression that Hazlitt is at last coming clean by explaining the political grounds of his savage attack on the Sage of Highgate. But Hazlitt's text is here riven with the paradox of his separation between imagination and power. Underlying the whole attack, and threatening to break in upon the writing at any point, is the very smack of power which such anti-Jacobin imaginations can conjure. Hazlitt's attack on Coleridge turns out to be a particularly contradictory affair: in order to preserve his own position as a cultural commentator he must marginalise Coleridge; and the most likely way of doing so is to confirm his public's sense of the unreality of the poet and the poetic imagination. Only by limiting the sway of imaginative power can Hazlitt envisage the scope for what he sees as the inevitably libertarian progress of letters. But to partition the republic of letters in this way is itself to betray his almost Paine-like optimism in the transparent openness of a rapidly increasing print culture. Ironically, in ridiculing the unreality of the poetic imagination, Hazlitt comes close to the project of Coleridge himself. Better to be master of the selected audience, to go for the partial truth, rather than the promise of the whole Truth.

A more exact measure of what is at stake in Hazlitt's attack on *Biographia Literaria* can be had from his review of *Lay Sermons*, published eight months earlier in the *Edinburgh Review*. Here Hazlitt had adopted a different strategy for consigning Coleridge to aesthetic oblivion: he characterises him as always falling between two stools: between theory and practice; fancy and reason. Where the great mediatory, esemplastic power should be there is only an absence of will. Coleridge is reduced by Hazlitt to the role of the Hamlet looker-on, possessed of the sensibility, but lacking the poems, the action, like Will Ladislaw in Eliot's *Middlemarch*. If, as Coleridge might insist, imagination is a faculty of possibilities, or promises, it is for Hazlitt, an emasculating aesthetic devoid of both real power and commonsense. Hazlitt's strategy, in short, is to turn Coleridge's experiment with audience against him. Just as in the case of the *Biographia*, Hazlitt takes the sting out of the text by relegating it to an aesthetic category of its own making, so too in his response to *Lay Sermons* he converts Coleridge's cleverly directed rhetoric into a waking dream of imagination. According to Hazlitt, the audience addressed here is *only* imaginary. He refers with characteristic mockery to: 'Mr Coleridge and his imaginary audience'.[26] Lacking will, Coleridge inevitably lacks power, Hazlitt insists. Coleridge's 'readiness of lending his imagination to every thing, prevents him from weighing the force of any one'.[27] Having compared Coleridge unfavourably with the 'vagaries, whimsies and pregnant throes of Joanna Southcote', Hazlitt soon reveals what it is that makes Coleridge's attempt at the 'rhematic'[28] no more than a waking dream: 'Plain sense and plain speaking would put an end to those "thick-coming fancies," that lull him to repose.'[29]

Hazlitt's review soon turns on the issue of the reading public itself.

Ultimately, the issue is seen to rest on the relation between public opinion and private conscience – that powerful, if problematic, combination formed from his dissenting inheritance and liberal hopes:

> Would he punish the *reading public* for their bad taste in reading periodical publications which he does not like, by suppressing the freedom of the press altogether, or destroying the art of printing? He does not know what he means himself. Perhaps we can tell him. He, or at least those whom he writes to please, and who look 'with jealous leer malign' at modern advantages and modern pretensions, would give us back all the abuses of former times, without any of their advantages... (*Works*, XVI, p. 106)

With angry disbelief, Hazlitt makes mock of the threat:

> The public is become a reading public, down to the cottager's child; and he thanks God for it – for that great moral steam-engine, Dr Bell's original and unsophisticated plan, which he considers as an especial gift of Providence to the human race – thus about to be converted into a great reading public; and yet he utters his Profaccia upon it with a desponding sigh; and proposes, as a remedy, to put this spirit which has gone forth, under the tutelage of churchwardens, to cant against 'liberal ideas', and 'the jargon of this enlightened age'; – in other words, to turn this vast machine against itself, and make it a go-cart of corruption, servility, superstition and tyranny. Mr Coleridge's first horror is, that there should be a reading public: his next hope is to prevent them from reaping an atom of benefit from 'reflection and stirrings of the mind, with all their restlessness'. (*Works*, XVI, p. 113)

Such vehement defences of the freedom of the press and the circulation of ideas belie Hazlitt's seemingly confident declarations earlier on in the review when he quotes Coleridge's own words: '*Implicite*, it is without the COPULA – it wants the possibility – of every position, to which there exists any correspondence in reality';[30] and that: 'It tends to produce a complete *interregnum* of all theory and practice'. Coleridge 'is always promising great things, in short, and performs nothing'.[31] Clearly, Hazlitt has much to fear from such Coleridgean meddling and perhaps he too recognises, like Jon Klancher more recently, the fact that Coleridge's attempts were the most sophisticated experiments in the construction of an audience to be found in the nineteenth century.[32] As a result, he is intent on consigning Coleridge's new science of the 'rhematic' to oblivion before it even gets off the ground.

Hazlitt's portrait of Coleridge in *The Spirit of the Age* also suggests that he is the victim of much too multifarious a genius, a man of potentialities rather than of achievements; but it is also willing to see him as the victim of 'the hag, Legitimacy'. Compared to the other apostates, Wordsworth and Southey, Coleridge has not, in the eyes of Hazlitt, taken that fatal step of becoming an establishment sinecure-man. In fact he remains in Hazlitt's view, poised – though slumped would be more accurate – on the margins of legitimacy, trapped by power into a lethargy and idleness of almost aesthetic proportions:

and so has [Coleridge] sunk into torpid, uneasy repose, tantalized by useless sources, haunted by vain imaginings, his lips idly moving, but his heart forever still, or, as the shattered chords vibrate of themselves, making melancholy music to the ear of memory! Such is the fate of genius in an age, when in the unequal contest with sovereign wrong, every man is ground to powder who is not either a born slave, or who does not willingly and at once offer up the yearnings of humanity and the dictates of reason as a welcome sacrifice to besotted prejudice and loathsome power. (*Works*, XI, p. 34)

Hazlitt's reviews of *Lay Sermons* and *Biographia* in 1817 provide ample evidence of a long established split between theory and practice. Recent criticism has drawn attention to the complex relativity of Hazlitt's texts, particularly in the case of *The Spirit of the Age*.[33] This squares well with his separatist line of thinking as far as the imagination is concerned. His articles and biographical portraits appear as discrete relativised units which suggest quite strongly that a more panoptic, overall view is actually unattainable. In other words, Hazlitt's relativity might well signal a cultural incapacity to perceive the 'spirit of the age'. Indeed, it could be argued that his division between imagination and reason is a means of coping with such cultural relativity. His vituperative attack on Coleridge in 1817 makes a particularly strong argument in favour of separating imagination from politics. Coleridge the poet is clearly thought of as a dangerous meddler in political affairs, particularly, one suspects, when so much is at stake for Hazlitt. Faced with Coleridge's attack on the force of public opinion and on the nature of the language which might be the vehicle of such opinion, Hazlitt is forced to sacrifice imagination for fear of losing the battle of words.

The same sacrifice or separation is apparent in Hazlitt's attitude towards the advance of print culture and the progress of letters. He can be excitedly optimistic and confident in expressing the liberalising and enlightening power of the press:

The gift of speech, or the communication of thought by words, is that which distinguishes man from other animals. But this faculty is limited and imperfect without the intervention of books, which render the knowledge possessed by every one in the community accessible to all. There is no doubt, then, that the press (as it has existed in modern times) is the great organ of intellectual improvement and civilization. (*Works*, XVIII, p. 38)

But such belief in the improving power of knowledge, circulating through the various organs of the press does not extend, in Hazlitt's view, to the fine arts. His brief attempt at a subject that had much exercised both Peacock and Shelley – 'Whether the Arts are Progressive?' – contains a familiar historical view: science may be liable to progress but the arts are not and characteristically have their finest flowering in their barbarous infancy. As a result, so Hazlitt argues (working on his favourite principle of the sympathetic imagination), the artists or creators are also their best consumers. Since 'the highest efforts of genius, in every walk of art, can never be properly understood by the generality of mankind', the fine arts operate at a distinct remove from the workings of liberal democracy:

> The principal of universal suffrage, however applicable to matters of government, which concern the common feelings and common interests of society, is by no means applicable to matters of taste, which can only be decided upon by the most refined understandings... It may be objected, that the public taste is capable of gradual improvement, because, in the end, the public do justice to works of the greatest merit. This is a mistake. The reputation ultimately, and often slowly affixed to works of genius is attempted upon them by authority, not by popular consent or the common sense of the world. (*Works*, IV, p. 164)

Such a claim for the recalcitrant aristocracy of letters should not surprise us after witnessing the ambivalence of his response to Burke.

Hazlitt's attack on Coleridge strategically deploys the idea of the new reading public in order to focus on its own agenda for reform. The distracting effect of Coleridge's political interventions must be undermined, even if that means a temporary relegation of poetry along with the figure of the dissolute poet. For Hazlitt, Coleridge threatens the idea of a unified common sense of reform by his explicit address to different classes of readers. He also threatens to mystify the particularity of action by his insistent recourse to abstraction. According to Hazlitt, Coleridge has this much in common with the new philosophers of utility.[34] But in his critique of them Hazlitt also faces an enemy whose popular identity is based on a thorough denial of the very idea of the aesthetic as existing in anything but the sum total of the general happiness. The new enemy also has the temerity to have appropriated for itself the very name of reform.

IV

One of Hazlitt's strategies for tackling this burgeoning ideology of utility is to deny its novelty and its originality. He claims it is doing no more than rehearse the dead philosophies of Mandeville, Helvetius, Paley, and Godwin. In joining together these philosophies, Hazlitt inadvertently constructs a powerful lineage for the new mode of thinking. Like Coleridge (as we shall see in the final chapter), he synthesises otherwise competing texts into a coherent philosophy of utility which crosses party lines. He makes it into a dominant ideological structure like the 'hag Legitimacy' so that he can rail against it by adopting the persona of an embattled outsider.

In many other respects, of course, there is a connection between the old and new philosophies of utility, and Hazlitt finds himself revisiting and revising the positions and arguments he had espoused much more optimistically twenty years earlier. And within British thinking, he returns to the debates on charity which had begun with Mandeville and which had found a theological and specifically Establishment basis in Paley's *Principles of Moral and Political Philosophy* (1785).[35] But by the mid 1820s Hazlitt finds himself a belated 'Jacobin' overtaken by the new reformers whose utilitarian ideology he attacks on the grounds that it is complicit with the old philosophies of selfishness. It is now apparent that the perfectibilist optimism of Godwin and what he considers to be the degrading threat posed by Malthus's essay on population share a common methodological and ideological axis. The legacy of the French Enlightenment which Hazlitt at one point saw in the imaginative sentiment of Rousseau has instead manifested itself in the secular materialism of Helvetius.[36] Not surprisingly, Hazlitt is in danger of being made to look superannuated by what he refers to as 'the new school of reform'. His old brand of libertarianism with Liberty as its watchword and 'Legitimacy' as its demon has been replaced by an ideology which can now be embraced by the establishment in the name of progress.

Exactly how Hazlitt perceived the change in political climate and culture is evident from 'On Jealousy and the Spleen of Party', the last essay in *The Plain Speaker*. Hazlitt clearly overplays the level of popularity, unanimity, and cohesion which once existed in the libertarian cause in order to emphasise the exclusive, elitist character of the new reformers:

The tone of politics and public opinion has undergone a considerable and curious change, even in the few short years I can remember. In my time, that is, in the early part of it, the love of liberty (at least by all those whom I came near) was regarded as the dictate of common sense and common honesty. It was not a question of depth of learning, but an instinctive feeling, prompted by a certain generous warmth of blood in every one worthy the name of Briton. A man would as soon avow himself to be a pimp or a pickpocket as a tool or a pander to corruption. This was the natural and at the same time the national feeling. Patriotism was not at variance with philanthropy. To take an interest in humanity, it was only thought necessary to have the form of a man . . . (*Works*, XII, pp. 372–373)

Hazlitt's nostalgic vision of the past takes the form of a Rousseauan transparency in which natural sentiment, political view, and national identity are one. Morality acts upon an almost prelapsarian 'instinctive feeling' and operates in true sentimental fashion through the pulsings of the bloodstream. All this only serves to highlight the change which has taken place: the schism in culture which has since been generated by the arrival of an intellectual elite whose arcane, technical knowledge claims to have replaced the old language of morality.

As he itemises the intellectual landmarks which betray the gradual deterioration from the popular cause of 'Liberty', the familiar and famous instances of apostasy combine with the methodological threat from the new philosophy:

Mr. Burke had in vain sung his *requiem* over the 'age of chivalry:' Mr. Pitt mouthed out his speeches on the existence of social order to no purpose: Mr. Malthus had not cut up Liberty by the roots by passing 'the grinding law of necessity' over it, and entailing vice and misery on all future generations as their happiest lot: Mr. Ricardo had not pared down the schemes of visionary projectors and idle talkers into the form of Rent: Mr. Southey had not surmounted his cap of Liberty with the laurel wreath; nor Mr. Wordsworth proclaimed Carnage as 'God's Daughter;' nor Mr. Coleridge, to patch up a rotten cause, written the FRIEND. (*Works*, XII, p. 374)

Now Hazlitt finds himself caught between the aristocractic, effeminate, dandy Whigs and the cynical, university educated, and puritanical new reformers. As a liberal journalist he is caught between the *Edinburgh* and *Westminster* reviews. Such sectarianism means that the cause of reform itself loses contact with 'the People' and that it, of course, loses out to the Tories who know their enemies and who are willing to use support from whatever rank or class it comes. Hazlitt's position in the mid 1820s, as he so graphically puts it, is to be squeezed between 'the painted booths of Whig aristocracy' and 'the sordid styes of Reform'.[37]

This is the context which imposes itself on the persona of *The Plain Speaker* and which generates the urgency of 'On Reason and Imagination', probably Hazlitt's most famous and most celebrated exposition of his literary aesthetics. This essay is certainly his most direct and explicit commentary on the vexed Romantic and literary faculty of the imagination. It is surprising then that even his best critics have underplayed the extent to which the aesthetic exposition here is driven by the need to resist the ideology of utility.[38] Hazlitt's article is a desperate attempt to deny the new epistemology and in particular its claim to a new mode of cognitive knowledge which incorporates ethics and bypasses the culture of feelings which Hazlitt had problematically inherited from Rousseau and which was, of course, central to his own subscription to literary culture – what he more pertinently describes as 'the aristocracy of letters'. The ethical capacity of imagination is much more to the fore in this article than any narrow literary understanding of the faculty; and Hazlitt's idea of imagination comes under pressure not just from the new philosophy but also from his own subscription to an empiricist form of individualism.

'On Reason and Imagination' opens with a typically barbed example of plain-speaking: 'I hate people who have no notion of any thing but generalities, and forms, and creeds, and naked propositions, even worse than I dislike those who cannot for the soul of them arrive at the comprehension of an abstract idea.'[39] Hazlitt pitches his aggression precisely: even though he might count himself among the readers and writers of philosophy, the very people who deal in abstract ideas, the new enemy comprises those whose exclusive focus on the ideology of utility rules out the very possibility of possessing a soul. The new philosophy takes no account of 'humanity', by which Hazitt means the evidence of the senses mediated and thereby humanised through passion, sympathy, and the imagination. An article which ostensibly subscribes to the complementarity of faculties – reason and imagination – finds it increasingly difficult to maintain such a happy fiction in the face of a mathematical methodology. Having stated that 'Logic should enrich and invigorate its decisions by the use of imagination; as rhetoric should be governed in its application, and guarded from abuse by the checks of the understanding', Hazlitt immediately goes on to announce that 'The mind can conceive only one or a few things in their integrity: if it proceeds to more, it must have recourse to artificial substitutes, and judges by comparison merely.'[40] These potentially contradictory statements set the terms for the ethical attack on utility which follows. At the same time as Hazlitt objects to the God-like panoptic view claimed by the philosophers of utility, he severely limits his notion of the sympathetic and empathetic imagination. Almost implicit in his critique of the panoptic view is a worry over its aesthetic freedom, its ability to deal in 'artificial substitutes'.[41] Hazlitt's empiricism and his associationism together ground his own aesthetic in a very empirical reality which has little truck with representation: 'There is no language, no description that can strictly come up to the truth and force of reality: all we have to do is to guide our descriptions and conclusions by the reality.'[42]

The defence of imagination which follows is similarly determined by the thinking of his opponents: 'all individual facts and history come under the head of what these people call *Imagination*'.[43] In response, Hazlitt draws powerfully and strategically on the recent historical debate over the slave trade in order to drive home his point about the ethical capacity of sympathy.[44] He quotes from *The Memoirs of Granville Sharp* in order to illustrate how, in the case of slavery, the individual is linked to the general, and how the appalled imagination is a sure test of morality:

If a man should try to kill me, or should sell me and my family for slaves, he would do an injury to as many as he might kill or sell; but if any one takes away the character of Black people, that man injures Black people all over the world; and when he has once taken away their character, there is nothing he may not do to Black people ever after. (*Works*, XII, p. 49)

This, for Hazlitt, represents incontrovertible experiential evidence of the inadequacy of utilitarian philosophy:

more real light and vital heat is thrown into the argument by this struggle of natural feeling to relieve itself from the weight of a false and injurious imputation, than would be added to it by twenty volumes of tables and calculations of the *pros* and *cons* of right and wrong, of utility and inutility, in Mr. Bentham's handwriting. (*Works*, XII, p. 49)

On the same principle, Hazlitt argues, 'an infinite number of lumps of sugar put into Mr. Bentham's artificial ethical scales would never weigh against the pounds of human flesh, or drops of human blood, that are sacrificed to produce them'.[45] Having dealt a severe blow to Bentham, Hazlitt next turns his attention to James Mill, knowing that the reader has already had the benefit of a moral reminder on the slave trade before he deals with utility's most able colonialist spokesman.

Hazlitt attacks James Mill for having 'declared that he was [better] qualified to write a History of India from having never been there than if he had'. Hazlitt's response is to stick to the 'local':

> I humbly conceive that the seeing half a dozen wandering Lascars in the streets of London gives one a better idea of the soul of India . . . than all the charts, records, and statistical reports that can be sent over, even under the classical administration of Mr. Canning. (*Works*, XII, p. 51)

Once again, Hazlitt circumscribes the efficacy of imagination at the same time as he champions it, resolute as he is in affirming that the individual is the source of knowledge. The precariousness of this sympathetic knowledge as a basis for ethical behaviour is revealed when he declares that: 'The imagination is an *associating* principle; and has an instinctive perception when a thing belongs to a system, or is only an exception to it.'[46] If there were doubts as to whether all instances provide the same clear-cut substitution of individual for general as in the case of slavery, this claim for 'instinctive perception' certainly confirms them. The epistemological certainty Hazlitt claims for the sympathetic imagination conflicts sharply with the complementarity between reason and judgement which he argues for elsewhere in the article; and his own argument is not particularly bolstered by the fact that he is also keen to articulate, albeit defensively, the dangers of the abuse and misuse of imagination in the case of Burke and in the massacres of the French Revolution.[47]

Hazlitt's portrait of Bentham in *The Spirit of the Age* as the arch philosopher of 'Utility' reinforces this sense of an alien and alienating methodology. In personal terms, his character study is of an isolated recluse whose reputation only exists at an abstracted international level. According to Hazlitt, Bentham is a virtual unknown in his own neighbourhood. Like the image of James Mill in 'On Reason and Imagination', Bentham's actual existence is symbolic of the new philosophy: deliberately abstracted from the particular and the local in its perverse quest for the intellectually remote and exotic. Even more significant is the way Hazlitt presents Bentham's writing. Instead of operating upon a principle of transparent mediation, it actually '*darkens knowledge*' by setting up a boundary between the vulgar and the learned: 'It is a barbarous philosophical jargon, with all the repetitions, parentheses, formalities, uncouth nomenclature and verbiage of law-Latin.'[48] Hazlitt's critique of Bentham's style operates a rhetoric of class and cultural difference in order to emphasise its foreign or alien culture. While he recognises some of the dangers of 'local and natural affection',[49] Hazlitt constructs Bentham's philosophy as an undermining of what is natural and civilised: 'Those who on pure cosmopolite principles or on the ground of abstract humanity, affect an extraordinary regard for the Turks and Tartars, have been accused of neglecting their duties to their friends and their neighbours.'[50] Too great a regard for abstract humanity, Hazlitt's implied argument runs, leads to barbarism. And at the same time as he mounts this attack, he foregrounds the limitations of his version of the imagination:

> Could our imagination take wing (with our speculative faculties) to the other side of the globe or to the ends of the universe, could our eyes behold whatever our reason teaches us to be possible, could our hands reach as far as our thoughts and wishes, we might then busy ourselves to advantage with the Hottentots, or hold intimate converse with the inhabitants of the Moon; but being as we are, our feelings evaporate in so large a space – we must draw the circle of our affections and duties somewhat closer – the heart hovers and fixes nearer home. (*Works*, XI, p. 10)

Hazlitt's affective bias provides the limit to his idea of imagination: feelings can only be stretched so far. Rather than mounting on the wings of speculation, Hazlitt's conception of this faculty is still very much circumscribed by natural ties and affections. He refuses to cut it off from either perception or the local.

If in his attempt to make strange the ideology of utility Hazlitt is led to parochialise the imagination, his countering the enemy with the power of the sympathetic imagination leads him into further difficulties. When he comes to tackle Utilitarianism's now famous involvement with the legal system and penal reform Hazlitt again reveals the limits of his imaginative sympathy. If he had great difficulty identifying with the Turk, the Tartar, and the Hottentot, he also has difficulty closer to home with criminals and murderers. In order to rescue the language of morality from what he considers to be a dehumanising, even degrading, mode of computation, Hazlitt is led to take a pessimistic view of human nature. If the philosophy of utility has taken for itself the side of perfectibilist optimism, Hazlitt, while decrying a methodology which he sees as reducing 'Man' to a mere animal, is forced to ground his social and psychological speculations on our baser desires and affections. Since he considers sentiment and sympathy to be part of a habitual moral reflex, acts of inhumanity are thought to tear through the fabric of social ties. One can be de-humanised, alienated from feeling. This is the down-side to the idea of 'an intercommunity of feeling'.[51]

One of Hazlitt's most trenchant and most interesting critiques of 'Utility' is to be found in his short article on 'The Late Murders' which responds to public opinion in the aftermath of the 'Burke and Hare' murder trial which took place in Edinburgh in 1828. Here Hazlitt's opening gambit is to correct the public's view that 'the shockingness of the crime' depends on 'the value of human life'. Rather, Hazlitt suggests, our attention should be on 'the value which every human being sets on it'. Immediately, he revolts against what he sees as the meaningless abstraction of 'human life' and replaces it with the experiential reality of human interaction. Such abstraction, he then goes on to argue, is as characteristic of the utilitarians as the body-snatchers. The suggestion is that not only will utilitarian thinking make us incapable of responding in a proper moral fashion to such events, but that its method itself constitutes an act of moral indifference. And once again, Hazlitt turns to Burke for a moral register of civilisation and barbarism in order to expose this latent inhumanity within the utilitarian methodology. Hazlitt's murderous utilitarians resemble Burke's depiction of barbaric French revolutionaries in the *Reflections*:

to take away life in order to *sell* the dead body, to be hacked and hewed, and turned to use that way – as if the vile carcass were of more value than the living soul – is the highest aggravation of the cruelty and insult; for it is placing the contrast between life and death in the extremist point of view, and still contemplating it with brutish indifference or fiend-like avarice. It is the worst kind of cannibalism: for that may be hunger or savage rage, this is cold-blooded calculation. We may see by this example (in spite of what the *Utilitarians* tell us) how impossible it is to sanctify the means by the end . . . (*Works*, xx, p. 192)

This passage confirms the threat posed by 'cold-blooded calculation' to Hazlitt's philosophy of the sympathetic heart and to his religious sense of the after-life. More problematically, it also reveals his own ambivalence towards the body, his squeamishness when faced with actual blood rather than the blood of sentimental discourse. The terrible social implications of such an indifferent mode of reckoning are made clear soon after in a scenario of degeneration often thought to be more characteristic of reactionary political commentators than liberal/radical ones like Hazlitt:

Harden the feelings, debase the imagination – and you strike at the root of all morality and at the whole social system. There is no answering for the consequences. From the resurrection-man with his yellow fingers and torpid load, the transition is obvious to the assassin with blood-stained hands and his struggling victim. By familiarity . . . he loses the repugnance due to death, and by degrees the reverence due to life. He looks at human bodies as containing so many bones and muscles, as so many moving anatomical preparations, and thinks that every pound of flesh, if it were *dead*, would be worth so much gold. This is a fearful train of ideas. The abstract utility does not purify these men's motives, as long as their imagination is a charnel-house, and they are accustomed to *stop the mouth* of all their own natural scruples . . . There is then something besides Utility. (*Works*, xx, p. 192)

This short article strikes at the heart of the moral issue informing the spirit of the age. By 1829 public perception can already be assumed to be moulded by and to be proceeding unconsciously according to utilitarian principles. Somewhat ironically, this alien, remote, and intellectually specialist mode of knowledge has begun to form the popular consciousness or at least to have infiltrated the language of moral judgement.

Hazlitt tries desperately to reintroduce a sense of ethical individualism into a situation where, he assumes, the dominant mode of philosophical thinking – utilitarianism – has captured the moral imagination of the public. Hazlitt's sense of this philosophy's pervasiveness is evident in the way in which his article ends: with a call for more passion and, consequently, for an ethical engagement of the sympathetic imagination in contemporary drama. It is implied that the spirit of the age has acceded to the utilitarian mode of representation. The article's earlier admission that 'We have been so used to count by millions of late, that we think the units that compose them nothing; and are so prone to trace remote principles, that we neglect the immediate results'[52] indicates that the utilitarian mode of thinking (or at least its agenda) has become such a habitual reflex of the cultural imagination as to infect the current state of the drama.

Hazlitt's aggressive response to the philosophers of utility is to offer an aggregative and repetitional form of individualism which, he claims, is capable of constructing a community of feeling and, even more problematically, a form of moral knowledge based on affective cognition:

Man is (so to speak) an endless and infinitely varied repetition: and if we know what one man feels, we so far know what a thousand feel in the sanctuary of their being. Our feeling of general humanity is at once an aggregate of a thousand different truths, and it is also the same truth a thousand times told . . . The boundary of our sympathy is a circle which enlarges itself according to its propulsion from the centre – the heart. (*Works*, xii, pp. 54–55)

'The New School of Reform' confirms Hazlitt's problem in articulating his critique of the new enemy. Even the dialogue he constructs between a Rationalist ('R') and the 'sentimentalist' ('S') is conceived in the terms of his opponents. ('Sentimentalist' is the term of abuse employed by the

Westminster against the belletristic faults of *The Edinburgh Review*.) Not only have they usurped his explicitly ideological position of radical reformer, they have banished aesthetics from their commonwealth.

Hazlitt's response is entirely characteristic: he equates their abstract philosophical pretensions with a narrowness of vision, and he debunks their claims to be new and original by comparing their ideas with stolen rags and iron. He presents them as no-sayers, fundamentalist philosophers who betray their origins in Scottish Calvinism. Instead of 'hellfire or the terrors of purgatory' these 'modern polemics set their disciples in the stocks of Utility, or throw all the elegant arts and amiable impulses of humanity into the Limbo of Political Economy'.[53]

Although the ostensible purpose of the dialogue is to require the reader to resist the terms of the debate by having them redefined by the Sentimentalist, the result is far from satisfactory. Asked by the Rationalist to accede to the distinction between utility and 'fanciful interest', the Sentimentalist only confirms the separation:

there are two standards of value and modes of appreciation in human life, the one practical, the other ideal, – . . . Why then force these two standards into one? Or make the Understanding judge of what belongs to the Fancy any more than the Fancy, judge of what belongs to the Understanding? Poetry would make bad mathematics, mathematics bad poetry: why jumble them together? Leave things, that are so, separate. *Cuique tribuito suum*. (*Works*, XII, p. 191)

This split in culture is then confirmed as a split identity when he announces: 'Besides my automatic existence, I have another – a sentimental one.'[54] Despite his later claim that he 'place[s] the heart at the centre of his moral system',[55] the ground has effectively been conceded to the more inclusive and therefore more ideologically potent philosophy of utility. The best that Hazlitt can do is to adopt Burke's stance in the *Reflections* with regard to the Enlightenment thinkers whom he argues are behind the Revolution. The new ideology, Hazlitt argues echoing Burke, turns 'Man' into 'a mere animal, or a mere machine'. 'To deprive man of sentiment, is to . . . turn him into a savage, an automaton, or a Political Economist.'[56] Hazlitt's moral rhetoric struggles with this dichotomy. His savage indignation at the 'sordid, squalid, harsh, and repulsive' vision produced by such a 'want of imagination' finds itself in a position which can only supplement the inadequacies or make good the deficiencies of this philosophy, rather than challenge its basic tenets head-on. The middle ground of the radical essayist has been taken way from him and the new philosophy exposes the tensions between his literary aesthetics and his social sympathies. The sentimentalist ideal of an aggregative community of feeling based on passion and the instinctive morality of the sympathetic imagination has been by-passed by a scientific calculation of happiness. Hazlitt's brand of individualism has to contend with the new idealism,[57] and it is made to look schizophrenic, even contradictory. A gap has opened up between social improvement and the elegant arts of literary culture.

For the next generation of utilitarians, which includes John Stuart Mill, the aesthetic is, ironically, only brought back into play after they have confidently imagined the success of the new ideology. As we shall see in the next chapter, the culture of feelings for which Hazlitt fights so doggedly reappears at the imaginative prospect of achieved social improvement. The repressed affect of the utilitarian project returns in the form of an alienated self-consciousness which desperately seeks to supplement itself with feeling.

5
Cobbett's imaginary landscape

I

To include Cobbett in a book on imagination might seem surprising. So much of his writing is contingent and of practical intent that its relationship to an aesthetic sense seems remote, for all his preoccupation with happiness, and his eulogising of the English countryside. Our sense of remoteness here is itself, of course, a measure of historical distance and of our dominant cultural inheritance from the last two centuries which, as Raymond Williams has pointed out,[1] has dissociated aesthetics and utility in this way. Just as twentieth-century accounts of Cobbett's politics need to be self-conscious about how his kind of political writing has, unlike Paine's, been discontinuous with progressive political histories, so too appreciating Cobbett's aesthetics must also involve, in part, an act of historical recovery.

Recent studies have significantly altered our perception of Cobbett as a writer by analysing the complexly strategic nature of his texts, the heterogeneous nature of his language, and the specifically rural nature of his cultural identity.[2] It is no longer possible to see Cobbett as some kind of literary primitive or ingenu who became one of the most influential and certainly voluminous publishers of his day almost despite himself. A new picture is beginning to emerge of a writer who successfully and intelligently exploited the new possibilities in audience and print culture. He is not simply 'authentic' or naive. As a consequence of such work, it is also no longer possible to take at face value the truth claims of his texts. Cobbett is emerging as a complex rhetorical strategist whose deployment of a plain style is both complex and sophisticated. Nevertheless, there are still ways in which his writings resist conventional literary analysis and demand a social semiotics which can appreciate the transmission of text and idea in a wider cultural and historical context.[3] My aim in this chapter, however, is not to provide a poetics of Cobbett's styles, but to expose the necessity for aesthetics at the heart of his apparent empirical transparency. My aim is to uncover the necessary connection betweeen beauty and utility in his writing, and, as in the chapter on Paine's literalism, to see how in a cultural crisis this apparent transparency actually depends upon a specific sense of the aesthetic and implies a role, however limited, for the faculty of imagination. In Cobbett's case, the threat posed by political economy leads him to a mode of representation which must transcend sense perception as well as the moment.

In terms of the wider perspective of this study, imagination here is, for the most part, conspicuous by its studied absence. Forms of polite aesthetic generally and imagination particularly are attacked and defined negatively before the term imagination reasserts itself at crucial moments in Cobbett's texts. Cobbett's example gives us a valuable opportunity to explore the figure of imagination as a putative entity and as a key word in his very distinctive debates about utility, aesthetics, and the visible truth of his England.

The subject of this chapter, therefore, is as much the avoidance of things imaginative as the existence of an aesthetic sense lurking on the periphery of Cobbett's work. Cobbett failed to rule imagination out of court because his preoccupations after his disillusionment with the present system of English government necessitated its use. Under pressure to describe the 'canker-worm' at the heart of English society, Cobbett is forced to make that which is invisible visible; that which is merely fictional a reality.[4] Even if the drive of his work is to expose and demystify, this process inevitably makes him accede to the existence of a power which he would otherwise deny; makes him defer to a whole series of categories which run counter to his apparently dogmatic materialism.

II

In his astute commentaries on Cobbett in *The Making of the English Working Class*, E. P. Thompson draws attention to his 'anti-intellectualism' and its legacy for future thinkers on the Left in British politics. In such a castigation Thompson revealed his own priorities in establishing a historical definition of working-class political culture and the role of the intellectual in the British labour movement in the late 1950s. This is even more apparent when he writes of Cobbett's legacy as 'theoretical opportunism (masked as "practical" empiricism)'.[5] Wishing to clear practical empiricism of a bad example, Thompson labels it 'theoretical opportunism' and effectively kills two birds with one stone. That, I assume, is the rationale of his remarks. For our purposes, Cobbett's anti-intellectualism, even what some may consider to be his philistinism, takes on a different identity when considered in the context of his infiltration of as well as his assault on polite culture.[6] Opportunistic and strategic Cobbett's writings certainly are, but, as we shall see, they demonstrate great difficulty in negotiating a culturally and historically determined shift in the theoretical and empirical grounds of knowledge.

Cobbett's attack on imagination can, in part, be explained by his wish to engage in a battle with polite culture. It stems from his equation of indolence with refinement. His description of the *Political Register* (the publication he set up, and which provided his major outlet for more than thirty years) glories in its refusal to eschew all forms of entertainment or association with leisure which characterise most other periodicals – even those which had a specific political identity. At the beginning of the first issue of the seventh volume in January 1805, he proudly announces that the pages of his publication 'sedulously excluded . . . every thing calculated to amuse the frivolous or to entertain the indolent' and that it was to be occupied 'entirely with dry political matter, requiring seriousness and reflection in the perusal to render it at all valuable'. Furthermore, it was not to be 'aided by the sprightliness of wit or the embellishments of style, but, in its unenticing garb, addressed directly to the understanding and the reason'.[7] Characteristically, Cobbett combines a moral, even puritanical, attack on polite society with an appeal to the directness of his writing, which claims to have freed itself from the clutter of taste by its singular concentration on seriousness and content. And, on a more pragmatic level, Cobbett's exclusion of aesthetic amusement means that he can proclaim the *Political Register*'s circulation to be a direct reflection of 'its principles and opinions'.[8]

The same sort of attacking bravado directed against refinement is evident in the following exchange on landscape:

I have, for *my part*, no idea of *picturesque* beauty separate from *fertility of soil*. If you can have *both*, as on the banks of CLYDE, and on the skirts of the *bays* and *inlets* in Long Island, then it is delightful: but, if I must have *one* or *the other*, any body may have the *picturesque beauty* for me.[9]

Here the importance of the contextual nature of polemic is brought to the fore: where there has to be a choice Cobbett plumps with relish for that which confirms his position as a parvenu in the refined world of letters.

Having allowed for Cobbett's undermining of the polite forms of culture, his assumption that refinement is automatically false and morally debilitating, and his consistent use of the word 'vulgar' to describe his adversaries, it soon becomes apparent that the distinction which supports and, indeed, premises this class warfare is a fundamental one between beauty and utility. And the attack is very specifically targeted according to social group and Cobbett's sense of the threat posed to it by his notion of refined beauty in the form of luxury, indolence, and effeminacy. This is obviously one of the determining factors in his *Advice to Young Men, and (Incidentally) to Young Women, in the Middle and Higher Ranks of Life, in a Series of Letters Addressed to A Youth, A Bachelor, A Lover, A Husband, A Father, and a Citizen or a Subject* (1830). It is significant that this book is aimed in part at men (and, to a lesser extent, women) in the middle ranks of life. In this respect, it registers one of Cobbett's preoccupations: that the yeoman farmers of England have diminished in number not only because of larger economic trends, but also because they have undermined their own position by adopting the manners and life-style of the gentry. They have exposed themselves to the dangers of luxury or what he calls 'imaginary wants'. With this in mind, Cobbett offers the following advice on education:

> It is impossible for me, by any words that I can use, to express, to the extent of my thoughts, the danger of suffering young people to form their opinions from the writings of poets and romances.[10]

That the danger springs from literature's dissociation from utility emerges when he offers this distinction:

> The difference between history and romance is this; that that which is narrated in the latter leaves in the mind nothing which it can apply to present and future circumstances and events; while the former, when it is what it ought to be, leaves the mind stored with arguments for experience, applicable, at all times, to the actual affairs of life. (Cobbett, *Advice*, p. 300)

This prepares the ground for the conclusive remark that 'In short, a young man should bestow his time upon no book, the contents of which he cannot apply to some useful purpose.'[11] The useful purpose of a young wife in this social group is even more limited, as one might expect. Having warned against the dangers of a girl with a boarding-school education, Cobbett instructs and reassures his prospective male lover that 'If she be good in her nature, the first little faint cry of her first baby drives all the tunes, and all the landscapes, and all the Clarissa Harlowes, out of her head for ever.'[12] That this bleak scenario represents a kind of freedom for Cobbett (a freedom from false refinement) is evident from his description of 'men of literary talent' who, he asserts, 'suffer from depression of spirit, of inactivity and of servility'. He even suggests that 'the evil arises from their own fault; from them having created for themselves, imaginary wants'.[13] Typically, Cobbett is not impressed by the power of this act of mind: the logic of his statements is clearly cautionary. One of the prerequisites for preserving the independence of the social classes he addresses is the eschewal of a whole range of cultural refinement which would undermine their financial base and make them servile to either landlords or the monied interest.

Cobbett's attitude towards polite culture is not so limited as to serve only the preservation of these predominantly agricultural social groups however: it extends beyond the context of audience to encompass a more universal belief in the power of utility. Even in his *Grammar of the English Language*, when attempting to explain the subjunctive to his reader, Cobbett takes the opportunity of affirming his belief in utility: 'Distinctions, without differences in the things distinguished, are fanciful, and, at the best, useless. Here is a real difference, a practical difference; a difference in the form of the word.'[14] In this particular instance the text hovers uneasily between its usual appreciation of language as something transparent, the invisible tool of ideas, and something which has an identity in its own right. More frequently in this text, Cobbett draws the distinction between beauty and utility by taking a swipe at both the establishment and the literary establishment in his choice of examples. When he comes to define the apostrophe, or mark of elision, he explains:

I have mentioned this mark, because it is used properly enough in *poetry*; but, I beg you never to use it in prose in one single instance during your whole life. It ought to be called the mark not of *elision*, but of *laziness* and *vulgarity*. (Cobbett, *Grammar*, p. 62)

And when in the same work Cobbett deals with prepositions joined to verbs, such as 'within' and 'without' – what he calls 'compound words' – he refuses to undermine the distinction between the vulgar and the refined by turning it on its head and instead pulls out of what he considers to be needless theorising. His appeal to the realistic expectations of his audience is far from defensive:

These are all *compound* words, but, of what *use* to us to enter on, and spend our time in, inquiries of mere curiosity? It is for monks, and for Fellows of English Colleges, who live by the sweat of other people's brows, to spend their time in this manner, and to call the result of their studies *learning*; for you, who will have to earn what you eat and what you drink and what you wear, it is to avoid every thing that tends not to real utility. (Cobbett, *Grammar*, p. 55)

The force of these last words – 'real utility' – is in their general application: Cobbett is not simply drawing up the limits of what is useful to a certain level of society. His disbelief in such learning extends far beyond that. Drawing the same distinction we have already witnessed between words and ideas, Cobbett once stated of Napoleon that if he considered a classical education as the 'greatest of human endowments, he never would have attained to so complete a mastery in that science, which, more than any other, perhaps, demands an extensive acquaintance with *men* and *things*'.[15] Bonaparte provides him with an example (and to Cobbett a particularly abhorrent one) with which to universalise his attack on polite learning. Indeed, his own grammar represents, even without its satirical use of examples, an enormous confidence in the possibility of access to power at the highest level, freed from the trammels of class distinction. (So too, of course, does his own turbulent career from plough-boy to a seat in Parliament.) His attitude to language is perhaps peculiar in this respect; that while constantly ridiculing the false forms of refinement it adheres to a belief in a language freed from a connection with social hierarchy.[16] This is, perhaps, the only thing which he could celebrate in the rise of Napoleon:

> The reader will recollect, that some time ago, the editors of some of the London papers treated us with an intercepted letter of Buonaparte; from which it was evident, that the poor little fellow was not only not a classical scholar, but that he was deficient even in that part of the art of grammar, which the 'learned' call orthography, and which the 'ignorant' call *spelling*. This letter was the subject of a good deal of merriment, which would have lasted for several days, and would, probably, have lasted much longer, had not the attention of the learned and witty been called off by the news of the battle of Austerlitz, which served, too, as a sort of practical illustration of the inutility of Latin and Greek, in the performances of great actions in the world.[17]

Such examples of his celebration of the criteria of hard work and usefulness, and his attack on idleness and uselessness, at most have the desired effect of making Cobbett's target look ridiculous. That the basis of his attack goes deeper than this would suggest is evident from those numerous occasions when his polemic is underscored not so much with a heavy moral argument as with a profound, even disturbing, moral disgust. This is compounded in the following example by a particularly perverse example of Cobbett's patriotism. Here again, we have the argument for utility and the onslaught against polite forms of culture, taken to the limit of its general application – the way in which it characterises, or, in his terms, 'infects' the identity of a whole nation. The issue arises when he describes Castlereagh's stripping of the museums of France after the demise of Napoleon:

> Viewed as an object of worth to a nation, the museums were worse than useless to France. It has always been seen, amongst nations as amongst individuals, that a proneness towards things of show; that a general taste for what are called the fine arts, tends to the degradation and slavery of a people. The countries of painters and poets have not been the countries of freedom; and it is very natural that they should not. A people will always be proud of something: one of military renown; another of naval renown; another of commercial greatness; another of excellence in the *fine arts*, as they are called, until every third man wishes to be a painter, a poet, or a musician; another will be proud of its good laws, its liberties, its good living. Now, unhappy is it for a nation, when it happens to make a choice of a thing to be proud of, which thing has a tendency neither to strengthen it against its foreign enemies, nor to make the people easy and happy at home. All the efforts which can be made will never make Englishmen painters and poets and musicians: bodies filled with beef and beer are not to carry throats and eyes and ears for singing and painting; lentils for dinner, a lettuce for supper, raw green peas and beans for a dessert, and vermicelli, snails, frogs and polenta, for days of feasting; these produce soft pipes, sharp eyes, and delicate ears, laziness, filth, and cunning too profound for Satan himself.[18]

Cobbett clearly uses his very specific sense of English identity to fend off the threat of what he sees as aesthetic degradation. His chauvinistic image of France provides helpful backing for his idea that the 'fine arts' are really a form of Satanic temptation capable of undermining hard-won British male liberty. And once again, he focuses on the corruptible/healthy body as the basis of his beliefs.

More strategically and more particularly, the distinction between beauty and utility here is drawn against the background of a stark choice. What might appear as Cobbett's bizarre anti-epicureanism is as much motivated by the fact that Parliament had just voted for a gallery costing £75,000. Cobbett's alternative for these funds is a stark reminder of conditions in 1833. This same money, he argues, would 'maintain four thousand families of labourers for one year; and the interest . . . would maintain one hundred and seventy-five labourers' families for ever'.[19] In the various statements that we have just considered, Cobbett's separation between the beautiful and the useful takes place as part of a more general assault on polite culture; in other words, where there is a conspicuous rank or class difference informing the distinction. The beautiful here is unqualifiedly alien: literature, novel, poetry, painting, and affected grammar can all be seen as clearly separate as well as unnecessary or artificial. As such, the distinction is perhaps easier to make; especially when, as we have seen, the exemplary nature of such forms of culture represents a terrible temptation to the upwardly-mobile farmers of the 1820s and 1830s. Cobbett's distinction in this respect charts, at the same time, a shift in social custom and economic grouping. But where landscape is concerned, the alien nature of the beautiful no longer holds good; or, more accurately, the infiltration of a polite perspective on the countryside is so much more pervasive. When, as we have already seen, Cobbett describes the choice between fertility of soil and a sense of picturesque beauty, the latter does form part of his vocabulary, even if it is reluctantly dismissed as secondary to fertility in the end.

III

It might be thought that in *Rural Rides* there can be no outright philistinism of the kind that we have already seen. Here, it might be assumed, the landscape holds good and gives no such opportunity to Cobbett's oppositional rhetoric. But *Rural Rides* is not only Cobbett's readings of agriculture through the state of the soil or the growth of trees or crops, it is at once the state as landscape and the state of 'man' in the landscape as a state of loss. Cobbett's empirically and sometimes imperiously presiding consciousness purports in no uncertain terms to give the reader things as they are, but the text is profoundly strategic and metonymic. England is read as and through the rural. The text itself has a dual status as picaresque autobiography and, supposedly, no text at all, only a quasi-Lockean travelogue giving direct access to empirical data.

Amid all its topographical details, its in-depth surveys of the productivity and make-up of different English soils, its resurfacing arguments on paper money, rural depopulation, poverty, and abuse of government pensions, *Rural Rides* characteristically defines the English landscape as either beautiful or ugly. In most cases a single word is all the text offers, and any link with the subsequent commentary is difficult to determine. But in those cases where there is more than an isolated adjective, where some connection with the surrounding commentary can be found, there would seem to be a direct link between either beauty or ugliness and the productivity which otherwise dominates the text. The ugly side of the equation is fairly straightforward: since Cobbett has little sense of wild nature, the unproductive landscape holds little interest for him; the heathlands of southern England, the tussocky pastures of the West Riding, lowland marshes or swamps, as he calls them, are all 'dreary wastes'. Throughout *Rural Rides*, in fact, the attention is agricultural and on the farmed landscape. This is the 'nature' within which Cobbett's use of the beautiful functions.

For the most part, Cobbett's designation of a place as beautiful in *Rural Rides* is an affirmation of its productiveness: there is no separation between the two, as he writes of Mr Drummond's park at Albury: 'Everywhere utility and convenience is combined with beauty.'[20] However, there does not appear to be an absolute correspondence between the two; for when he deals with the fertile lands of East Anglia, Cobbett celebrates their productivity, but witholds some of his usual enthusiasm: 'But alas! what, in point of beauty, is a country without woods and lofty trees!' He explains that 'the great drawbacks on the beauties of these counties are their flatness and their want of fine woods'.[21] These two typical objections – a flat and treeless landscape – suggest that the ideal haven for this 'most itinerant of writers' should possess some topographical variation between hill and dale. Indeed, it soon becomes apparent in *Rural Rides* that Cobbett's beauty is premised on a 'beautiful variety of hill and dale'.[22] An extended passage of the same kind reveals a more rational explanation than variety for its own sake:

This country, though so open, has its beauties. The homesteads in the sheltered bottoms with fine lofty trees about the houses and yards, form a beautiful contrast with the large open fields. The little villages, running straggling along the dells (always with lofty trees and rookeries) are very interesting objects, even in the winter. You feel a sort of satisfaction, when you are out upon the bleak hills yourself, at the thought of the shelter, which is experienced in the dwellings in the valleys. (Cobbett, *Rural Rides*, I, p. 115)

Despite the idealised picture of a home nestling amongst trees in a nook between meadow and downland pasture, there still remains the possibility that this too is predetermined by an all-pervasive sense of usefulness. The satisfaction referred to here and on other occasions – the reason the scene impresses itself upon the mind pleasurably – depends on an act of association which is governed by the idea of shelter. In the following passage, it can be seen that even Cobbett's trees – the guarantors of beauty in his idyll – are still specified according to their useful purposes:

I love *the downs* so much that, if I had to choose, I would live even here . . . I have now seen . . . what are deemed the richest and most beautiful parts of England;

and if called upon to name the spot which I deem the brightest and most beautiful and, of its extent, *best* of all, I should say the villages of *North Bovant and Bishopstrowe* between Heytesbury and Warminster in Wiltshire; for there is, as appertaining to rural objects, *everything* that I delight in. Smooth and verdant downs in hills; valleys of endless variety as to height and depth and shape; rich common-land, unencumbered by fences; meadows in due proportion, and those watered at pleasure; and, lastly, the homesteads, and villages, sheltered in winter and shaded in summer by lofty and beautiful trees; to which may be added roads never dirty and a stream never dry. (Cobbett, *Rural Rides*, II, p. 135)

Even when, as here, Cobbett's trees are referred to in terms of shelter, it is easy to make a connection between their beauty and their indirect value as timber or their importance in a subsistence economy. Throughout *Rural Rides* the point is made that rural poverty in the labouring classes is at its least severe in forested or wooded districts. Here fuel, game, and the possibility of forage for pigs is sufficient to offset the worst consequences of the economic shift in agricultural relations. And, as Ian Dyck has pointed out, even *Cottage Economy* could be read as a cleverly veiled incitement to poaching.[23] Even in this approximation to a rural idyll we are not far removed from Cobbett's requisites of shelter and sustenance – the basis for his ultimate goal of material happiness. The most that can be claimed is that the sense of a pleasurable appeal to the senses is still very much contained within the physical conditions of productivity. Usefulness and happiness are directly connected with a sense of beauty unproblematically situated in the connection between these two.

On a few relatively isolated occasions in *Rural Rides* the landscape, in contrast to what we have just seen, impresses itself upon Cobbett in such a way as to offer a dislocation between utility and beauty. One such occasion is a description of a remembered scene in Pennsylvania. Temporarily, Cobbett's text allows metaphor a freer range, albeit in a restricted context. Typically, trees and a sense of visual variety are the locus of Cobbett's beautiful apprehension; but here the visual scene is uncharacteristically obscure, indeterminate – almost an illusion:

I remember a valley in Pennsylvania, in a part called *Wysihicken*. In looking from a hill, over this valley, early in the morning, in November, it presented one of the most beautiful of sights, my eyes ever beheld. It was a sea bordered with beautifully formed trees of endless variety of colours. As the hills formed the outside of the sea, some of the trees showed only their tops; and, every now-and-then, a lofty tree growing in the sea itself, raised its head above the apparent waters. Except the setting-sun sending his horizontal beams through all the variety of reds and yellows of the branches of the trees in Long Island,

and giving, at the same time, a sort of silver cast to the verdure beneath them, I have never seen anything so beautiful as the foggy valley of Wysihicken. (Cobbett, *Rural Rides*, I, p. 4)

Before we are tempted to translate this brief interlude into a parallel to Wordsworth's climactic ascent of Snowdon in *The Prelude* (after all, the weather conditions and the sea analogy are present here too), Cobbett's text pulls back into a reliance on country lore and then returns to the political cement of the whole series – an attack on the advocates of the paper-money system:

But, I was told, that it was very fatal to the people; and that whole families were frequently swept off by the '*fall-fever*', – Thus the *smell* has a great deal to do with health. There can be no doubts that butchers and their wives fatten upon the smell of meat. And this accounts for the precept of my grandmother, who used to tell me to *bite my bread and smell to my cheese*; talk much more wise than that of certain *old grannies*, who go about England crying up 'the *blessings*' of paper-money, taxes, and national debts. (Cobbett, *Rural Rides*, I, p. 4)

The beautiful turns out in the end to be rather dangerous and the delicate indeterminacy of the visual landscape is replaced by a firm trust in a rural reading of sense perception.

A similar passage of apparent aesthetic appreciation occurs when Cobbett describes his visit to a 'hanger', or wood on the side of a steep hill or bank, in Sussex. Rather than the potentially eerie tranquillity of the previous scene, here the sense of beauty is supplemented by the emotions of surprise and apprehension. Once again the fairly obvious substitution of land for sea is present:

The lane had a little turn towards the end; so that, out we came, all in a moment, at the very edge of the hanger! And never, in all my life, was I so surprised and so delighted! I pulled up my horse, and sat and looked; and it was like looking from the top of a castle down into the sea, except that the valley was land and not water . . . Those who had so strenuously dwelt on the dirt and dangers of this route, had said not a word about beauties, the matchless beauties of the scenery . . . I came to the edge of the hanger, which was on the south. The ends of these promontories are nearly perpendicular and their tops so high in the air, that you cannot look at the village below without something like a feeling of apprehension. The leaves are all off, the hop-poles are in stack, the fields have little verdure; but, while the spot is beautiful beyond description even now, I must leave to imagination to suppose what it is when the trees and hangers and hedges are in leaf, the corn waving, the meadows bright, and the hops upon the poles! (Cobbett, *Rural Rides*, I, pp. 138–39)

Ironically, just at the moment when the text hovers on the verge, not only of a hanger, but of the beautiful and of a transformation into a literary moment, Cobbett pulls himself up short by reference to the imagination. As Cobbett leaves the scene to imagination, he leaves the scene of imagination behind. The potential moment ends with agricultural productivity: the sense of surprise and apprehension is left behind.

That Cobbett's sense of the beautiful is dependent on variety has been briefly noted in a suggestive essay by John Barrell, where he reads a polite sense of beauty into *Rural Rides* by comparison with Burke's idea in his *Enquiry into the Origin of our Ideas of the Sublime and Beautiful*.[24] Further comparisons are made possible as Cobbett moves beyond a perception of smooth contours to include a sense of apprehension and surprise, as well as an act of association stemming from feelings of self-preservation, into his definition of the relationship between beauty and utility in *Rural Rides*. But there is little coordination or integration of these factors sufficient to allow one to promote them to the status of an important component of his work. At best it could be argued that at the margins of his text on landscape there is a certain seepage from the more general discourse of aesthetics which mixes uneasily with his own drier discourse of particularist rural political economy.

And when Cobbett has the opportunity to write about landscaped gardens in *Rural Rides* it provides him with yet another means of attacking the new monied interest. In the 'improved' parks and estates he encounters head-on the impact of taste upon the landscape. Just how much it differs from his version of the natural can be gauged when he describes Moore Park, a place he had known from his childhood:

the exquisitely beautiful little lawn in which the seat stood was turned into a parcel of diverse-shaped cockney-clumps, planted according to the strictest rule of artificial and refined vulgarity. (Cobbett, *Rural Rides*, 1, p. 287)

In this particular instance the attack is generated by the intrusive taste and the economic and social threat of London's monied society; but it is typical of Cobbett's evaluations in this area in its reference to artificiality. The same explanation can be offered of his mocking description of Mr Montague's park (October 1831). After making the statement 'what I disliked most was the apparent impiety of a part of these works of refined taste',[25] Cobbett's objection turns out to be more specific than one had imagined, and he is ultimately willing to separate the issues of piety and taste because of his pro-Catholic reform activities. As a result, he concentrates his ridicule and his indignation on the 'meek' nature of the whole enterprise. But there is a suggestion here that refined taste mocks nature because of its artificiality and is therefore 'impious' in that it challenges God's creation. As we shall see, a displaced Christian metaphysics feeds into Cobbett's critique of the changing face of the landscape.

As a final illustration of the way in which a strand of the beautiful is woven into the mixed bag of *Rural Rides*, I wish to return to Cobbett's obsession with trees. In this instance it can be seen how a celebration of beauty in nature can be used to reinforce the vehemence of the political argument; and more importantly, how the beautiful in this work, at the point where it separates itself off from utility, lines up, not so much with the polite discourse of aesthetics as with a moral discourse based on Christian providence. What appears to be Cobbett's man-made sense of the natural turns out to be at least partly inspired by a belief in God-made nature:

Woodland countries are interesting on many accounts. Not so much on account of their masses of green leaves, as on account of the variety of sights and sounds and incidents that they afford. Even in winter, the coppices are beautiful to the eye, while they comfort the mind with the idea of shelter and warmth. In spring they change their hue from day to day during two whole months, which is about the time for the first appearance of the delicate leaves of the birch to the full expansion of those of the ash; and even before the leaves come at all to intercept the view, what in the vegetable creation is so delightful to behold as the bed of a coppice bespangled with primroses and bluebells? The opening of the birch leaves is the signal for the pheasant to begin to crow, for the blackbird to whistle, and the thrush to sing; and just when the oaks-buds begin to look reddish, and not a day before, the whole tribe of finches burst forth in songs from every bough, while the lark, imitating them all, carries the joyous sounds to the sky. These are amongst the means which Providence has benignantly appointed to sweeten the toils by which food and raiment are produced; these the English Ploughman could once hear without the sorrowful reflection that he himself was *a pauper*, and that the bounties of nature had, for him, been scattered in vain! And shall he never see an end to this state of things! Shall he never have the due reward of his labour! Shall unsparing taxation never cease to make him a miserable dejected being, a creature famishing in the midst of abundance, fainting, expiring with hunger's feeble moans, surrounded by a carolling creation! O! accursed paper-money! Has hell a torment surpassing the wickedness of thy inventor! (Cobbett, *Rural Rides*, 1, p. 64)

It is difficult to determine the extent to which this passage and others like it are strategic. The God-given adornments of nature very characteristically lead on to a sense of paradise lost as Cobbett brings forcibly home to his reader the current state of things and their cause. The passage in this sense is more interested in damning Pitt's government than in singing the praises of 'carolling creation', more interested in the present state of loss than in the quality of an Edenic past.

IV

Partly as a result of the popularity of *Rural Rides*, Cobbett has become associated, with good justification, with landscape; a figure whose writings and political views, too, are anchored in that landscape, as if it were the basis of all arguments on taxation, corruption, parliamentary reform, and paper money. After all, his practical handbooks such as *Cottage Economy* (1822) depend on that landscape for their existence. From his experiments in animal and plant husbandry spring his passionate statements in favour of independence; Cobbett moves from subsistence to mainstream political representation.[26] Such a straightforward transition is in danger of being unable to account for the nature of Cobbett's writing, the very medium which makes such a transition possible. It is also in danger of undervaluing the representational crisis which Cobbett's radical critique undergoes in its engagement with political economy and population theory. The connection between landscape and economics is more complex than one might think. It certainly challenges the notion of a transparent empirical aesthetic.

The turning point in Cobbett's career as a political journalist occurs around 1804–5 and can be measured by a series of articles styled as letters addressed to Pitt.[27] From a belief in political independence and a hope that this can be brought about by the present administration, Cobbett suddenly becomes disillusioned. Rather than equate this with personal relationships – his falling out with Windham and other government ministers, and his first real experience of electioneering in the English system – I want to concentrate on the connection between this turn-about in political loyalties (if such it should be called) and Cobbett's reading of a pamphlet by Tom Paine, originally published in 1796 and entitled, rather grandiosely, *The Decline and Fall of the English System of Finance*. Typically, the change in direction comes with Paine the economist rather than with Paine the revolutionary.[28] As a result of contact with this brief tract the rather naive materialism and literalism of Cobbett's writing is challenged. It is not the self-evident, read-at-a-glance text of the English landscape that matters so much now as the way a corrupt system of government has insidiously and invisibly altered the straightforward nature of the landscape. Perversely, the logic of *Rural Rides* is not the description or manifestation of England but a desperate means of indirectly portraying decades of corrupt government.

As I have already suggested, the transition in Cobbett's political career is at least partly inspired by his championing of independence: independence for politicians being freed from bribery, corruption, and the pocket borough system; freedom for the yeoman farmer from overbearing landlords; freedom for the agricultural labourer from highly-taxed consumer goods. This belief in independence is a manifestation of his own particular version of the landed interest. But the more one probes the idea that land is the foundation for this belief the more one finds other things – invisible things – premising a political argument which permeates all levels of society. When nudged by Rousseau to consider the basis of social relations, Cobbett has something else to offer:

Rousseau observes, that men are happy, first, in proportion to their virtue, and next, in proportion to their independence; and that of all mankind, the artisan, or craftsman, is the most independent; because he carries about, in his own hands and person, the means of gaining his livelihood . . . Aye, and this is the reason why shoe-makers are proverbially the most independent part of the people, and why they, in general, show more public spirit than any other men. He who lives by a pursuit, be it what it may, which does not require a considerable degree of bodily labour must from the nature of things, be more or less, a dependent; and this is, indeed, the price which he pays for his exemption from that bodily labour. (Cobbett, *Advice*, p. 307)

In the invisible property of skills and ideas Cobbett clearly has a rival to the idea of the productivity of the English soil as the basis of his political position. This squares uneasily with numerous statements throughout his writings, including a notorious article in the guise of the antirevolutionary Francophobe Peter Porcupine published in 1794 and entitled 'Observations on the Emigration of Priestley'. In this venomous attack on Painite radicals, Jacobins, and francophiles which is motivated by a ferocious patriotism, Cobbett typically opposes universal theories:

System-mongers are an unreasonable species of mortals: time, place, climate, nature itself, must give way. They must have the same government in every quarter of the Globe; when perhaps there are not two countries which can possibly admit the same form of Government at the same time. A thousand hidden causes, a thousand circumstances and unforeseen events, conspire to the forming of a government. It is always done little and little.[29]

In adopting and adapting to Paine's economic critique therefore,

Cobbett seems to be responding not so much to the principles of political economy evident in it so much as to its applicability to England. Paine's universalist Enlightenment text can be assimilated to Cobbett's sense of particularity and national difference. He need not respond to Paine the advocate for international free trade or Paine the spokesman for abstract revolutionary principles.

It is difficult to overestimate the significance of Paine's economics in the second half of Cobbett's career. This is the act which has not only threatened to break up the social relations of his agricultural England, but also the one which breaks up his idea of agricultural England. The reader who opens his *History of the Regency and the Reign of George the Fourth* expecting to find detailed surveys of that mountain of flesh will be severely disappointed. Cobbett turns very quickly from the embarrassing immoralities and injustices of the Regency. Instead, the reader is frequently presented with declarations as to the primary significance of Cobbett's favourite economic argument:

I shall here leave this affair of the paper-money at present; not however without beseeching the reader to let it remain deeply imprinted on his mind, because he will have to recur to this transaction, as to the root of these numerous legislative proceedings which have related and which relate to the currency of the country, which have produced so much distress and so much confusion, and which, of all the causes which have been at work, has been the most conspicuous and the most powerful in the producing of those great changes in the beginning of which we are now living in the year one thousand eight hundred and thirty-one. (Cobbett, *History*, para. 123)[30]

At the same time as he argues for its abiding significance, Cobbett's concern is to support this with a desperate plea for its conspicuousness. The problem is, as we shall see, that it is precisely its inconspicuousness which dictates to the nature of his texts. As a result, Cobbett here wittily asks his reader to 'deeply imprint' the issue of paper money on 'his mind', thus foregrounding the need to imagine this new form of representation. In the same work, he has to face up to his peculiar problem: his being the advocate of a cause that no-one can see. Isolated in this dilemma the spokesman for the working people self-consciously explains:

The mass of mankind cannot, without a cessation of the pursuits necessary to carrying-on of the affairs of the world, acquire that knowledge which is necessary to make them understand the real cause of effects like these. All at once, prices fell: rents were, in fact, nearly doubled in real amount . . . *credit*, is, in ordinary circumstances, of great value to a nation, as well as to an individual:

the solidity of every thing in England; the confidence between man and man; these, to which may be added the very character of the people, have made England a country of credit: the great object here, amongst tradespeople, seems to be, to get you to take their things away, without hardly an inquiry as to the time of payment: almost all is credit; and, let the reader observe, that this change, with regard to the currency, nearly doubled the amount of every debt in reality: let him further observe, that it is the poorer part who are the debtors, and the richer part who are the creditors . . . (Cobbett, *History*, para. 291)

The movement or slippage from visible to invisible, from physical to mental realities is evident throughout the range of Cobbett's writing. Raymond Williams might confidently announce that 'Cobbett's central idea of freedom is always material, even physical. This is the firm ground of his political sanity',[31] but this sanity is in need of invisible support. Cobbett himself can argue as vehemently in favour of the simply physical as he can against the artificiality of polite culture:

Now, I am for no visionary, no fanciful, no refined benefit; no mental advantage; nothing so very fine that we can neither see, hear, feel, nor touch, it; and, if it could be proved to me that this reform would bring no real, substantial, aye, and bodily, good to the millions of the people, I should say, at once, that it was good for nothing. The *words* rights, liberty, freedom, and the like; the *mere words*, are not worth a straw; and very frequently they serve as a cheat. What is the sound of liberty to a man who is compelled to work constantly and who is still, in spite of his toil, his vigilance, his frugality, half naked and half starved![32]

This is the popular, well-advertised version of the Cobbett whose style itself is 'tactile' and whose criteria are primitively empirical, the Cobbett who announces at the opening of *Journal of a Year's Residence in the United States of America* (1819), 'The account which I shall give, shall be that of actual *experience*. I will say what I *know* and what I have *seen* and what I have *done*',[33] and the Cobbett who can turn even things spiritual into more solid realities:

The *Christian religion*, then, is not an affair of preaching, or prating, or ranting, but of taking care of the bodies as well as of the souls of the people; not an affair of belief and of faith and of professions, but an affair of doing good, and especially to those who are in want; not an affair of fire and brimstone, but an affair of bacon and bread, beer and a bed.[34]

Running counter to this well publicised strand in Cobbett's work is the evidence of the necessity to deal in the intangible realities of his opponents. If you rail against the so-called system-mongers you have to deal in the reality of their system. It has to be admitted, with the intrusion of an overtly political argument in *A Year's Residence*, that 'in the word England, many things are included, besides climate and soil and seasons, and eating and drinking'.[35] Similarly, in *Rural Rides* the reading of the landscape stops and Cobbett announces: 'It is time for me now, withdrawing myself from these objects visible to the eye, to speak of the state of *the people*, and of the manner in which their affairs are affected by the workings of the system.'[36] On such occasions one wonders whether the transition from one to the other is as easy as was at first envisaged:

at the end of a tramp like this, you get impressed upon your mind a true picture, not only of the state of the country, but of the state of the people's minds throughout the country. (Cobbett, *Rural Rides*, I, p. 159)

Even the physical model of his idea of economic exchange gives way when, in his *Advice*, he goes back for once to first principles: 'the great purpose of human art, the great end of human study, is to obtain *ease*, to throw the burden of labours from our own shoulders, and fix it on others'.[37]

Indeed the more one pursues Cobbett back to first principles the more one encounters the invisible property of the country people: their labour, wisdom, skill, and thought. 'Happiness, or misery', he wrote in his *Grammar*, 'is in the *mind*. It is the mind that lives; and the length of life ought to be measured by the number and importance of our ideas; and not by the number of our days.'[38] Such invisible qualities are, in fact, the guarantors of their freedom or independence, and not the land conceived as inviolable private property. True to his roots, Cobbett claims that 'Property sprang from labour, and not labour from property.'[39]

Even within these intangible experiential qualities there are inherent conflicts. Measuring life and happiness by ideas challenges the culture of rural labour which would recognise a day's work, and would also go against the idea that at all points Cobbett's radicalism is underscored by 'the great "instrument" of "daily experience"'.[40] Cobbett's own negotiation with vulgar and refined forms of culture necessarily implicates his own texts and his own practice of writing. To speak for rural popular culture in the mainstream of print and political representation is inevitably to become different. This is one area where Raymond Williams's analysis is particularly helpful. As he charts the progress of Cobbett's career after the move to Kensington in 1820 he makes the following suggestive, if rather cryptic, comment: 'It is at once a consciously examined renewal of the elements of a subsistence economy, and yet in the practice and in the writing an enterprise beyond subsistence.'[41] I would like to take up Williams's suggestion by considering Cobbett's role as writer when he goes beyond subsistence in his assault on the issue of paper money.

v

When Cobbett rhapsodises on his project to increase the planting of his beloved locust tree across England, he encapsulates his sense of the best kind of economic transaction and compares it with the worst:

It would be a prodigious creation of real and solid wealth. Not such a creation as that of paper money, which only takes the dinner from one man and gives it to another, which only gives an unnatural swell to a city or a watering place by beggaring a thousand villages; but it would be a creation of money's worth things. (Cobbett, *Rural Rides*, II, p. 16)

This peculiarly contracted phrase – 'money's worth things' – is precisely that natural physical model of exchange which first Paine and then Cobbett argue has been undermined by the artificiality of a fictional invisible currency. It is the description of paper money as unnatural and invisible in Paine's work which appeals to Cobbett.

The force of Paine's argument in 1796 that a 'failure of finances' in every case has produced 'a revolution in government'[42] is much less attractive: even in moments of despair in 1817 Cobbett's position is one of reluctance rather than whole-hearted support.[43] Paine's argument depends upon an analogy of the body: the dying state being eaten away by debt is unnatural in that it does not manifest its decline. The demise of this 'modern complicated machine', as he calls it, is not as predictable or self-evident as that of the natural human body:

When I said that the funding system had entered the last twenty years of its existence, I certainly did not mean that it would continue twenty years and then expire as a lease would do. I meant to describe that age of decrepitude in which death is every day to be expected, and life cannot continue long. But the death of credit, or that state that is called bankruptcy, is not always marked by those progressive stages of visible decline, that mark the decline of natural life. In the progression of natural life, age cannot counterfeit youth nor conceal the departure of juvenile abilities. But it is otherwise with respect to the death of credit; for though all the approaches to bankruptcy may actually exist in circumstances, they admit of being concealed by appearances. Nothing is more common than to see the bankrupt of today a man of credit but the day before; yet no sooner is the real state of his affairs known, than every body can see he had been insolvent long before. In London, the greatest theatre of bankruptcy in Europe, this part of the subject will be well and feelingly understood. (Paine, *Decline and Fall*, p. 15)

As one would expect of Paine, he consolidates his sense of the natural here by attacking the system as insubstantial and imaginative. His argument builds up to a tremendous crescendo in which he brings in another of his main ideas, familiar to any reader of *Rights of Man*, that each new generation must politically reconstitute itself. When this is added to the comparison with the body, his argument is complete:

Do we not see that Nature, in all her operations disowns the visionary basis upon which the funding system is built? She acts always by renewed successions, and never by accumulating additions perpetually progressing. Animals and vegetables, men and trees, have existed ever since the world began; but that existence has been carried by succession of generations, and not by continuing the same men and the same trees in existence that existed first, and to make room for the new she removes the old. Every natural idiot can see this. It is the stock-jobbing idiot only that mistakes. He has conceived that art can do what Nature cannot. He is teaching her a new system – that there is no occasion for man to die – that the scheme of creation can be carried on upon the plan of the funding system – that it can proceed by continual additions of new beings, like new loans, all live together in eternal youth. Go, count the graves, thou idiot, and learn the folly of thy arithmetic! (Paine, *Decline and Fall*, p. 16)

The extent to which the argument about visibility here is important is made all the more obvious to Cobbett (and at the same time, one suspects, more attractive) by the fact that Paine sees this as the distinguishing characteristic of the English system: 'The English system', he claims, 'differs from that of America and France in this one particular, that its capital is kept out of sight; that is, it does not appear in circulation.'[44]

If we return now to Cobbett's own obsession with a self-evident or visible world, the desperate nature of his pleas for the validity of his argument is easy to see. To his modern unsympathetic critics this process of earnest justification for the pernicious effect of a system which is hidden from view has looked a bit like paranoia; a number of them have argued that he suffered from an identity crisis which made him all too easily subscribe to a conspiracy theory, particularly on the vexed issue of population.

In Cobbett's writings the attack on the new system of finance manifest symbolically in the issue of paper money combines powerfully with his assault on population theory.[45] And for Cobbett they share the same ideological power base and the same representational mode. They impose the same dehumanised abstract – 'the system' – upon the people. Their mode of operation, Cobbett insists, is itself immoral and unethical because it challenges the very basis of his notion of Christianity evident in the harmonious relationship between human and natural fertility. As their abstractive utility supplants his particularist utility, it forces him into a moral and spiritual rhetoric. But even here, where Cobbett seems at times to be most exposed and open to ridicule, his arguments can carry a strategic force which should not be underestimated. Defending and politicising the rural poor takes many different, sometimes surprising, forms.

Cobbett's infamous commentaries on population in which he calculates the inhabitants of rural southern England to have been significantly greater in number in the Middle Ages on account of the size and congregation capacity of churches and cathedrals have, not surprisingly, attracted much ridicule and scorn. But not all of it is deserved. In his construction of the invisible populous past, Cobbett's strategic purpose is to undermine the political economists and population theorists on the basis of his own rival empirical observation. He is also led to defend the inherent fertility of the land as well as the inherent fertility of the people in order to challenge the basis of Malthusian theory and its consequences for the poor as utilitarian thinkers take charge of the reform of poor relief and charity. That he chooses places of Christian worship as the sign of his methodology is entirely fitting. Malthus and the political economists are thereby defined as ungodly and as spoilers of God's fecund creation. Throughout his writings, in fact, Cobbett demonises Malthus by repeatedly referring to him as a satanic apostate preaching a false gospel. He is 'the monster Malthus' who with 'the Scotch *feelosofers*' form a satanic 'crew' who peddle a 'mixture of madness and blasphemy'.[46] Even the central tenet of Malthus's population theory is conceived in these damning terms: it is a 'diabolical assertion ... that the human kind have a natural tendency to *increase beyond the means of sustenance for them*'.[47]

The immorality and blasphemy lurking within Malthusian theory forms the substance of Cobbett's three act comic drama, *Surplus Population: or Poor Law Bill* (1831),[48] in which Squire Thimble's population theory is exploited by the lecherous Squire Grindum in order to prevent the marriage and aid the seduction of young Betsy Birch. The play makes clear the extent to which, in practice, population theory deriving from the '*hell-featured brawling Scotch vagabond*'[49] could be used by the gentry to carry out new forms of exploitation in the very name of 'Reform'.

Cobbett's assault on the abstractive ideology of Malthusian theory and its attendant claim to social utility is met not only with claims of its blasphemous immorality, but also by his own belief in the possibility of a transparent mode of economic exchange. But the blasphemy, to Cobbett's eyes, of utilitarian discourse still looks like a mode of critique and not like a commonsensical perception. In the following extract from *Rural Rides*, for example, the first sentence – indeed, the first clause – belies the ease of interpretation which is claimed as he urges us to an immediate shared visual perception:

Does not everyone see, in a minute, how this exchanging of fairs and markets for shops creates IDLERS AND TRAFFICKERS; creates those locusts called middlemen who create nothing; who add to the value of nothing, who improve nothing, but who live in idleness and who live well, too, on the labour of the producer and the consumer – The fair and the market, those wise institutions of our forefathers, and with regard to the management of which they were so scrupulously careful; the fair and the market bring the producer and the consumer into contact with each other. Whatever is gained is, at any rate, gained by one or the other of these. The fair and the market bring them together, and enable them to act for their mutual interest and convenience. The shop and the trafficker keeps them apart: the shop hides from both producer and consumer the real state of things ... The fair and the market lay everything open: going to either you see the state of things at once; and the transactions are fair and just, not disfigured, too, by falsehood and by those attempts at description which disgrace trafficking in general. (Cobbett, *Rural Rides*, II, p. 195)

It is easy to see in such an instance how Paine's powerful arguments in favour of free trade can be adapted to support Cobbett's passionate belief in the traditional rural modes of exchange. What this passage also suggests, however, is that once such transparency is lost it is difficult to see how it might be restored without the aid of another kind of middleman: Cobbett the social critic. The loss of openness generates the need for the mediation of representation in the form of critique.

This is most apparent when Cobbett combines his hatred of the paper-money system with his disbelief in the population statistics. On the question of rural depopulation and the growth of Regency London Cobbett stretches his belief in self-evident truth to the limit. Here the emphasis is very much on the need and the capacity to interpret:

It is the destructive, the murderous paper-system, that has transferred the fruit of the labour, and the people along with it, from the different parts of the country to the neighourhood of the all-devouring *Wen*. I do not believe one word of what is said of the increase of the population. All observation and all reason is against the fact; and, as to the *parliamentary returns*, what need we more than this: that *they* assert that the population of Great Britain has increased from ten to fourteen millions in the last *twenty years*! That is enough! A man that can suck that in will believe, literally believe, that the moon is made of green cheese. Such a thing is too monstrous to be swallowed by anybody but Englishmen, and by any Englishman not brutified by a Pitt-system. (Cobbett, *Rural Rides*, I, p. 136)

Here Cobbett characteristically writes about the transmission of information in terms of sustenance for the working body. Underscoring his points about immediate and visible truth is a moral register of degeneration and the corruption of that working body into the brutish form of a passive political subject. As he ridicules the voice of the establishment with its abstract statistics, his own language of 'literal belief' begins itself to look suspect. The opposition to his commonsense is conceived of as ideological indoctrination tantamount to moral depravity. The terms of the debate about knowledge and experience have polarised.

In the light of this stark portrayal of opposed kinds of truth, and the position thus generated for the social critic who must now represent a commonsense which may no longer be taken as common, even for his own target audience, it is, I think, pertinent to ask: what is the enterprise of *Rural Rides*? Is it an open manifestation of the real state of things or an exposé of the hidden state of things? Is it a strategically indirect description of the system or the visible effect of that system? That Cobbett in the last two quotations admits that the real 'state of things' can actually be hidden, casts an interesting light on his writings – as acts of interpretation feeding off a system he finds abhorrent.[50]

The same kind of desperation which prefaced the last quotation is evident in one of his series of articles on paper money which appeared in the *Political Register*. In the first sentence here there is, again, a fascinating fluctuation between the visible and the invisible:

It was impossible to conceive how a paper-money, a fictitious currency, could cause the grass to grow or the grain to kern or the cattle to fat; but, here we have the plain visible fact, stated in so many words, that this paper-money did render it *difficult to procure provisions* for the people of the county towns of England, and that in consequence thereof, *numbers of women and children were seen in a deplorable condition*. Women and children! Aye, and *men* too, I warrant you; for men cannot live without eating and drinking any more than women and children.[51]

Given the contradiction of representation that *Rural Rides* and many of the other writings are up against, one of Cobbett's typical responses is metaphorically to mount his horse and survey the scene, a position which is, in fact, impossible. This is his reaction to a colonial conquest in the West Indies during the Napoleonic era. His way out of the problem betrays his pastoral origins:

> I thought, that, the other day; or, at most, but a few months ago, I heard the cannon fire for the taking of Guadaloupe. And so I did. And I heard of new governors and judges and officers without end, appointed to rule this new conquest. Well, and what does it bring us? What is our gain in it? More sugar and more coffee to be added to the immense loads already rotting in our warehouses, and the want of a market for which is, as we are told, one of the causes of the blowing up of the Wiltshire paper-money. Yes, we fire cannons; we make bonfires; *we rejoice* at the taking of an island, the produce and the inhabitants of which must perish, or the former must be brought to England to assist in producing the effects now witnessed at Salisbury and in Ireland. – This is taking a very narrow view of the subject. It is *muddling* along half blind and half seeing. It is like a view of a chase through hollow ways and thickets. Let us, therefore, mount the eminence, and see the whole thing clearly at once.[52]

Cobbett's iconoclastic version of 'an equal wide survey' implies a panoptic and instantaneous vision of the singular 'thing'.

The same metaphorical deployment of this transfigured countryman's perspective is evident in the following passage on the paper-money system and the budget of 1805, but now it is even more problematic. Cobbett's claim for straightforward transparency is betrayed by the need to image the unseen. It is, one might suggest, difficult to see a 'canker-worm' from the top of an eminence:

> To hear people talk upon this subject, a total stranger to our situation and circumstances, would think the national debt to be something belonging to the soil or the atmosphere of the country. We look at its progress with apprehension and even with terror; but we seem to wait for its final effects with that sort of feeling that malefactors wait for the day of execution. Here! here! and nowhere else, is the canker-worm that is eating out the heart of England! And until that ever-gnawing worm be killed, one moment's real peace she will never know.[53]

As with the artificiality of polite culture and its ridiculous imposition on the landscape which we saw earlier, the act of introducing a paper-money system is seen as a fall from grace: it has travestied the material laws and relations of exchange laid down by a peculiarly materialist God. That loss seems to have made representation and critique necessary. Cobbett seems to see even his most egoistic mode of writing as a moral duty incapable of causing him embarrassment. There is also, as this passage indicates, a suggestion of morally justified violence at work in Cobbett's text. Such 'killing' is characteristic of his rhetoric and bears an interesting relationship to it. The suggestion is that once the invisible worm has been destroyed there will no longer be any need for the rhetoric. At the same time, however, Cobbett himself operates upon an idea of knowledge which cuts through the middle-ground of representation to claim an almost prelapsarian, even God-like, immediacy in a scene where simply to perceive is to know. All one needs are self-evident sense perceptions. In this peculiar way, Cobbett's own text takes on this privileged role of being able to see the thing itself. Cobbett's opponents could exploit this paradox at the heart of his form of critique. In such works as *The Book of Wonders* (1820 and 1821) and *The Beauties of Cobbett* (1820?),[54] they reprinted selections designed to expose the absurd contradictions lurking within his voluminious publications and at the same time reintroduced the very sense of the aesthetic which he had attempted so sedulously to exclude.

V

In dealing with paper money and from then on in his attack on the 'system', and the 'thing', Cobbett wages war with what appears to be an invisible enemy and has to make it visible. In his voluminous writings he attempts to reconstruct or read a system from visible clues. An empirical, physical, and visible set of criteria premised on a belief in present happiness being brought about by concentrating on things useful, is forced to coexist with a sense of past happiness based on something approaching spiritual values. His deployment of an idealised version of rural England – whether it be pre-Reformation, or the England of his childhood – is founded upon a fiction of England as a beautiful imagined paradise. The disbelief in metaphor and his attack upon refined culture take place alongside a much less prosaic act of construction and idealisation than one might expect. An Edenic world of visible value has been lost and must be restored.[55]

This forlorn yearning for a lost Arcadia informing Cobbett's radical writing has often puzzled and disappointed his Left-wing admirers. While admitting the force of his writings and recognising his ability to represent the mass of the people by instinct, Marx also castigates him as 'an inveterate John Bull' whose 'revolution was not innovation, but restoration, not the creation of a new age, but the rehabilitation of the "good old times"'.[56] In contrast, one of his most admiring literary critics refers us to his 'landscape of memory' which is founded on a 'sentimentalised retrospective Arcadia',[57] while an economic historian reinforces the sense of a displaced aesthetic at work in this most strategic and practical of writers:

> Historians who have written about the period in which Cobbett lived have not been able to agree upon a classification for him. Perhaps if a label is desired, 'utopian reactionary' is as close as one might come to identifying Cobbett in a word or two. Reactionary because his ideal was fixed firmly in the past, utopian because it was visionary, basically a product of his imagination. For all his jokes at the dreamers of his day, Cobbett himself was thoroughly romantic.[58]

In foregrounding the strategic nature of Cobbett's writings my analysis has resisted grounding his texts by reference to this belief in the past. The past is a rhetorical figure deployed to incite a reaction in order to change present conditions. Only by maintaining this sense of rhetorical persuasion in relation to change can we do justice to the meaning of Cobbett's texts, for there is a real danger that in labelling him a 'utopian radical' we bypass his writing altogether and cannot account for the nature or status of the texts themselves.

As is so often the case, Raymond Williams offers a deceptively simple and rich suggestion in his account of Cobbett's response to growing industrialisation and the new means of factory production. According to Williams, the following perception is at the heart of all Cobbett's writing: 'the natural relation between labour and sufficiency has been destroyed, and an unnatural relation between labour and property established. Accordingly, the unnatural relation must be destroyed and the natural relation restored.'[59] This captures the rhetorical violence of Cobbett's texts as well as their contextual complexity. In this chapter I have attempted to address the contradictions in Cobbett's writings which stem from this change in relations. Unlike most of his other commentators I have approached this from the unlikely perspective of aesthetics in an attempt to see how Cobbett's own brand of literalism and utility needs the aesthetic and the beautiful as an integral component in his idea of representation. Cobbett's combination of the particular and the useful forms an ideological and epistemological position which struggles to deal with the threat of the new utilitarian modes of social critique ranging across political economy, demography, and morals. In the next chapter we shall see how a writer from a different social background and with a much heavier investment in literary culture also struggles to find a place for the particularity offered by imagination – both to aid his own liberal individualism and to fend off the rise of utilitarianism.

6
Coleridge and the afterlife of imagination

I

The imagination is the distinguishing characteristic of man as a progressive being; and I repeat that it ought to be carefully guided and strengthened as the indispensable means and instrument of continued amelioration and refinement. Men of genius and goodness are generally restless in their minds in the present, and this, because they are by a law of their nature unremittingly regarding themselves in the future, and contemplating the possible of moral and intellectual advance towards perfection. Thus we live by hope and faith; thus we are for the most part able to realize what we will, and thus we accomplish the end of our being. The contemplation of futurity inspires humility of soul in our judgement of the present.[1]

In his 1818 lecture on the subject of European literature Coleridge confidently announces the pride of place which should be afforded to imagination in the education of children. In this context the faculty is firmly linked to ideas of individual, historical, and social progress. Seen from this optimistic progressivist perspective, imagination is the mainstay, the primary and central principle onto which other faculties and their methodologies can fruitfully be grafted. The very nature of the subjectivity produced by imagination is thus prospective and propulsive, a selfhood based, as Coleridge makes clear, on faith and hope. Keeping such hope alive in the face of what he perceives to be the pervasive and dominant ideology of utility is no easy matter and it leads Coleridge to view the present with anything but humility of soul. The gap between future and present registered in Coleridge's description of the workings of imagination becomes the very means of marking the difference between his Christian optimism and what he sees as the impious, mechanistic, and materialistic manifestations of this alternative vision of social improvement. The population theory of Malthus, the ethics of Paley, political economy, and the 'progress' of England's commercial development are joined together in Coleridge's swingeing attack upon the contemporary.

In such texts as the *The Statesman's Manual, A Lay Sermon, Biographia Literaria, On the Constitution of the Church and State,* and *Table Talk,* Coleridge opens up a debate about the condition of England which will define in British cultural thinking the idea of a schism between utility and imagination.

In turn, this provides us with another way of viewing a schism in Coleridge's own thinking. It has been convincingly argued that by 1817 Coleridge had given up on any attempt to mediate the split between perception and writing, that optimistic belief in the idea of the 'One Life' which he had espoused so enthusiastically in the 1790s.[2] By the time of *Biographia Literaria* and the *Lay Sermons,* Coleridge had renounced the mediatory power of imagination or had, at least, consigned it to a more circumscribed and limited realm of the aesthetic. This is supported by Jon Klancher's vision of Coleridge as the most gifted theoriser of audience in the whole of the nineteenth century, whose rhetorical engagement with different audiences on the basis of class amounts to a desperate and forlorn attempt to maintain a lost hegemony.[3]

Describing the 'retreat' of imagination in Coleridge's later writings almost inevitably involves a consideration of the considerable threat posed to his ideas by print culture. In the battle over the sign, his subscription to the 'Idea' puts a particular squeeze on imagination. Faced with an increasingly materialistic culture, Coleridge's dilemma is that he needs to provide an explanation of how the most precious faculty of perception and of poetic creation manifests itself in language: how the esemplastic power becomes writing. At the same time, imagination must always be held in reserve: its potential kept intact. Coleridge's deployment of imagination in his later writings is characterised by a separation between its potential or promissory function and its manifestation in words.[4] This is how it figures in his response to the increasingly materialist nature of English society and the rival claims of a dominating utilitarian movement.[5]

Coleridge's reaction to the philosophy and practices of 'utility' is characteristically vague, though Malthus and Paley are his most explicit targets. But specific texts and authors are not the point. The reason for what appears to be a specific and deliberate rhetorical strategy is that Coleridge perceives the threat of utilitarianism as an emergent dominant ideology. By the time he writes *Table Talk* in May 1834, Coleridge's worst fears seem about to be realised: the House of Commons is, he thinks, dominated by Malthusian thinking. Referring to 'this infidel and politico-economy Parliament',[6] he laments the fact that 'the monstrous sophism of Malthus should now have gotten possession of the leading men of the Kingdom!'[7] And in a manner which anticipates Mill's essays on Bentham and Coleridge, Coleridge himself sees utilitarianism as the manifestation of some of the seminal philosophical ideas of the eighteenth century: 'The histories and political economy of the present and preceding century partake in the general contagion of its mechanistic philosophy, and are the *product* of an unenlivened generalizing Understanding.'[8]

The force of this alien ideology lies not simply in its manifestation across the disciplines of history, philosophy, politics, and economics, nor in its popularity and therefore manifestation in the public works, committees, and opinions of those in office. As an ideology, its power resides in its capacity to link such external and physical manifestations to the life of the mind, even of the soul. And for Coleridge, Paley's ethics demonstrate this terrible continuum between the privacy of conscience and the external life of the English nation.

Coleridge had mounted an attack on Paley in essay XV of *The Friend* where he poses his own conscientious morality against what he sees as the false abstraction of Paley's 'systematic comprehension' and his 'cold ideal calculation of imaginary GENERAL CONSEQUENCES'.[9] The 'cold ideal' constitutes a self-interestedness masquerading as benevolence. Selfishness is the hallmark of the new philosophy's ethics. For Coleridge, Paley's ethics threaten the role of the will in morals by moving from a consideration of 'inward motives' to 'the outward act'. According to Coleridge, Paley has substituted a form of legality and a requirement of intelligence – 'comprehension' – for such intuitive moral impulses. In Coleridge's view, this makes 'understanding' the test of morality.

As a result of this 'general contagion', Coleridge finds his idea of a Christian nation governed according to the 'living educts of the imagination' or Reason replaced by an age of 'understanding'. Even the physical realm of progress is thoroughly permeated by the ideology of this lesser faculty:

My eye at this moment rests on a volume newly read by me, containing a well-written history of the Inventions, Discoveries, Public Improvements, Docks, Rail-ways, Canals, &c. for about the same period, in England and Scotland. I closed it under the strongest impressions of awe, and admiration akin to wonder. We live, I exclaimed, under the dynasty of the understanding: and this is its golden age.

It is the faculty of means to medial ends. With these the age, this favoured land, teems: they spring up, the armed host, ('seges clypeata') from the serpent's teeth sown by Cadmus: 'mortalia semina, dentes'. In every direction they advance, conquering and to conquer. Sea, and Land, Rock, Mountain, Lake and Moor, yea Nature and all her Elements, sink before them, or yield themselves captive! But the *ultimate* ends? By what name shall I seek for information concerning these? By what name shall I seek for the historiographer of REASON? Where shall I find the annals of *her* recent campaigns? the records of her conquests? In the facts disclosed by the Mendicant Society? In the reports on the increase of crimes, commitments? In the proceedings of the Police? Or in the accumulating volumes on the horrors and perils of population? (*CW*, x, pp. 59–60)

Coleridge's impassioned declamation ends, significantly, with a grotesque parodic rewriting of *Paradise Lost*:

> O voice, once heard.
> Delightfully, *Increase and multiply!*
> Now death to hear! For what can we increase
> Or multiply, *but penury, woe and crime?* (*CW*, x, p. 60)

Nothing could better demonstrate Coleridge's sense of the impiety and blasphemy contained in what he has constructed as the monster of utility. Not only has it challenged the moral integrity of conscience, it also threatens to bring sin and death into his beloved country by radically altering the essential Christian idea of hope. And in this respect the new philosophy goes against Coleridge's very belief in the divine status of 'Man':

Our Maker has distinguished man from the brute that perishes, by making hope first an instinct of his nature; and secondly, an indispensable condition of his moral and intellectual progression:
   For every gift of noble origin
   Is breathed upon by Hope's perpetual breath. WORDSWORTH
(*CW*, x, p. 73)

II

The famous description of imagination in the action of a water insect 'winning its way up against the stream' in *Biographia Literaria* best captures this required combination of propulsion and ground-edness which characterises the mediatory role demanded of imagination in Coleridge's aesthetics of Christian optimism. In particular, it illustrates how identity, for Coleridge, is premised on intuitive hope. As the insect uses the surface tension of the water to make its way up the rivulet, it illustrates how the creative life-force of the mind works in conjunction with the recalcitrance of matter.

> Most of my readers will have observed a small water-insect on the surface of rivulets, which throws a cinque-spotted shadow fringed with prismatic colours on the sunny bottom of the brook; and will have noticed, how the little animal *wins* its way up against the stream, by alternate pulses of active and passive motion, now resisting the current, and now yielding to it in order to gather strength and a momentary *fulcrum* for a further propulsion. This is no unapt emblem of the mind's self-experience in the act of thinking. There are evidently two powers at work, which relatively to each other are active and passive; and this is not possible without an intermediate faculty, which is at once both active and passive. (In philosophical language, we must denominate this intermediate faculty in all its degrees and determinations, the *IMAGINATION*. (*CW*, VII, vol. 1, pp. 124–25)

In this description Coleridge indicates the promissory, narrative propulsion of the imaginative faculty at the same time as declaring its realisation in the world of time and matter. The claim is that imagination is here the implied ghost in the machine: the soulful premise on which such action takes place. The passage ends up as a statement of faith rather than an analogy.

Coleridge had already indicated the nature of this instinctive and self-conscious reflex in his outline of the principles of method in *The Friend* nearly eight years earlier. Using the Aristotelian axiom that the whole is of necessity prior to its parts, he attempts to identify 'the instinct in which humanity itself is grounded'.[10] Taking as his example 'the enlightened naturalist' (a figure, one presumes, likely to have been influenced by French materialism) he proceeds to a Kantian assumption of purpose in nature:

> Yet even he admits to a teleological ground in physics and physiology: that is, the presumption of a something *analogous* to the causality of the human will, by which, without assigning to nature, as nature, a conscious purpose, he may yet distinguish her agency from a blind and lifeless mechanism. Even he admits its use, and, in many instances, its necessity, as a regulative principle; as a ground of anticipation, for the guidance of his judgement and for the direction of his observation and experiment: briefly in all that preparatory process, which the French language so happily expresses by *s'orienter*, i.e. to find out the east for one's self. (*The Friend*, *CW*, IV, vol. 1, pp. 498–99)

There is a confidence in this example from *The Friend*; Coleridge takes on the enemy and demonstrates the instinctive life-force necessarily informing all human activity.

In contrast, the opening to *A Lay Sermon* (1817) seems much more anxious and desperate: a last test of one's Christian faith in the face of adversity. It begins in high Romantic fashion with the invocation of a blessed breeze of inspiration, derived in this instance from the prophet Isaiah: 'Blessed are ye that sow beside all waters.'[11] This breeze, Coleridge informs us, is

> at once our Guide and our Pioneer! – a Breeze from Heaven, which at one and the same time determines our path, impels us along it, and removes beforehand, each overhanging cloud that might have conspired with our own dimness to bewilder or to dishearten us. Whatever our own Despondence may whisper, or the reputed Masters of Political Economy may have seemed to demonstrate, neither by the fears and scruples of the one, or by the confident affirmations of the other, dare we be deterred. They must both be false if the Prophet is true. We will still in the power of that faith which can *hope even against hope* continue to sow beside all waters: for there is a Blessing attached to it by God himself, to whose eye all consequences are present, on whose will all consequences depend. (*A Lay Sermon*, *CW*, VI, p. 140)

Once again, Coleridge indicates his anxiety at the apparent secularisation of society evident in the discourse of utilitarianism. Coleridge's own language is forced to reassess the meanings now ascribed to 'ultimate ends' and 'consequences'.

In these commentaries on the instinctive nature of hope it is possible to observe how Coleridge's theory of imagination passes into the private zone of the individual. The culture of the individual is now the focus of his concern rather than the confident progressivism of imagination's role in civilisation and education with which I began this chapter. Coleridge's battle with utility and its redefinition of consequences pushes him towards a defence of individual conscience and threatens to open up a gap between it and the realm of social improvement and the advance of material technologies.

In this context of the threat of utilitarian thought it is perhaps not surprising that Coleridge's grand project in *Biographia Literaria* to expound a theory of imagination should take an autobiographical form. Coleridge's aim is to reaffirm the link between author and text, both in the sense of the creative power of imagination encapsulating a conscientious act of will and through his own personal address to the next generation of aspiring authors.

III

[H]e wishes nevertheless to open out his heart to such as he either knows or hopes to be of like mind with himself, but who are widely scattered in the world: he wishes to knit anew his connections with his oldest friends, to continue those recently formed, and to win other friends among the rising generation for the remaining course of his life.

(*CW*, VII, vol. 1, 3)

That the *Biographia* might be read as a writing from the heart seems to have been lost in recent critical discussions of Coleridge's most famous exposition of literary theory. My aim in this section of the chapter is to show how Coleridge's language of personality combines with his literary theory in the more general attempt in *Biographia Literaria* to offer up imagination in the face of utilitarian thinking.

Coleridge's epigraph to *Biographia Literaria* is indicative of the anxiety of authorship which haunts its pages.[12] One of the pressing concerns of the book is to rescue the possibility of an author maintaining a particular, creative connection with the words on the page. Faced with the commercialisation of literature, the savage personal attacks of the new journalism, and, as we have seen, a philosophy of utility which challenges the conscientious choice of the author, Coleridge looks for a mediatory agent which can stave off the threat of alienation and self-destruction. In this sense, Coleridge's literary life depends upon his famous definitions of imagination and fancy which are mustered to make good this connection and thereby secure the unity of literary identity. The singular 'biographia' of Coleridge's title is threatened with disconnection and the very real possibility that a literary life in this unified sense may no longer be possible in an age of mass readership. *Biographia Literaria* may be seen as an attempt to explain and reveal the 'one life' through which the author is connected spiritually and morally to the words on the page and to the ideal reader. Coleridge's selection of the epigraph from Goethe shows him once again attempting to control and focus the potential chaos which results from publication and the trade of literature through the rhetorical device of addressing a friend as he had done in the subscription journal of that name earlier in his career.

Chapter II of the *Biographia* consists of Coleridge's refutation of the popular conception of the irritability of genius. It does so by demonstrating the link between genial feelings and genius. Coleridge counters the reading public's aggression towards authors not by severing the link between author and text, but by confirming it. The 'character' of genius is here being used to supplant other notions of 'character' current in British society. Possessing a character, having a consistency of character, in these more popular senses, is being undercut by Coleridge's articulation of this deeper, more moral, less fashionable and, it is claimed, more integrated notion of the identity of genius.

A savage attack on the current state of society and its relationship to literature surrounds and supports this defence of genius. Coleridge's anxious joke at the end of the chapter that 'the original sin of my character consists in a careless indifference to public opinion'[13] registers those other charges on the grounds of indolence and the sins of omission which we have already witnessed in Hazlitt's reviews, as well as the more general threat resident in the very idea of 'public opinion'. According to Coleridge, 'the multitude of books and the general diffusion of literature' have produced 'lamentable effects in the world of letters'[14] which have reduced the rare and privileged communication between writers to a common and superficial language: 'a still greater diffusion of literature shall produce an increase of sciolists; and sciolism bring[s] with it petulance and presumption'.[15] As a result of 'the more artificial state of society and social intercourse, language, mechanized as it were into a barrel-organ, supplies at once both instrument and tune'.[16] What had been beautiful music between poets is now a free-for-all cacophony. Coleridge takes the point even further by suggesting that, as a result of this debasement brought about by mass communication, society and language are also radically changed in their nature. Society is now 'artificial' and language has been not just mechanised, but reduced to material fragments:

I have attempted to illustrate the present state of our language, in its relation to literature, by a press-room of larger and smaller stereotype pieces, which, in the present anglo-gallican fashion of unconnected, epigrammatic periods, it requires but an ordinary portion of ingenuity to vary indefinitely, and yet still produce something which, if not sense, will be so like it as to do as well . . . Hence of all trades, literature at present demands the least talent or information; and, of all modes of literature, the manufacturing of poems. (*CW*, vii, vol. i, p. 39)

This fashionable, but ultimately mechanistic, use of language which Coleridge characteristically identifies with the French, disconnects words from truth. There is no spirit in this showy materialism which can link the units of language together. An artificial style produces an artificial literature in which the genius of composition has been replaced by the mechanical combinations of the compositor.

Such statements about the state of the language and the state of literature being reflective of the commercialised spirit of society are replicated in many of Coleridge's most aggressive statements in *Biographia Literaria*. They are motivated by an assumption that popularity or the greater dissemination of literature will inevitably lead to its debased commercialisation or 'plebification' as he terms it at one point in *On the Constitution of the Church and State*.[17] Coleridge repeatedly advises the aspiring authors in his readership – those of the 'rising generation' – not to pursue literature exclusively or as a trade. His advice is that they should cut themselves off from the market-place of literature and forego the opportunities now opening up for pursuing a career as a professional man of letters. '[B]e not *merely* a man of letters!' he urges, 'Let literature be an honourable *augmentation* to your arms; but not constitute the coat, or fill the escutcheon!'[18] Coleridge then concludes his chapter with similar advice from Herder which he translates as:

With the greatest possible solicitude avoid authorship. Too early or immoderately employed, it makes the head *waste* and the heart empty; even were there no other worse consequences. A person, who reads only to print, in all probability reads amiss; and he, who sends away through the pen and the press every thought, the moment it occurs to him, will in a short time have sent all away, and will become a mere journeyman of the printing-office, a *compositor*. (*CW*, VII, vol. 1, p. 231)

In this way, Coleridge focuses his attack on the self-conscious and market-oriented nature of publishing which he sees as a dangerous form of alienation. The public opinion now being referred to in the age of the steam-press is itself an idea which smacks of utilitarian modes of thinking: an indiscriminate mass of individuals reified by the discourse of population into the respectability of an idea, or, as he puts it himself: 'the multitudinous PUBLIC, shaped into personal unity by the magic of abstraction'.[19] In this way abstraction constructs a new, false form of subjectivity. The resultant 'personal unity' is a mockery of the integrated, moral self. The dissemination of literature has not only transformed personality into celebrity; it has fabricated a personality for the public itself.

Against this false and alienating zeitgeist, Coleridge offers a natural form of spirit and communion. He poses 'the naked eye of our common consciousness'[20] against the artificiality of public opinion and writes, more famously, of a 'collective, unconscious good sense working progressively to desynonymize'.[21] At such moments Coleridge still retains the possibility of a radical common sense and an almost primitivist belief in the transparency of representation. This supports his view of genius as cutting through custom, convention, and opinion to reveal a natural morality and with it the possibility of an integrated, conscientious selfhood whose actions resist measurement by a mathematical scale of abstraction.

In the middle of this 'exhortation' to younger readers not to follow the exclusive trade of writing Coleridge articulates his belief in the connection between genius and virtue. He advocates a separation of activity which corresponds to his distinction between genius and talent. Maintaining or operating upon this distinction guarantees the possibility of keeping in touch with the progressive, noble ends of 'literature'. Two chapters before he outlines his definition of imagination, Coleridge is careful to define the practical ends of genius and to assert the link which exists between it and virtue.

Money, and immediate reputation form only an arbitrary and accidental end of literary labor. The *hope* of increasing them by any given exertion will often prove a stimulant to industry; but the *necessity* of acquiring them will in all works of genius convert the stimulant into a *narcotic*. Motives by excess reverse their very nature, and instead of exciting, stun and stupify the mind. For it is one contradistinction of genius from talent, that its predominant end is always comprized in the means; and this is one of the many points, which establish an analogy between genius and virtue. (*CW*, VII, vol. 1, p. 224)

For Coleridge, it is precisely the ulterior motive of utilitarian ethics – certainly in the case of Paley – which represents a threat to his idea of a moral act, including the conscientious act of writing. Like Godwin, he views as pernicious the idea that one's actions are motivated by self-interest in the face of a system of rewards and punishments, by the abstraction of benevolence, rather than by the spontaneous benevolence of the sympathetic imagination.

At this point in the *Biographia* Coleridge might be seen as consigning literary production and the workings of genius to the realm of leisure. He presents his aspiring literati with a vision of domestic tranquility enhanced by its separation from the hard-nosed world of work. (In many ways, this domesticity is reminiscent of his efforts to find tranquility or at least moments of repose in the supportive framework of family and friends in the turmoil of the 1790s.) More importantly, Coleridge establishes at this moment a key aspect of the power of his aesthetic. The self-sufficing nature of genius and its productions is central to both his sense of art and his Christianity. This is the moment at which he can confidently differentiate himself from the competing and, for him, life- and soul-threatening ideology of utility and its attendant methodologies. At the same moment as he guarantees the morality of genius – the conscientious nature of unconscious genius – he has to sever its links with economics and the external manifestations of social progress.

As a result, it could be argued that Coleridge played into the hands of his utilitarian enemies: by limiting the scope of the imagination to a discrete and mystificatory realm, he consigned it to the sidelines of power, or, at least, made it an easy, albeit precious, target. Coleridge's development of 'the Idea' at the expense of the mediatory imagination in his later writings can be construed as a giving up on the notion of 'the One Life', as Nigel Leask suggests, which makes it sound like a retreat.[22] Imagination ceases to be the battleground of cultural conflict, the one power thought capable of solving, albeit miraculously, a dichotomous culture. Perhaps with hindsight it might look more like a strategic withdrawal: imagination remains to fight another day. The aesthetic reservoir can be drawn upon when required. The retreat might even act in favour of the power of the aesthetic: to make the aesthetic a discrete zone might provide it with all the power of the repressed, or even of the unconscious, which is well capable of making its return at moments of cultural crisis. In this scenario it might be denied power of the overt and supposedly real empiricist kind described by Hazlitt, but it retains a power within the culture which is not susceptible to the conscious political ideology of utilitarianism. It has all the force of a power which resists the definition of the centre.

In the last sections of this final chapter I would like to outline some of the implications of this 'retreat' of the imagination in the face of what Coleridge considers to be an increasingly materialist culture and the counter claims of utilitarianism. Coleridge's legacy to John Stuart Mill and I. A. Richards suggests very different ways in which that unconscious of the imagination could be tapped and could itself speak. Not least among these is its capacity to announce the incapacity of utility from within the enemy camp.

IV

Coleridge's appropriation by utilitarians was already under way before the publication of *On the Constitution of the Church and State*. In January 1830 *The Westminster Review*, mouth-piece of the utilitarians led by James Mill and Jeremy Bentham, published a review of the second edition of Coleridge's *Poetical Works* now thought to have been written by W. J. Fox. Even at this stage, the *Westminster* is clearly keen not to be identified as anti-literary and antipathetic to poetry. Only 'dunces', the reviewer announces pugnaciously, would suggest that there is 'any natural incongruity between the reasoning and imaginative faculties'.[23] After this rather defensive opening which declares the harmonious joining together of utility and poetry, the reviewer boldly announces:

Thus Mr. Coleridge is a Benthamite in his poetry; a Utilitarian; a 'greatest happiness' man; for, as a poet, he writes under the controlling and dictating power of truth and nature, under the inspiration of his own profound convictions and emotions.[24]

But even as the reviewer attempts to incorporate the poetic in the truth of utility by sounding the praises of Coleridge's poems, he enacts the split between the logical, discursive nature of prose and the intuitive, imaginative nature of poetry by declaring that Coleridge in his prose 'is not his own man'.[25]

An anonymous reviewer in the *Athenaeum* only days later takes up the challenge of this description of Coleridge as an unconscious utilitarian and focuses particularly on the threatening suggestion of a split in Coleridge's psyche between the imagination and reason:

Can such a critic have any idea of a human being as a complex, but homogeneous whole? Is it possible to conceive all the poetry-making part of a mind as sound, and the prose-making part as corrupt, through the whole of life; and to fancy that the health shall not heal the disease, nor the malady infect the health? Is there nothing at first sight astounding in such a notion? Is it not certain, that the very same faculties are employed in both these mental occupations?[26]

Both men in their different ways prefigure later debates involving the utilitarian appropriation of Coleridge, not least in their desperate attempts to maintain a unified and sane self in a contest of faculties haunted by the spectre of break-down. The more they struggle to unify, the more their cultural values come apart at the seams.

V

The afterlife of Coleridge's definitions of imagination in *Biographia Literaria* and his application of the related concepts of the 'Idea' and 'Reason' in *The Lay Sermons* and *On the Constitution of the Church and State* finds perhaps its most famous manifestation in John Stuart Mill's two celebrated and influential essays on Bentham and Coleridge published in 1838 and 1840 respectively. The role played by imagination in these paired studies of the 'two most seminal figures of the present age', as Mill calls them, could easily be overlooked as it plays second fiddle to more pressing concerns about the nature of progress and the need for systematic, impartial thinking. The way in which Mill deploys the idea of imagination is entirely characteristic of the complex and skilfully imbricated nature of these essays, but it is also, I think, indicative of an unanswered question about the relationship between aesthetics and psychology at the heart of his thinking.

Here once again the imagination signals a deep-seated anxiety about the nature of culture precisely because it is deployed to cover up the gap; and in the case of Mill a gap – or a vacancy left in the wake of negative sceptical thought – is viewed with something akin to horror. The main purpose of these two essays is, of course, to heal a breach in the thinking of the age by taking these two opposed thinkers and showing how their philosophies contain a complementary truth: that together they represent the current peak of achievement in the history of ideas. Mill urges his reader to rise above sectarian, party-led oppositions to appreciate the truth in rational thought even when carried out by the opposition – in this case the Idealist and 'Conservative' Coleridge. According to Mill, Bentham and Coleridge are 'each other's "completing counterpart"'[27] and he goes on in typical liberal fashion to apply the Whig notion of the constitution to the history of ideas and sees Bentham and Coleridge as exhibiting 'antagonist modes of thought . . . as necessary to one another in speculation, as mutually checking powers are in a political constitution'.[28] Mill's adhesion to the combined 'truth' of these competing philosophies is equivalent to his attachment to his more famous paradoxical notion of 'liberty'. Both essays manifest a desire to rise above division, but their arguments very much depend upon it. Indeed it could be said that the very notion of complementarity draws attention to difference in order to contain it.

In his essay on Coleridge Mill appears to be categorical in denying the claims made for the Coleridgean imagination or anything resembling it.

Above all others it is the point at which he openly expresses his opposition. After dispassionately offering the competing views of the rival camps in which 'the school of Locke, Hartley, and Bentham' are seen to allege 'that the transcendentalists make imagination, and not observation, the criterion of truth'[29] he makes a point of leaving objectivity behind and announces:

> we here content ourselves with a bare statement of our opinion. It is, that the truth, on this much-debated question, lies with the school of Locke and Bentham. The nature and laws of Things in themselves, or the hidden causes of the phenomena which are the objects of experience, appear to us radically inaccessible to the human faculties. We see no ground for believing that anything can be the object of our knowledge except our experience, and what can be inferred from our experience by the analogies of experience itself; nor that there is any idea, feeling, or power in the human mind, which, in order to account for it, requires that its origin should be referred to any other source. We are therefore at issue with Coleridge on the central idea of his philosophy . . .
> (Mill, *Collected Works*, x, pp. 128–29)

Such a forthright denunciation of the Coleridgean imagination and in particular the claims made for its metaphysical and divine origins does not, as one might expect, signal the end of the issue. As the essay develops, the realm of imagination maintains an unsettling presence at the margins of Mill's thought.

Mill sides sympathetically once more with the 'truthful' side of Coleridge's thinking as he rehearses the reaction against what he sees as the necessary response to eighteenth-century British philosophy and to philosophe thinking more generally. It soon becomes apparent that Coleridgean Germanic thought was a response to a real psychological need. (Mill has already subtly addressed this in the first sentence of the essay where he refers to the 'inward workings of the age manifest[ing] themselves more and more in outward facts'.) The reaction against the eighteenth century signalled, according to Mill, the fact that 'the age of real psychology was about to commence'.[30] As he outlines the limitations in French thinking on the subject of 'the essential requisites of civil society'[31] he alludes to the gap created by the wholesale revolutionary sweeping away of the vestiges of civilisation – what we have seen Hazlitt refer to as the 'gew-gaws of legitimacy'. The conservative philosophers such as Coleridge are to be applauded, argues Mill, for appreciating the psychological role played by 'institutions and creeds' in binding civil society together. These 'had rendered essential services to civilization, and still filled a place in the human mind, and in the arrangements of society, which could not without great peril, be left vacant'.[32] Similarly, when it comes to epitomising the Coleridgean version of history, exemplified by Herder and Michelet, imagination is an important psychological component in the transmission of this new history. The new historians, 'by making the facts and events of the past have a meaning and an intelligible place in the gradual evolution of humanity, have at once given history, even to the imagination, an interest like romance, and afforded the only means of predicting and guiding the future'.[33] As Mill introduces a sense of the aesthetic into history on the grounds of psychological need, he also extends his encomium on this new philosophy. It is more than a 'philosophy of history'; it is 'the philosophy of human culture'.[34] Out of the need to address the issue of civil society Mill recognises the ideological pull of the aesthetic and extends the Coleridgean understanding of inwardness to his own sense of national identity. Even for Mill, then, Coleridge represents an opportunity for avoiding the gap in the cultural apparatus. As much as he wishes to demystify Coleridge's assigning of a divine or at least metaphysical origin to imagination he recognises how the schism between inward mind and outward fact can be spanned by Coleridge's attention to education and the role of the intellectual in the form of the clerisy which had been outlined in *On the Constitution of Church and State* and the *Lay Sermons*.

If the reference to the Coleridgean imagination appears to be veiled or at least indirect in the essay on Coleridge it is perhaps because it is so explicit in the earlier essay on Bentham. In the first part of this essay Mill offers a devastating attack on Bentham's philosophy and psychology which despite brave efforts cannot quite be redeemed in the second half when he comes to praise Bentham's achievement. Mill's critique centres on Bentham's 'want of imagination', a phrase which reverberates throughout the essay.[35]

After drawing attention to Bentham's scorn for the opinion of previous thinkers which he considers to be the first of his 'disqualification[s] as a philosopher', Mill turns to the second: 'the incompleteness of his own mind as a representative of universal human nature'.[36] For the new age of real psychology this is a pretty damning disqualification, especially since imagination is thought to be the key not just to experiencing, but also for understanding the new territory, as Mill's explanation reveals:

In many of the most natural and strongest feelings of human nature he had no sympathy; from many of its graver experiences he was altogether cut off; and the faculty by which one mind understands a mind different from itself, and throws itself into the feelings of that other mind, was denied him by his deficiency of Imagination. (Mill, *Collected Works*, x, p. 91)

That Mill has in mind something more than a popular sense of imagination as florid style or even a glib sense of the sympathetic imagination is immediately made apparent in the next paragraph:

With Imagination in the popular sense, command of imagery and metaphorical expression, Bentham was, to a certain degree, endowed. For want, indeed, of poetical culture, the images with which his fancy supplied him were seldom beautiful, but they were quaint and humorous, or bold, forcible, and intense: passages might be quoted from him both of playful irony, and of declamatory eloquence, seldom surpassed in the writings of philosophers. The Imagination which he had not, was that to which the name is generally appropriated by the best writers of the present day; that which enables us, by a voluntary effort, to conceive the absent as if it were present, the imaginary as if it were real, to clothe it in the feelings which, if it were indeed real, it would bring along with it. This is the power by which one human being enters into the mind and circumstances of another. This power constitutes the poet, in so far as he does anything but melodiously utter his own actual feelings. (Mill, *Collected Works*, x, pp. 92–93)

While Mill is certainly deferring to a specialised 'Romantic' version of the imagination here his statements are also underscored with potential critique. The tone is grudging, to say the least. There is no recognition that the realm of imagination has any status as reality, and the description of the poet as only melodiously uttering his own actual feelings maintains the sense that Mill's capacity for critique in this area is stronger than his professions of sympathy. But the tension in his position is registered in the adjective of 'actual feelings'. If he does not go so far as to endorse the reality of imagination, he does seem to subscribe to the reality of feelings. Indeed the realm of the psychological accessed through the imagination, is not only considered to be real, it also occupies a special place in the history of the present and has developed a language of its own.

Imagination's key role in the production of this new sense of identity, in tune with the spirit of the age and its attendant metalanguage, emerges as Mill pursues Bentham's deficient empiricism. Without the power of imagination, Mill argues, 'nobody knows even his own nature, further than circumstances have actually tried it and called it out; nor the nature of his fellow-creatures, beyond such generalizations as he may have been enabled to make from his own observation of their outward conduct'.[37]

As a result, Bentham simply does not qualify as a man of the age; he has not attained that paradoxical manhood produced out of agonised self-reflection which is the hallmark of greatness:

> He knew no dejection, no heaviness of heart. He never felt life a sore and a weary burthen. He was a boy to the last. Self-consciousness, that daemon of the men of genius of our time, from Wordsworth to Byron, from Goethe to Chateaubriand, and to which this age owes so much both of its cheerful and its mournful wisdom, never was awakened in him. (Mill, *Collected Works*, x, p. 92)

This description of an experiential knowledge which has a psychological life of its own does not simply complement the observations of an unfeeling empiricism, it challenges them. The subtle workings of 'the mind upon itself'[38] and 'the distinctions which are legible in the hearts of others' are unavailable to Bentham for he possesses no 'self-culture'.[39] The resultant isolated position which Bentham occupies, for all its achievement in the field of careful juridical observation and codification, cannot properly connect the isolated individual to the civic or national community. For this to take place, imagination is necessary.

According to Mill, it is Bentham's very identity as a moralist which accounts for this 'one-sidedness'. When he comes to address 'the popular idea of a Benthamite' as 'cold, mechanical, and ungenial',[40] he is careful to distinguish this from utilitarianism. As a moralist, Bentham fails to appreciate human action from a 'sympathetic' and an 'aesthetic' perspective. Once again it is the want of imagination which cuts him off from the idea of culture which means he cannot bridge the gap between individual and nation. Bentham cannot connect his sceptical individualism with popular opinion; he cannot envisage how others can see themselves in relation to the civic polity; and taking 'no account of national character and the causes which form and maintain it, he was precluded from considering . . . the laws of the country as an instrument of national culture'.[41]

Mill's critique of Bentham draws attention to the dangers, particularly the resultant myopia, of materialism. Throughout the essay, the attack on Bentham's narrowness is premised on a belief in the complexity and the power of psychology; and the agent which can mediate between the otherwise isolated individual and the general good of the nation is the imagination. At times, this seems to be no more than an extension of Adam Smith's notion of the sympathetic imagination; at others, there is a recognition of its connection with a new discourse and knowledge of inward, self-culture. Mill seems to recognise, albeit grudg-

Coleridge and the afterlife of imagination 183

ingly at times, the experiential reality and ideological implications of this connection. Coleridge's linking of the imagination with the Idea and with the clerisy, once cleared of its dangerously metaphysical origins and tendency towards mystery, can thus be appropriated by Mill's own brand of psychologically bolstered utilitarianism.

Mill's famous description in his *Autobiography* of the 'crisis' in his 'mental history' contains an equally complex rehabilitation of the imagination in order to make it compatible with the philosophy of utility. As he begins to explain the vacuum in his psychic development Mill draws attention to the split between 'logic and analysis' and his tendencies towards 'sympathy with mankind' and 'genuine benevolence' whose 'natural aliment' is 'poetical culture'.[42] His education has led him to 'neglect both in theory and in practice ... the cultivation of feeling' which results in 'an undervaluing of poetry, and of Imagination generally as an element of human nature'.[43] Mill's solution to this dichotomy of value is to present the problem as a false opposition which can be resolved through balance. But the way he presents his crisis suggests a more complex and certainly more unresolvable nature to his culture debate.

Mill's mental crisis, he tells us, comes from imagining that the reform of society through the philosophy of social utility has actually been completed. This scenario exposes the surplus nature of his own identity. By imagining the end of the narrative Mill's mind exposes the extent to which his own self has been suppressed, even erased, by subjection to this narrative of reform and improvement. The meaning of his existence as self-abnegating, puritanical struggle is immediately called into question. The terms in which Mill describes the state of mind brought on by this realization are Coleridge's. He quotes from both 'Dejection: an Ode' and 'Work without Hope'.[44] The way he does so is curious. Referring to the opening lines of 'Work without Hope' he comments:

Two lines of Coleridge, in whom alone of all writers I have found a true description of what I felt, were often in my thoughts, not at this time (for I had never read them), but in a later period of the same mental malady:

> Work without hope draws nectar in a sieve
> And hope without an object cannot live.
> (Mill, *Autobiography, Collected Works*, 1, pp. 143–44)

As well as belying the idea of a single crisis which has been overcome, this statement accords the lines an uncanny force. Coleridge's words are a retrospective imposition upon the experience, but their power to articulate the experience means that they seem to have actually infiltrated Mill's past. In this way, the discourse of self-hood, even negative self-hood haunted by the daemon of self-consciousness, has a life and power of its own. Attention is more usually focused on Wordsworth's role in effecting a healing solution to Mill's problem, but Coleridge, I would argue, plays an equally interesting role – both as a poet and as a thinker. As Mill indicates in the essay on Bentham, dejection constitutes knowledge ('wisdom') as well as a distinct psychological language of the mind.

Understanding this deployment of Coleridge also helps us to appreciate the more celebrated role played by Wordsworth's poetry in Mill's recovery. In broad terms, the popular view is that poetry translated into feeling makes good the limitations of a life devoted to utility. Supplementing analysis with a culture of feeling remedies the alienated subjectivity of our autobiographer. But the more one looks at the detailed explanation of how reading Wordsworth's poems effects a restoration, the less satisfying is this story of supplementation. Although Mill is careful to rehearse a story of complementarity, his description of the restorative effect of Word-sworth's poetry reveals only another separation. The imaginative and consolatory aesthetic which he finds in the poems of 1815 cannot connect with social improvement and progress: it threatens to emerge as a self-sufficing, autotelic zone. This is apparent from the way Mill dismisses both the philosophical content of the poems and their referentiality. He is quick to tell us that the 'Immortality Ode' contains 'bad philosophy' and that a second-rate landscape painting could accomplish much more in terms of mimesis than any of these poems. What these poems do offer Mill, however, is the 'culture of feelings'.[45] In this powerful and enigmatic phrase the poetic and the psychological have become one and the result appears to be a separation off from the world of social improvement.

At one point in his argument it is as if the aesthetic has actually been absorbed by the psychological. Mill values Wordsworth's poetry not as poetry, but as 'medicine':

What made Wordsworth's poems a medicine for my state of mind, was that they expressed, not mere outward beauty, but states of feeling, and of thought coloured by feeling, under the excitement of beauty. (Mill, *Autobiography, Collected Works*, I, p. 151)

Following Wordsworth's own wording in his 'Preface to the second edition of the Lyrical Ballads', Mill manages to de-aestheticise Wordsworth, or, at least, to focus on psychology rather than art. According to Mill, Wordsworth is 'the poet of unpoetical natures' and he maintains that he 'long continued to value Wordsworth less according to his intrinsic merits than by the measure of what he had done for me'.[46]

What Mill seems to have in mind here is a form of parallelism in which one side can respond to, or reflect, the other even if there is no actual connection. It is as if the realm of inward feelings can exist side by side with the world of external facts. The following sentence (which refers to Wordsworth's poems) enacts this ambivalence; it announces separation, but is never quite prepared to let go:

In them I seemed to draw from a source of inward joy, of sympathetic and imaginative pleasure, which could be shared in by all human beings; which had no connexion with struggle or imperfection, but would be made richer by every improvement in the physical or social condition of mankind. (Mill, *Autobiography*, Collected Works, I, p. 151)

The same tension reappears later in the same chapter of the *Autobiography* when Mill outlines his arguments and debates with Roebuck. Having characterised Roebuck as a cultured Benthamite with a typical Englishman's resistance to and mistrust of feeling, Mill explains how, after his recovery through reading Wordsworth's poetry in the summer of 1828, he is now able to advocate this inward culture of feeling to his opponent:

He saw little good in any cultivation of the feelings, and none at all in cultivating them through the imagination, which he thought was only cultivating illusions. It was in vain I urged on him that the imaginative emotion which an idea when vividly conceived excites in us, is not an illusion but a fact, as real as any of the other qualities of objects; and far from implying anything erroneous and delusive in our mental apprehension of the object, is quite consistent with the most accurate knowledge and most perfect practical recognition of all its physical and intellectual laws and relations. The intensest feeling of the beauty of a cloud lighted by the setting sun, is no hindrance to my knowing that the cloud is vapour of water, subject to all the laws of vapours in a state of suspension; and I am just as likely to allow for, and act on, these physical laws whenever there is occasion to do so, as if I had been incapable of perceiving any distinction between beauty and ugliness. (Mill, *Autobiography*, Collected Works, I, p. 157)

This rosy picture of easy coexistence between science and aesthetics is hardly convincing especially when, in the final quoted sentence, Mill, perhaps pleading too hard in the face of Roebuck's opposition, represents scientific explanation as his second nature, aesthetic perception as a possibility he can easily imagine losing. Here Mill has taken the material language of empiricism and transferred it to the mind. Rather than challenging the world of fact, this replicates facts in the realm of feeling. It is also difficult to ascertain the temporal nature of Mill's psychologised aesthetic. This too seems to have it both ways: it is both timeless and a culture susceptible to improvement. It is composed of what is common and permanent in human nature, yet represents an opportunity for the process of civilisation.

These desperate attempts by Mill to reconcile beauty with utility clearly delineate the territory already inhabited by Coleridge's ideas of the imagination. As we have seen, Mill's troubled engagement with the aesthetic in his *Autobiography* takes the form of a quasi-scientific psychologising rather than a championing of art or artifice. He is more interested in the reality of feelings than the medium of poetry. His aesthetics is likely to take the form of a psychological realism which can neatly parallel the world of objects in scientific observation. At least, this is the impression to be had from his reading of Wordsworth. Wordsworth offers him this possibility of 'recompense'. Coleridge, on the other hand, precisely because he contains no medicine, offers him – like the other agonised literary idols of the age – a more troubling language of disconnection which contains a disabling truth for the improver and reformer: the awareness of loss which exposes the status of restored equilibrium as mere recompense.

On the one hand, Mill's idea of the 'culture of feelings' suggests that feelings are culture; but on the other he is equally intent on making the link with the nation and on finding a means by which the inward culture of feelings can find a manifestation in the life of the nation through education. Mill's use of the word 'culture' is illustrative of this divide.

VI

The legacy of Mill's encounter with Bentham and Coleridge haunts the work of I. A. Richards. Just as the full significance of Coleridge's production of imagination in the face of the threat from utilitarianism can only be fully understood by analysing the role it plays a generation later in the life and work of John Stuart Mill, so its twentieth-century meaning must include an understanding of Richards's own attempt to straddle the great divide between imagination and utility. Richards's ambitious project is at once the last attempt to solve a nineteenth-century schism in British intellectual culture and an illuminating and rare twentieth-century British attempt at a systematic criticism. At the end of the line of utilitarian thought, Richards returns us to the critical problems which inform and structure our current understanding and evaluation of the Coleridgean imagination.

Richards's 1934 study *Coleridge On Imagination* occupies a central place in the development of his critical position and exposes the nature of his struggle to resolve the nineteenth-century cultural crisis over the relationship between aesthetics and utility. This particular connection with Mill complements and complicates his more obvious Arnoldian inheritance.[47] In *Science and Poetry* (1926) Richards had already drawn attention to what he felt to be the dichotomous nature of culture and the inadequate means commentators like himself had of addressing it. Although he quotes Matthew Arnold in his epigraph,[48] the fact that none of the arguments attempting to use poetry as 'a denial or as a corrective of science' can match 'Mill's *Logic*' seems equally important to him.[49] Arguing that poetry is 'capable of saving us' or at least of 'preserving us or rescuing us from confusion and frustration', Richards's concern is to expound the argument in the positivist terms of the supposed enemy. In short, Richards attempts to collapse the dichotomy by declaring it false.

Half-way through his book on Coleridge, in a chapter entitled 'Good Sense', Richards poses the question that had already preoccupied him in *Science and Poetry* (1926) and which was to recur throughout his career:[50]

What, after all, is the practical utility of literary theory? There are a number of sound enough answers. One is that we shall in any case use theories, and that good theories will protect us from worse. Another is that persons with literary interests to-day frequently suffer from lack of exercise in careful and sometimes arduous thinking. And this the understanding of a good theory entails. A third is that the theory of literary analysis is at an extremely interesting point in its development, on the point of making, through experiment, those contacts with actuality that would transform it into a science, and a science from which very important practical utilities may be expected to result. (Richards, *Coleridge On Imagination*, p. 137)

Coleridge's exploration of imagination provides Richards with precisely the example he needs in order to further his dream of a scientific criticism. It gives him the crucial link between language and psychology and in particular an understanding of language which is at once abstract and specific, linguistic and experiential, philosophical and poetic.[51] Operating within an empiricist position, Richards's liberal humanism discovers itself in the encounter with Coleridgean idealism. As a result, for Richards, Coleridge's idea of imagination seems to have an almost salvific potential. Threatened on the one hand by the emergence of fascism in central Europe[52] and on the other by the pervasive unthinking snobbery of English literary culture,[53] Richards turns to Coleridge's theory of imagination as the last great chance for a systematic and scientific criticism.

In *Coleridge On Imagination* Richards describes himself as a Benthamite attempting to find, in true liberal fashion, the truth within the opponent's position. In this agonised and embattled text Richards reads Coleridge against the grain, translating where he can his subject's idealism into a more manageable and familiar form of empiricism. He presents Coleridge as a 'semasiologist', one who is aware that to ask questions about the meanings of words is to ask questions about everything; and he sees the primary purpose of his study as taking Coleridge's lead and pushing on one step further with semasiology (or semantics) which he describes at one point as the 'most central incipient science of the future'.[54]

Defending Coleridge against Victorian charges of addiction and muddle, Richards offers instead a story of intellectual 'crisis' and 'conversion' as Coleridge moves from Hartley to Kant in order to formulate his idea of imagination. He then approaches Coleridge through Mill, claiming that the latter's terms come 'naturally to me – writing here as a Benthamite also'.[55] He then replicates Mill's rhetorical strategy of learning from the opposition. Maintaining such a liberal objectivity when posing his own materialism against Coleridge's 'repugnant' idealism is, as he admits, not 'an easy aim'.[56] As one might expect, Richards not only keeps Coleridge's thought at arm's length, he also tames it and translates it so that it can be accommodated within his own value-system. As part of the apparently healthy process of self-consciousness the reader is immediately alerted to the fact that he intends to describe Coleridge's key distinctions between different kinds of imagination as 'machinery': convenient fictions in the service of truth.[57] With these admissions of difficulty and with a paradoxical combination of detachment and appropriation Richards sets about his rehabilitation of Coleridge's imagination. Having set up the idea of a conversion from Hartley to Kant, Richards's attempt is to go beyond the apparent schism in culture between a Lockean and an idealist epistemology, to find no conflict of interest between Coleridge's idea of mind as 'self-realizing activity' and the Lockean or utilitarian view of it as 'a combination of impressions, ideas, and movements'.[58] If Coleridge's theory of imagination is the particular historical example that can be thus extended and modified to suit his purposes, it is Richards's own extended semasiological view of language which ultimately provides the opportunity for a new criticism. Coleridge's repugnant idealism has been turned into a 'refreshed atomism'[59] and his own literary principles have been described as providing a 'charter of technological liberty'.[60]

Despite its metaphysical and even religious connections, Richards manages to turn Coleridge's idea of imagination to account in his mission to bridge the gap in English culture between two philosophical traditions and two forms of literary criticism. Even allowing for the elements of translation and absorption in Richards's argument, Coleridge's idea serves Richards's purpose because it enables him to straddle critical theory and practical criticism. Coleridge's definitions of primary and secondary imaginations provide him with precisely the base he needs. The primary imagination gives him the psychological foundation he requires and the secondary enables him to project his own peculiar justification of culture and the link between poetry and civilisation.

As with Mill, such accommodation of an apparent intellectual opponent comes at a price. The claim to reason and objectivity evident in the following first person address – 'I write then as a Materialist trying to interpret before you the utterances of an extreme Idealist'[61] – at once announces and belies Richards's own conversion and crisis of belief. The terms in which he draws attention to the agonised philosophical truth of Coleridge's existence reflect powerfully on his own predicament:

The contrast between living power and lifeless mechanism was no abstract matter with him, but a daily torment. Recognizing this more clearly as the 'years matured the silent strife', refusing the comfort of forgetfulness, he had to extricate himself from the Locke tradition, not because it was 'false', but because for himself, at some hours, it was too painfully true. It was the intellectual equivalent of his uncreative moods, and of the temper of an uncreative century.[62]

At times, Richards seems to be a reluctant utilitarian desperate to find a way of including the aesthetic within the prevailing scientific culture. His adoption of the terms 'scientific', 'technological', and 'mechanism' appears almost parodic of the dominant position of facts and actuality and sits uneasily by the side of his calls for psychological relativity and provisional truths. His agonised attempt to reconcile the antagonist forces of English intellectual culture – poetry and science, utility and imagination – forces him to a paradoxical limit where rigorously reasoned argument and clarification of terms actually depend for support upon the prescient structures of contemporary English poetry and the eastern mysticism of his poetic epigraphs and illustrations from the works of Omar Khayyam, Isa Upanishad, and Chuang Tzu. In such ways Richards offers his own version of the 'unsayable' to match Coleridge's disproved metaphysics and discredited idealism.

By the time he writes the introduction to his edition of the *Viking Portable Coleridge* in 1950 Richards appears to have undergone something of a conversion. In the conclusion to that introduction he represents all Coleridge's activities, from 'the local act of critical choice' to the systematic philosophising, as part of a quest for 'authority'. Here Richards offers a Platonic reading of Coleridge's emphasis on the activity of mind and 'the mind's self-experience in the act of thinking' in order to illustrate his own self-confessedly paradoxical form of liberty. In this combination of Plato and Coleridge Richards illustrates his view that 'authority' is premised on 'dependence'. This combination affords him the opportunity of healing the cultural schism so famously experienced as a personal crisis by Mill and which is all too apparent in his own wrestling with the Coleridgean imagination and the question of utility. Typically, Richards's proffered solution, quoting Coleridge, is a psychologising of actuality:

We know this paradox well: What should rule, in the individual – torn between Science and Poetry or between any others of the warring 'subjects' – and in a world of Nations so unable to become United? 'The perfect frame of a man is the perfect frame of a state.'[63]

Even in the 1960s Richards returned in a tone of resignation to the question of Mill on Coleridge and Bentham as something of a test-case for an understanding of the state of culture and civilisation. True to form, he suggests the antidote to the cultural divide is to be found in Coleridge:

That there are Coleridgeans and anti-Coleridgeans (by nature or nurture) is notorious. Few as yet can follow Mill and combine their admirations for S. T. C. and Bentham. The sad probability still is that whoever esteems the one will despise the other. For these outdated oppositions *The Friend* offers innumerable occasions and the remedy.[64]

As a whole, Richards's book on Coleridge seems to replicate the structure of the *Biographia* as the general linguistic and ontological theory of the first half becomes manifest in the second in the practice of contemporary poets (Eliot, Auden, Yeats, and Empson) and the problem of readership. In many ways Richards's 1930's study of Coleridge illustrates many of the recent arguments of the last fifteen years[65] about the *Biographia* which have been concerned with the suppression of a radical theory of language in the process of desynonymisation and the gap between theory and practice. It also provides an interesting example of an early twentieth-century appreciation of Coleridge as an intellectual whose example could still be mustered in support of systematic theory despite the dominant disclaimers of the Victorians.

In effect, Richards's study of Coleridge's imagination by-passes it as a mediatory faculty credited with a different degree of perceptive or constitutive power. Imagination in Richards's terms is infinite: apparent everywhere in the sublimely interconnecting network of language and the mind. Hence the focus on detail as well as the reader's reaction to it, as well as the fact that his particular attention to the language of poetry is accompanied by calls for a new systematic science combining semantics and psychology. Richards's invocations to a new science are, from this perspective, thrillings to the infinity or limitlessness of his object of study rather than (as in the case of Mill) excitement at the prospect of a new systematic theory or philosophy.

In these last two sections of this chapter I have been following in the footsteps of Raymond Williams whose influential 1958 study *Culture and Society* identified in Mill's essays on Bentham and Coleridge the origin of the social idea of 'Culture'. This was evident in Mill's call for a 'system of action' to form a process of civilisation. Williams exposes how 'Culture' in this sense could be used by Mill (or Coleridge) to act as a judge upon the shortcomings of the so-called industrial civilisation. In the following passage, he identifies the construction of an ethico-aesthetic position which allows the social commentator a vantage-point from which to speak:

The social idea of Culture, now introduced into English thinking, meant that an idea had been formulated which expressed value in terms independent of 'civilization', and hence, in a period of radical change, in terms independent of the progress of society. The standard of perfection, of 'the harmonious development of those qualities and faculties that characterize our humanity', was now available, not merely to influence society, but to judge it.[66]

Williams is careful to demystify Mill's claim to objectivity at the same time as he is desperate to preserve Mill's belief in the efficacy and need for 'system' or systematic thinking. Paradoxically, Coleridge emerges from Williams's chapter as the figure who offers the longed-for possibility of culture and systematic thinking as a process rather than a product. Attentive to the dangers of false synthesis and the myth of organic community, Williams's handling of Coleridge here reveals a figure interestingly caught between lived experience and theory.

What I have attempted to draw attention to in the cases of both Mill and Richards in my own analysis is the way in which the origins of this key stage in English thinking on the nature of culture and the state of the nation concern themselves with the territory of imagination: the hinterland of aesthetics and psychology. In particular, both Mill and Richards offer a very specific and urgent insight into the relationship between language and the mind. In this reappropriated property of the faculty of imagination they speak not only of a level of alienation, but a further worrying level of existential reality. In Mill's response to the reality of feeling and the language of dejection, and in Richards's obsession with the specifics of poetic discourse and his dream of semasiology, we see both writers demonstrating their belief in a further level of schism which cannot be confidently relied upon to stand as a moral testing-ground for 'civilisation'. Following the role of imagination in their different brands of utilitarianism reveals another kind of alienation operating within their constructions of the self. In their self-consciousness about the relationship between language and the mind they touch on a new language of subjectivity which is as likely to provide angst as legislative power.

Tracing the afterlife of Coleridge's ideas of imagination in John Stuart Mill and I. A. Richards indicates just how susceptible and malleable a cultural commodity imagination is. Its role in the larger nineteenth-century and early twentieth-century cultural debate over utility reveals the part it plays in giving a name to the schism in English culture. Given that Coleridge's production of his famous definitions in *Biographia Literaria* was, as we have seen, produced out of his debate with Malthusian and utilitarian forms of thought and their incipient mechanistic ideology, it is somewhat ironic to see how much Mill needs imagination to bolster his utilitarianism and his own construction of himself. Equally, Richards's attempts to break down the barriers between science and poetry reveal the necessity of imagination for the production of a new kind of criticism. Both examples might be described as ways of killing off the metaphorical threat of Coleridge's idealism. Mill invokes imagination only to dissipate it into a rarefied and at times rather vague form of sympathetic feeling while his generous treatment of Coleridge is never repeated. Richards's too is a demystification of the Coleridgean imagination: by invoking and asserting its presence in every minute form of the interface between mind and language, he too dissolves and dissipates it. And given the degree of mutation we have seen operating in this very specific example of the Coleridgean imagination's involvement with utilitarian thought it is not so much imagination's content that is important as its presence.

Although imagination has often been conjured as itself constituting the antithesis to utility, my description of its genesis in reaction to utilitarian culture suggests that, for all the schism in the British nation and the emergence of 'the two cultures', imagination is a product of that schism, itself the name given to the fracture in culture. Taking its origin from the threat from utility, imagination is in many ways collusive with it. For both Mill and Richards, it figures as the psychological link which makes good utility's inadequacy.

Richards's heroic and ambitious attempt to find a systematic and scientific criticism based on a conjunction of psychology and semantics provides an illuminating alternative to the often crude binarism informing much recent criticism, its too easy acceptance of the difference between theory and practice. Richards's own position in these debates on the validity of theory is, in the circumstances, rather ironic: vilified as the arch exponent of an Arnoldian moralism manifested in a practical criticism rather than a failed exponent of a scientific and systematic criticism. Not surprisingly then, Richards's own involvement with Coleridge exhibits the fraught antagonisms of much Coleridge criticism over the last two decades. His work desperately seeks in the Coleridgean imagination a way of straddling the terrible divide between system and practical criticism, between theory and practice.

Afterword

> Meanwhile, the Moon look'd down upon this shew
> In single glory, and we stood, the mist
> Touching our very feet; and from the shore
> At distance not the third part of a mile
> Was a blue chasm; a fracture in the vapour,
> A deep and gloomy breathing-place thro' which
> Mounted the roar of waters, torrents, streams
> Innumerable, roaring with one voice.
> The universal spectacle throughout
> Was shaped for admiration and delight,
> Grand in itself alone, but in that breach
> Through which the homeless voice of waters rose,
> That dark deep thoroughfare had Nature lodg'd
> The Soul, the Imagination of the whole.[1]

Wordsworth's celebrated depiction of the restoration of the imagination in Book XIII of *The Prelude* might seem to stand as an antithesis to the case I have argued for this most celebrated of faculties. Wordsworth's solution to a crisis which is at once personal, historical, and national is, characteristically, to describe imagination in all its glory, simultaneously located in the landscape and in the psyche. Imagination is made synonymous with 'Soul' and the apprehension of its location and its origin which the poem effects has, in itself, the status of a proof or demonstration of its existence. In this way, of course, imagination's restoration emerges redeemed, with the aid of hope and faith, from its previous impairment. But Wordsworth's text also continues to draw attention to the problem it has apparently solved. For all the political and historical referents which surround it, the imagination is still haunted by the spectre of its fissured constitution. In the dominantly celebratory depiction of its location, imagination is figured to the last as a paradoxical gap which resists definition – 'a fracture in the vapour'. Even when it is finally announced it slips into view on the back of 'Soul'. True to form, and to the nature of this speculative faculty, Wordsworth's blank verse renders it discursively.

In my account of six different manifestations of imagination in Wordsworth's period I have attempted to focus on its discursively rendered identity within cultural critique. I have been more concerned with the paradoxical position it occupies within aesthetic and political discourse – the 'fracture in the vapour' – than with the reassuring presence of 'Soul'. I have been concerned to focus on its capacity to act as a mediatory agent through which the competing voices of revolution and utilitarianism can be heard roaring. But as we have seen, imagination also inhabits a particularly moral and ethical space in the texts I have analysed. More particularly, it functions as the means of connection between secular and religious modes of thought. It is, if you like, the figure which provides the metaphysical backing for forms of social improvement. This is fairly well documented and expected in the case of Coleridge, but for the other five writers I have dealt with in this study this might come as something of a surprise. Burke, Paine, Wollstonecraft, Cobbett, and Hazlitt all use the imagination as a means of accessing ethical and religious power in order to bolster their ideological positions. And precisely because it performs this function, imagination takes on a peculiar and distinct status in writings of this period. It forms a middle ground between the secular and the religious. Indeed in the case of Mill (and certainly Richards) it begins to look as if imagination actually enables them to form a new and separate ethical zone of the psychological. In Mill's case this still retains elements of the old literary aesthetic, but it now mutates into a form of linguistic psychology to which the literary poetic has become a mere adjunct. The beginnings of such a process can be seen to be taking place in the writings of Hazlitt as his struggle with utility reveals not only his distrust of the established literary culture and its meddling poets, but also a deep-seated anxiety about the limits of social sympathy and the possibilities of ethical feeling.

There is a peculiar collusiveness between imagination and utility. This is not only the case in the figures of Paine and Cobbett where a sense of the aesthetic is seen to be inescapable, but also in those writers for whom the ideology of utility is the great enemy. This is perhaps the ultimate irony of the Coleridgean imagination: that perhaps its most famous twentieth-century proponent should use it for quasi-utilitarian purposes. As my study has suggested, this is not simply a misapplication on Richards's part; on the contrary, he might be said to have drawn on the inherent complicity between imagination and utility in Coleridge's thinking. Indeed it is precisely this kind of collusion or, more pertinently, cross-over which emerges from my account of the six selected writers. In every case their critique crosses over into the enemy territory and is changed by the experience. At key moments, all six writers are forced to recognise how they have absorbed the values or the forms of representation of their opponents. Burke cedes imagination to his French revolutionary opponents; Wollstonecraft struggles to free herself from the attraction of Rousseauvian feeling; Paine finds himself very selfconsciously entangled in Burke's *Reflections*; Cobbett sides with Paine's economic history when he recognises the limits of the sensible world; Hazlitt has to contend with the enemy in the cause of reform and must join with them in his attack upon the poets; Coleridge constructs the various utilitarian writers and methodologies into a single powerful identity. In inhabiting the gap in culture imagination often negotiates with both sides.

My account also suggests that imagination is an inescapable and essential element in cultural critique. This is not to suggest, in the manner of some other well established histories of the Romantic Imagination, that it is an essential human characteristic always there as a shaping presence and informing all our actions. In the more discursive and strategic version of imagination which I have put forward in this book it is as if the figure of imagination is immediately summoned to fill a void left by materialism or a thoroughgoing literalism. Even when a writer pushes extremely hard to eradicate polite aesthetics from his discourse as in the cases of Paine and Cobbett, there is still a need for this spectral or figurative capacity, if only to make the absent present, especially if this is convenient as part of the strategic business of social critique.

The creativity and resourcefulness which these six writers demonstrate in their various negotiations with 'imagination' is sufficient testimony to the term's historical significance in the fields of social and political critique. At the same time their work reveals the pervasive force of the figure across economic, social, spiritual, philosophical, and theological domains rather than letting it remain confined to the sacrosanct province of the poets. It should also make us rethink our understanding of the poets' versions of imagination. And, beyond the realm of literary criticism, there is also a strong case for harnessing and celebrating the resourcefulness and potential within the figure of imagination, a figure which still has such capacity and potential to act as as a point of ethico-political resistance and as a form of critique.

Notes

INTRODUCTION

1 For an account of the various manifestations of imagination in the eighteenth century and Romantic period, see James Engell, *The Creative Imagination: Enlightenment to Romanticism* (Cambridge, Mass. and London: Harvard University Press, 1981). Engell's study confidently argues for a coherent, identifiable idea of imagination which reached maturity in the later eighteenth century when it enjoyed its 'brilliant romantic expression'. His preface concludes with the claim that: 'The idea has since been rediscovered a number of times, and each time it has been given even greater value and hope, until imagination is now considered, without question, the supreme value of art and literature' (p. x.).

2 The imaginative creativity and variety within radical culture is evident from the following studies: Iain McCalman, *Radical Underworld: Prophets, Revolutionaries, and Pornographers in London, 1795–1840* (Cambridge University Press, 1988); Marcus Wood, *Radical Satire and Print Culture 1700–1822* (Oxford: Clarendon Press, 1994); Jon Mee, *Dangerous Enthusiasm: William Blake and the Culture of Radicalism in the 1790s* (Oxford University Press, 1992); David Worrall, *Radical Culture: Discourse, Resistance, and Surveillance, 1790–1820* (Hemel Hempstead: Harvester/Wheatsheaf, 1992).

3 See Jerome Christensen, *Coleridge and the Blessed Machine of Language* (Ithaca: Cornell University Press, 1981); Alan Richardson, *Literature, Education, and Romanticism: Reading As Social Practice 1780–1832* (Cambridge University Press, 1994); Josephine McDonagh, *De Quincey's Disciplines* (Oxford: Clarendon Press, 1994); John Whale, *Thomas De Quincey's Reluctant Autobiography* (Beckenham and Totowa, N.J.: Croom Helm and Barnes and Noble, 1984), pp. 40–77.

4 See Don H. Bialostosky, *Wordsworth, Dialogics, and the Practice of Criticism* (New York and Cambridge: Cambridge University Press, 1992), pp. 1–22; Jonathan Arac, *Critical Genealogies: Historical Situations for Postmodern Literary Studies* (New York: Columbia University Press, 1986), pp. 11–113; Clifford Siskin, *The Historicity of Romantic Discourse* (New York and Oxford: Oxford University Press, 1987) pp. 3–14, 15–36. In his chapter entitled 'The Un-Kind Imagination' Siskin's attempt at a new literary history which severs the coincidence between Romantic text and Romantic criticism defines

197

itself in terms of a formal self-consciousness. He refers to critics who 'privilege Imagination, neglect form, and produce Romantic literary histories rather than literary histories of Romanticism: developmental tales of individual and social epiphanies that replicate the narrative turns of the texts they canonize' (p. 18). He also refers to 'the way in which critical fascination with Imagination as an actual (physiological?) faculty of mind, or psychological truth, or locus of discursive or tropological activity, has led to scores of articles and books evaluating literature according to kinds of Imagination, rather than analyzing imagination as a historical *construct* having specific formal functions within literary kinds' (p. 16).

5 See Richard Kearney, *The Wake of Imagination: Towards A Postmodern Culture* (London: Routledge, 1994). Kearney is careful to give this 'wake' of imagination in the face of postmodernity the status of possibility. He describes its 'imminent demise' in the following terms: 'One of the greatest paradoxes of contemporary culture is that at a time when the image reigns supreme the very notion of a creative human imagination seems under mounting threat. We no longer appear to know who exactly produces or controls the images which condition our consciousness. We are at an impasse where the very rapport between imagination and reality seems not only to be inverted but subverted altogether. We cannot be sure which is which. And this very undecidability lends weight to the deepening suspicion that we may well be assisting at the wake of imagination' (p. 3). His monumental and self-confessedly pluralist study of imagination in Western culture reserves, in its coda, 'the model of a poetical-ethical imagination' which can perform a 'poetics of the possible' (p. 32).

6 Jonathan Bate, *Romantic Ecology: Wordsworth and the Environmental Tradition* (London: Routledge, 1991), p. 6.

7 Alan Liu, *Wordsworth: The Sense of History* (Stanford University Press, 1989), p. 39.

8 See, for example, Frances Ferguson, *Solitude and the Sublime: Romanticism and the Aesthetics of Individuation* (London and New York: Routledge, 1992).

9 Marilyn Butler, *Romantics, Rebels, and Reactionaries: English Literature and Its Background 1760–1830* (Oxford University Press, 1981), pp. 184 and 185.

10 David Simpson's *Wordsworth's Historical Imagination: The Poetry of Displacement* (New York and London: Methuen, 1987) is one of the most important studies to tackle this problem of an ideologically determined imagination and, symptomatically, Wordsworth's historical imagination is, according to Simpson, characterised by 'incoherence', 'displacement and alienation'. Most interestingly, its achievement can only be rendered as failure: 'It is a writing that continually falls short of what it aspires to be, but reveals in that falling short its greatest intelligence' (p. 2).

11 For an intelligent account of the nature and of the limits of 'new historical' methodologies, see Philip Martin, 'Romanticism, History, Historicisms', in *Revolution in Writing: British Literary Responses to the French Revolution*, Kelvin Everest (ed.) (Milton Keynes: Open University Press, 1991), pp. 9–26.

12 Terry Eagleton, *The Ideology of the Aesthetic* (Oxford: Basil Blackwell, 1990), p. 37.
13 Peter De Bolla, *The Discourse of the Sublime: Readings in History, Aesthetics and the Subject* (Oxford: Basil Blackwell, 1989).
14 Nigel Leask, *The Politics of Imagination in Coleridge's Political Thought* (Basingstoke: Macmillan, 1988), p. 1.
15 Richard Bourke, *Romantic Discourse and Political Modernity: Wordsworth, the Intellectual and Cultural Critique* (Hemel Hempstead: Harvester Wheatsheaf, 1993), p. 21.
16 Richardson, *Literature, Education, and Romanticism: Reading As Social Practice 1780–1832* (Cambridge University Press, 1994), p. 270.
17 Richardson, *Literature, Education, and Romanticism*, p. 261.
18 Kurt Heinzelman, *The Economics of the Imagination* (Amherst: University of Massachusetts Press, 1980), p. 8.
19 See Richardson, *Literature, Education, and Romanticism*; and Josephine McDonagh, *De Quincey's Disciplines* (Oxford: Clarendon Press, 1994).
20 Heinzelman, *The Economics of the Imagination*, p. 275.
21 Forest Pyle, *The Ideology of Imagination: Subject and Society in the Discourse of Romanticism* (Stanford University Press, 1995).
22 Pyle, *The Ideology of Imagination*, p. 22.
23 Pyle, *The Ideology of Imagination*, p. 3.
24 Mary Warnock, *Imagination and Time* (Oxford: Basil Blackwell, 1994).
25 This is the study's most problematic aspect: its Enlightenment wish to impose a single secular version of imagination across cultural, class, and gender differences.
26 Kieran Egan and Dan Nadamer (eds.), *Imagination and Education* (Milton Keynes: Open University Press, 1988).
27 In this respect I am indebted to the following works in this field: Ronald Paulson, *Representations of Revolution (1789–1820)* (New Haven and London: Yale University Press, 1983); Steven Blakemore, *Intertextual War: Edmund Burke and the French Revolution in the Writings of Mary Wollstonecraft, Thomas Paine, and James Mackintosh* (Madison, Teaneck: Fairleigh Dickinson University Press; London: Associated University Presses, 1997); Olivia Smith, *The Politics of Language, 1791–1819* (Oxford: Clarendon Press, 1984); Kelvin Everest and Alison Yarrington (eds.), *Reflections of Revolution: Images of Romanticism* (London: Routledge, 1993); Kelvin Everest (ed.), *Revolution in Writing: British Literary Responses to the French Revolution* (Milton Keynes: Open University Press, 1991); Barton R. Friedman, *Fabricating History: English Writers on the French Revolution* (Princeton University Press, 1988), esp. pp. 3–38.
28 This case is made out forcibly by Paulson in *Representations of Revolution*, esp. pp. 1–7. For the context of the so-called 'revolution controversy' see Marilyn Butler, *Burke, Paine, Godwin, and the Revolution Controversy*, Cambridge English Prose Texts (Cambridge University Press, 1984).
29 This aspect of Burke's *Reflections* is argued for in terms of an explicitly

poststructuralist model by Steven Blakemore in *Burke and the Fall of Language: The French Revolution as Linguistic Event* (Hanover and London: University Press of New England, 1988), esp. pp. 90–107.

30 See Kevin Gilmartin, 'Burke, Popular Opinion, and the Problem of a Counter-Revolutionary Public Sphere', in *Edmund Burke's Reflections on the Revolution in France*, Texts in Culture Series, ed. by John Whale (forthcoming from Manchester University Press, 2000).

31 See Blakemore, *Burke and the Fall of Language*, pp. 19–30.

32 For a brief consideration of the dangers of Paine's system of representation and its relation to a state of justice and a Benthamite panopticism, see my 'Literal and Symbolic Representation: Burke, Paine and the French Revolution', *History of European Ideas*, 16 (1994), pp. 343–49.

33 For competing accounts of Wollstonecraft's rationalism and its consequences see Jane Moore, 'Unseating the Philosopher-Knight' in *Political Gender: Texts and Contexts*, Sally Ledger, Josephine McDonagh, and Jane Spencer (eds.) (New York and London: Harvester/Wheatsheaf, 1994), pp. 71–84; Timothy J. Reiss's 'Revolution in Bounds: Wollstonecraft, Women, and Reason', and Frances Ferguson's powerful riposte 'Wollstonecraft Our Contemporary', both in *Gender and Theory: Dialogues on Feminist Criticism*, Linda Kauffman (ed.) (Oxford and New York: Basil Blackwell, 1989), pp. 11–62. David Simpson also discusses Wollstonecraft's 'balance between the rational and the emotional' in a short section entitled 'The Case for Female Reason', in *Romanticism, Nationalism, and the Revolt Against Theory* (Chicago and London: University of Chicago Press, 1993), pp. 104–12.

I   BURKE AND THE CIVIC IMAGINATION

1 My account of Burke's politicisation of imagination in this chapter is, in part, a response to the following suggestion Tom Furniss makes at the end of his influential study of Burke's aesthetics: 'This means that the question of false and true imagination . . . is urgently repoliticised in the *Reflections* (and in radical responses which seek to eliminate the imagination altogether). Yet the distinction between sound and corrupt imagination (between imagination and fancy) remains a problem internal to Britain's political economy and the texts which defend it. This irreducible problem constitutes, I suggest, the politicized discursive network within which English Romanticism's obsession with the imagination and its distinction from other, more dangerous, modes of thought and composition needs to be theorized.' See *Edmund Burke's Aesthetic Ideology: Language, Gender and Political Economy in Revolution* (Cambridge University Press, 1993), pp. 241–2. Furniss is, in turn, responding to Paul Hamilton's argument articulated in 'Keats and Critique', in *Rethinking Historicism* by Marjorie Levinson, Marilyn Butler, Jerome McGann, and Paul Hamilton (Oxford and New York: Basil Blackwell, 1989), pp. 108–42.

2 Work on Burke by literary historians and critics over the last two decades

has largely been concerned with the relationship between aesthetics and politics and has been dominated by attempts to read the *Reflections on the Revolution in France* through the categories set up by Burke's *Enquiry into the Origin of Our Ideas of the Sublime and Beautiful*. Burke's aesthetics have been a major concern of literary specialists in the field of Romanticism, not only for defining the nature of the *Reflections*, but also for understanding the gendered nature of the aesthetics informing Romanticism and the Gothic. My own account owes much to the following important contributions to this debate: Tom Furniss, *Edmund Burke's Aesthetic Ideology*, W. T. J. Mitchell, *Iconology: Image, Text, Ideology* (Chicago and London: University of Chicago Press, 1986); Frances Ferguson, *Solitude and the Sublime: Romanticism and the Aesthetics of Individuation* (New York and London: Routledge, 1992). See also Neal Wood, 'The Aesthetic Dimension of Burke's Political Thought', *Journal of British Studies*, 4 (1964), pp. 41–64; Frans De Bruyn, *The Literary Genres of Edmund Burke: The Political Uses of Literary Form* (Oxford: Clarendon Press, 1996); Christopher Reid, *Edmund Burke and the Practice of Political Writing* (Dublin and New York: Gill and Macmillan, 1985).

3 Terry Eagleton offers a powerful description of 'the aesthetic' more generally as a 'contradictory, double-edged' concept which is both emancipatory and regulatory as a result of its origin in the hegemonic power of bourgeois democracy: 'If the aesthetic is a dangerous, ambiguous affair, it is because ... there is something in the body which can revolt against the power which inscribes it; and that impulse could only be eradicated by extirpating along with it the capacity to authenticate power itself (*The Ideology of the Aesthetic*, p. 28). For Eagleton, the Burkean realm of sentiment, imagination, and custom, and late eighteenth-century sensibility more generally, point only to an originating inherent contradiction within 'the middle class' order: '"Deep" subjectivity is just what the ruling social order desire, and exactly what it has to cause to fear.' Eagleton's historically located origin of 'the aesthetic' is, symptomatically, in the absolutism of eighteenth-century German states (p. 28).

4 Edmund Burke, *Enquiry into the Origin of Our Ideas of the Sublime and Beautiful*, ed. by J. T. Boulton (London: Routledge and Kegan Paul, 1958), p. 17. All references to Burke's *Enquiry* are to this text. Where possible, reference to Burke's oeuvre is made to the authoritative edition currently in progress under the general editorship of Paul Langford: *The Writings and Speeches of Edmund Burke* (Oxford: Clarendon Press, 1981–). In the case of the *Reflections on the Revolution in France* reference is made to both the edition of Conor Cruise O'Brien (Harmondsworth: Penguin Books, 1968) and that in *The Writings and Speeches of Edmund Burke*, vol. VIII, *The French Revolution*, edited by L. G. Mitchell (Oxford: Clarendon Press, 1989). References to the latter are given in square brackets.

5 Burke, *Enquiry*, p. 17.

6 The phrase is taken from Jerome McGann's ground-breaking study of the early 1980s, the issues of which dominated discussion of the aesthetics of British Romanticism for at least the rest of the decade, and formed the

focus for subsequent methodological debates between its competing forms of historicism. See Jerome J. McGann, *The Romantic Ideology: A Critical Investigation* (Chicago and London: University of Chicago Press, 1983).

7 For an interesting Freudian analysis of these images, see Ronald Paulson, *Representations of Revolution (1789–1820)* (New Haven and London: Yale University Press, 1983), esp. pp. 57–73. See also Tom Furniss's 'Stripping the Queen: Edmund Burke's Magic Lantern Show', in *Burke and the French Revolution: Bicentennial Essays*, Steven Blakemore (ed.) (Athens and London: The University of Georgia Press, 1992), pp. 69–96.

8 Burke's phrase forms the title of James Chandler's important and influential study of the relationship between Burke and Wordsworth. See James K. Chandler, *Wordsworth's Second Nature: A Study of the Poetry and the Politics* (Chicago and London: University of Chicago Press, 1984).

9 Burke's complicated and, in many ways, humane response to state violence was, in part, the subject of a very powerful unpublished paper by Luke Gibbons entitled 'Customs in Contention: Burke, Ireland and the Colonial Sublime', delivered at 'Our Present Discontents: A Conference to Mark the Bicentenary of Edmund Burke's Death', Goldsmiths College, University of London, July 1997.

10 Burke, *Enquiry*, p. 57.
11 Burke, *Enquiry*, p. 157.
12 Burke, *Enquiry*, p. 92.
13 Burke, *Enquiry*, p. 110.
14 Burke, *Reflections*, pp. 101–2 [68].
15 Burke, *Reflections*, p. 113 [78].
16 Burke, *Reflections*, p. 116 [80].
17 Burke, *Reflections*, p. 178 [134].
18 Burke, *Reflections*, p. 150 [110].
19 Burke, *Reflections*, p. 194 [146].
20 Burke, *Reflections*, p. 196 [148].
21 J. G. A. Pocock has an interesting commentary on Burke in relation to Marx and energy in 'The Political Economy of Burke's Analysis of the French Revolution', in *Virtue, Commerce and History: Essays on Political Thought and History, Chiefly in the Eighteenth Century* (Cambridge and New York: Cambridge University Press, 1985), pp. 207–9; and Paulson's account of Burke in *Representations of Revolution* is a study of repression and energy. See pp. 64–73.
22 Burke, *Reflections*, pp. 171–72 [128].
23 See Tom Furniss, *Edmund Burke's Aesthetic Ideology*, pp. 41–67.
24 Burke, *Reflections*, p. 172 [129].
25 Burke, *Reflections*, p. 151 [111].
26 Burke, *Reflections*, pp. 152–53 [112].
27 Burke, *Reflections*, p. 133 [95].
28 For a specific account of the literary genre of the liberal perspective of the gentleman in Burke's writings, see De Bruyn, *The Literary Genres of Edmund*

Burke, pp. 111–64, where he draws on James Thomson's *The Seasons* and John Barrell's thesis in *English Literature in History: An Equal Wide Survey* (London: Hutchinson, 1983).

29 J. G. A. Pocock has addressed Burke's ideas on the constitution from the perspective of two very different traditions in 'The Political Economy of Burke's Analysis of the French Revolution', in *Virtue, Commerce, and History*, pp. 193–212; and 'Burke and the Ancient Constitution: A Problem in the History of Ideas', *The Historical Journal*, III, 2 (1982), pp. 125–43, reprinted in *Politics, Language and Time: Essays on Political Thought and History* (New York: Atheneum, 1971). See also Steven Blakemore, *Burke and the Fall of Language: The French Revolution as Linguistic Event* (Hanover and London: University Press of New England, 1988), esp. pp. 5–18; F. P. Lock, *Burke's Reflections on the Revolution in France* (London: Allen and Unwin, 1985); Gregory Claeys, *Political Writings of the 1790s* (London: Pickering and Chatto, 1995), vols. 1 and 2, esp. pp. xxii–xxx; Peter J. Stanlis, *Edmund Burke and Natural Law* (Ann Arbor, Mich.: University of Michigan Press, 1958).

30 Burke, *Reflections*, p. 115 [80].
31 Burke, *Reflections*, p. 121 [84].
32 Burke, *Reflections*, p. 231 [176].
33 Burke, *Reflections*, p. 314 [244].
34 Burke, *Reflections*, p. 278 [215].
35 Burke, *Reflections*, p. 296 [229].
36 Burke, *Reflections*, p. 374 [291].
37 See David Simpson, *Romanticism, Nationalism, and the Revolt Against Theory* (Chicago and London: University of Chicago Press, 1993), esp. pp. 57–63; and also his article 'Coleridge on Wordsworth and the Form of Poetry', in *Coleridge's Theory of Imagination Today*, Georgia State Literary Studies 4, Christine Gallant (ed.) (New York: AMS Press, 1989), pp. 211–25.
38 See Simpson, *Romanticism, Nationalism, and the Revolt Against Theory*, pp. 57–63.
39 See Eagleton, *The Ideology of the Aesthetic*, esp. pp. 31–69.
40 This is characteristic of Burke's attack upon Enlightenment thinking. See Seamus Deane, *The French Revolution and Enlightenment in England 1789–1832* (Cambridge Mass. and London: Harvard University Press, 1988), pp. 4–20.
41 Burke, *An Appeal from the New to the Old Whigs, The Works of the Right Honourable Edmund Burke in Twelve Volumes* (London: John C. Nimmo, 1899), vol. IV, pp. 80–81.
42 Burke, *Writings and Speeches of Edmund Burke*, vol. III, p. 765. As the editors point out, the last sentence of this passage reads like an adaptation of Vergil's *Aeneid*, VI, ll. 726 ff.
43 Burke, 'Speech on a motion for leave to bring in a Bill to Repeal and alter certain acts respecting religious opinions, upon the occasion of a petition of the Unitarian Society, May 11 1792', *The Works of the Right Honourable Edmund Burke*, vol. VII, p. 41.
44 Burke, *A Letter to a Noble Lord, Writings and Speeches of Edmund Burke*, vol. IX, pp. 155–56.

45 Burke, *Reflections*, p. 136 [99].
46 Burke, *Reflections*, p. 137 [99].
47 Burke, *Reflections*, p. 139 [101].
48 Burke, *Reflections*, p. 272 [210].
49 Burke, *Reflections*, p. 272 [211].
50 Burke, *Appeal from the New to the Old Whigs, The Works of the Right Honourable Edmund Burke*, vol. IV, pp. 212–13.
51 Burke, *Reflections*, p. 156 [115].
52 Burke, *Reflections*, pp. 122–23 [86].
53 Burke, *Appeal from the New to the Old Whigs, The Works of the Right Honourable Edmund Burke*, vol. IV, p.192.
54 In an unpublished paper entitled 'Burke's Mixed Systems: The Political Economy of Burke's *Reflections*' presented at 'Our Present Discontents: A Conference to Mark the Bicentenary of Edmund Burke's Death', Goldsmiths College, University of London, July 1997.
55 See Gregory Claeys (ed.), *Political Writings of the 1790s* (London: Pickering and Chatto, 1995), 8 vols., esp. vols. 1 and 2, 'Radicalism and Reform: Responses to Burke 1790–91' and 'Responses to Burke 1791–92' respectively.
56 More recently David Fairer has read Burke's *Reflections* in the context of debates in English poetry post–1744 with the result that Burke's deployment of the idea of an organic constitution can be seen only as a very problematic precursor to Romantic poets, his own poetics signalling the belatedness of an earlier 'romanticism' formed out of debates, such as those involving Thomas Warton, Chatterton, and the history of English poetry, about the relationship between romance, the Gothic, and history. From such a perspective, Burke's organicism takes on a very different form from Coleridge's: Burke's organically 'organized' constitution allows for 'order in variety' and is distinctly relational rather than essential in nature. See David Fairer, 'Organizing Verse: Burke's *Reflections* and Eighteenth-Century Poetry', *Romanticism*, 3:1 (1997), pp. 1–19.

2 PAINE'S ATTACK ON ARTIFICE

1 Paine, *Age of Reason, The Writings of Thomas Paine*, ed. by Moncur Daniel Conway (New York: Burt Franklin, 1969; first published 1902), vol. IV, p. 63. References to Paine's writings are to this edition hereafter abbreviated to *PW*. In the case of *Rights of Man* and *Common Sense* reference is also made to popular editions: *Rights of Man*, ed. by Henry Collins (Harmondsworth: Penguin Books, 1969); *Common Sense and The Crisis* (New York: Anchor Books, 1973), p.59.
2 Paine, *PW*, II, p. 70.
3 Paine, *PW*, II, 'The Magazine in America', p. 16.
4 Paine, *PW*, III, 'Letter to Thomas Jefferson', p. 377.

5 Paine, *PW*, III, 'Letters Addressed to the Addressors of the Late Proclamation', p. 45.
6 Paine, *Rights of Man*, p. 61 [*PW*, II, p. 275].
7 Paine, *Rights of Man*, p. 61 [*PW*, II, p. 275].
8 Paine, *Rights of Man*, p. 73 [*PW*, II, p. 288].
9 See Eric Foner, *Tom Paine and Revolutionary America* (Oxford and New York: Oxford University Press, 1976), esp. 'The Problem of Thomas Paine', pp. xvi–xx; and A. Owen Aldridge, *Thomas Paine's American Ideology* (Newark, London, and Toronto: Associated University Presses, 1984). Gregory Claeys's more recent study *Thomas Paine: Social and Political Thought*, (Boston: Unwin Hyman, 1989), is an attempt, in part, to redress the mistaken view that Paine is a mere populariser with scant intellectual forbears and traditions. Claeys locates Paine's thought and writings in their complex tradition of republicanism and natural law. Mark Philp's *Paine*, Past Masters, (Oxford and New York: Oxford University Press, 1989) takes the contrary view, preferring to concentrate instead on Paine's rhetorical skill. For recent studies of Paine dealing with the representation of revolution, the construction of audiences, and the role of language in the revolution controversy of the 1790s, see Paulson, *Representations of Revolution*, esp. pp. 73–79; Jon P. Klancher, *The Making of English Reading Audiences*, esp. pp. 18–46; Olivia Smith, *The Politics of Language 1791-1819*, esp. pp. 35–68. For the Anglo-American context of Paine's thought, see David A. Wilson, *Paine and Cobbett: The Transatlantic Connection* (Kingston and Montreal: McGill-Queen's University Press, 1988).
10 This can be gauged from Bishop Watson's reply: 'What I have written will not, I fear, make any impression on you; but I indulge an hope, that it may not be without it's effect on some of your readers. Infidelity is a rank weed, it threatens to overspread the land; its root is principally fixed amongst the great and opulent, but you are endeavouring to extend the malignity of its position through all the classes of the community. There is a class of men, for whom I have the greatest respect, and whom I am anxious to preserve from the contamination of your irreligion – the merchants, manufacturers and tradesmen of the kingdom. I consider the influence of the example of this class as essential to the welfare of the community' (G. Ingli James (ed.), *William Blake's Annotations to Richard Watson's 'An Apology for the Bible in a Series of Letters Addressed to Thomas Paine'*, eighth edition, London 1797, Regency Reprints III (University College Cardiff Press, 1984), pp. 119–20. See also pp. 65, 118).
11 For other accounts of Paine's critique of Burke, see Tom Furniss, 'Rhetoric in Revolution: The Role of Language in Paine's Critique of Burke', in *Revolution and English Romanticism: Politics and Rhetoric* (London: Routledge, 1990), pp. 23–48; and John Turner, 'Burke, Paine, and the Nature of Language', *Yearbook of English Studies* 19 (1989), pp. 36–53.
12 See J. T. Boulton, *The Language of Politics in the Age of Wilkes and Burke* (London: Routledge and Kegan Paul, 1963); Olivia Smith, *The Politics of*

Language 1791–1819, pp. 1–34. For another account of Paine's style in relation to audience, see Klancher, *The Making of English Reading Audiences*, pp. 27–28, 105–11.
13 Paine, *Rights of Man*, p. 86 [*PW*, II, p. 302].
14 Paine, *Rights of Man*, p. 189 [*PW*, II, p. 410].
15 Paine, *Rights of Man*, p. 96 [*PW*, II, p. 313].
16 Paine, *Rights of Man*, p. 73 [*PW*, II, p. 288].
17 Paine, *Rights of Man*, p. 73 [*PW*, II, p. 288].
18 Paine, *Rights of Man*, p. 73 [*PW*, II, pp. 288–89].
19 Paine, *Rights of Man*, p. 86 [*PW*, II, p. 302].
20 Paine, *Rights of Man*, p. 138 [*PW*, II, p. 357].
21 For example: 'A regency is a mock species of republic, and the whole of monarchy deserves no better description. It is a thing as various as imagination can paint' (Paine, *Rights of Man* p. 204 [PW, II, p. 425]); and: 'By engendering the church with the state, a sort of mule-animal, capable only of destroying, and, not of breeding up, is produced, called *The Church established by Law*. It is a stranger, even from its birth, to any parent mother on which it is begotten, and whom in time it kicks out and destroys' (*Rights of Man*, p. 109 [*PW*, II, 327]). For a brief, but lively account of Paine's organic metaphors, see Paulson, *Representations of Revolution*, pp. 73–79.
22 For commentary on Paine's theology and *The Age of Reason*, see J. Mackie, *The Miracle of Theism* (Oxford University Press, 1982); Mark Philp, *Paine*, pp.94–114; and Robert N. Essick, 'William Blake, Thomas Paine, and Biblical Revolution', *Studies in Romanticism* 30 (1991), pp. 189–212.
23 C.-F. de Volney, *The Ruins* (translated from the French, first impression 1847, second impression, London 1853), pp. 127–28.
24 'In the infancy of language nearly every word is a metaphor and every phrase an allegory. The mind grasps the figurative and the literal sense simultaneously. The word evokes the idea and at the same time the appropriate image by which the idea is expressed; but after a time the human mind becomes so accustomed to using the word in this figurative sense that by a process of abstraction it tends to fix on this alone and to lose sight of its original meaning; and so the secondary and metaphorical sense of the word gradually becomes its ordinary, normal meaning' (Antoine-Nicolas De Condorcet, *Sketch for a Historical Picture of the Progress of the Human Mind*, trans. June Barraclough (New York: Noonday Press, 1955), p. 37).
25 Paine, *Age of Reason*, *PW*, IV, p. 83.
26 Paine, *Age of Reason*, *PW*, IV, p. 188.
27 'The American constitutions were to liberty, what a grammar is to language: they define its parts of speech, and practically construct them into syntax' (Paine, *Rights of Man*, p. 117 [*PW*, II, p. 336]).
28 Paine, *Age of Reason*, *PW*, IV, p. 84.
29 'A universal language is that which expresses by signs either real objects themselves, or well-defined collections composed of simple and general ideas... the formation of such a language... is no chimerical scheme; that

even at the present time it be readily introduced to deal with a large number of objects; and that indeed, the chief obstacle that would prevent its extension to others would be the humiliation of having to admit how very few precise ideas and accurate, unambiguous notions we actually possess' (Condorcet, *Progress of the Human Mind*, pp. 197–98); and: 'So the need for writing was first, and the writing was invented. It seems to have been at first a genuine system of representation, but this gave way to a more conventional representation which preserved merely the characteristic features of objects. Finally, by a sort of metaphor analogous to that which had already been introduced into language, the image of a physical object came to express moral ideas' (*Progress of the Human Mind*, p. 7).

30 Paine, *Rights of Man*, p. 124 [*PW*, II, p. 343].
31 See, for example, the following distinction: 'a scene so new, and so transcendentally unequalled by anything in the European world, that the name of Revolution is diminutive of its character, and it rises into a Regeneration of man' (Paine, *Rights of Man*, p. 136 [*PW*, II, p. 355]).
32 Paine, *Age of Reason*, *PW*, IV, p. 239.
33 Paine, *PW*, II, p. 110.
34 Paine, *Rights of Man*, p. 86 [*PW*, II, p. 302].
35 Paine, *PW*, III, p. 400.
36 Paine, *Age of Reason*, *PW*, IV, p. 156.
37 Paine, *Rights of Man*, p. 102 [*PW*, II, p. 320].
38 Paine, *PW*, III, p. 271.
39 Paine, *Rights of Man*, p. 146 [*PW*, II, p. 365].
40 Paine, *Common Sense* p. 59 [*PW*, I, p. 118].
41 Paine, *Rights of Man*, p. 105 [*PW*, II, p. 323].
42 Paine, *PW*, III, p. 265.
43 Paine, *PW*, III, p. 263.
44 Paine, *PW*, III, p. 349.
45 Paine, *PW*, II, pp. 147–48.
46 See 'Letters Addressed to American Citizens': 'The boldness ... with which I speak on any subject, is a compliment to the judgment of the reader. It is like saying to him, *I treat you as a man and not as a child*' (Paine, *PW*, III, p. 404).
47 Ingli James (ed.), *William Blake's Annotations to Richard Watson's 'An Apology for the Bible in a Series of Letters Addressed to Thomas Paine'*, pp. 111–12.
48 Jean-Jacques Rousseau, *The Social Contract and Discourses*, trans. by G. D. H. Cole, (London: Dent, 1973; revised and augmented by J. H. Brummett and John C. Hall, 1973; first published 1913), p. 120.
49 Rousseau, *The Social Contract and Discourses*, p. 235.
50 For an extended example of Paine's deployment of the body analogy, see 'The Decline and Fall of the English System of Finance', Paine, *PW*, III, pp. 286–312.
51 Thomas Paine, *Common Sense*, in *Common Sense and The Crisis* (New York: Anchor Books, 1973), p. 59 [*PW*, I, p. 118].

3 WOLLSTONECRAFT, IMAGINATION, AND FUTURITY

1 Some of the most exciting recent accounts of Wollstonecraft's work have focused on the different ways in which she renegotiates the cultural construction of subjectivity. The two most influential accounts are Cora Kaplan's in *Sea Changes: Essays in Culture and Feminism* (London: Verso, 1986), where she helpfully draws attention to Wollstonecraft's puritanical suppression of sexuality in *A Vindication of the Rights of Woman* and to the illicit Gothic pleasure that haunts the text (pp. 45–46), and Mary Poovey's in *The Proper Lady and the Woman Writer: Ideology as Style in the Works of Mary Wollstonecraft, Mary Shelley, and Jane Austen* (Chicago and London: University of Chicago Press, 1984). In her essay 'Mary Wollstonecraft and the Wild Wish of Early Feminism', *History Workshop Journal*, 33 (1992), pp. 197–219, Barbara Taylor defines the tensions, repressions, and 'transgressive inspiration' in Wollstonecraft's writings. Frances Ferguson cleverly examines Wollstonecraft's revision of the 'culturally determined sexual division of reason and pity' in 'Wollstonecraft Our Contemporary', in Linda Kauffman (ed.), *Gender and Theory: Dialogues on Feminist Criticism* (Oxford and New York: Blackwell, 1989), pp. 51–62. Vivien Jones offers an illuminating account of the ways in which Wollstonecraft's response to the French revolution struggles to escape from the strangle-hold of Richardsonian Gothic and sentimental romance in 'Women Writing Revolution: Narratives of History and Sexuality in Wollstonecraft and Williams', in Stephen Copley and John Whale (eds.), *Beyond Romanticism: New Approaches to Texts and Contexts 1780–1832* (London and New York: Routledge, 1992), pp. 178–99. Jones also develops Kaplan's argument as she addresses the possibility of rewriting the dominant narratives which structure sexuality and pleasure in '"The Tyranny of the Passions": Feminism and Heterosexuality in the Fiction of Wollstonecraft and Hays', in Sally Ledger, Josephine McDonagh, and Jane Spencer (eds.), *Political Gender: Texts and Contexts* (New York and London: Harvester Wheatsheaf, 1994), pp. 173–88. In *Equivocal Beings: Politics, Gender, and Sentimentality in the 1780s* (Chicago and London: University of Chicago Press, 1995) Claudia L. Johnson considers Wollstonecraft's inheritance of a Burkean sentimentalism and a radical rhetoric which scorns effeminacy. As a result, she argues, Wollstonecraft becomes 'in her own manliness' an 'isolated and highly "equivocal being' (p. 25).
2 Mary Wollstonecraft, *Collected Letters of Mary Wollstonecraft*, ed. by Ralph M. Wardle (Ithaca and London: Cornell University Press, 1979), p. 263, hereafter cited as *Letters*.
3 See G. J. Barker-Benfield, 'Mary Wollstonecraft: Eighteenth-Century Commonwealthwoman', *Journal of the History of Ideas*, 50 (1989), pp. 95–115.
4 References are to *The Works of Mary Wollstonecraft*, 7 vols., ed. by Janet Todd and Marilyn Butler (London: Pickering and Chatto, 1989), hereafter cited as *WW*. See Wollstonecraft, *Rights of Woman*, vol. 5, esp. pp. 93–94, 108–12,

147–62. For an alternative account of Wollstonecraft's interaction with Rousseau, see Virginia Sapiro, *A Vindication of Political Virtue: The Political Theory of Mary Wollstonecraft* (Chicago and London: University of Chicago Press, 1992), esp. pp. 167–72, 282–87, 293–94. See also Kaplan, *Sea Changes*, pp. 39–42.

5 'It is imagination which enlarges the bounds of possibility for us, whether for good or ill, and therefore stimulates and feeds desires by the hope of satisfying them. But the object which seemed within our grasp flies quicker than we can follow; when we think we have grasped it, it transforms itself and is again ahead of us' (Jean-Jacques Rousseau, *Émile*, translated by Barbara Foxley (London and Melbourne: Dent, 1974; first published 1911), p. 44). The French reads: 'l'imagination, la plus active de toutes, s'éveille et les devance. C'est l'imagination qui étend pour nous la mesure de possibles soit en bien soit en mal, et qui par consequent excite et nourrit les desirs par l'espoir de les satisfaire. Mais l'objet qui paroissoit d'abord sous la main fuit plus vîte qu'on ne peut le poursuivre; quand on croit l'atteindre il se transforme et se montre au loin devant nous' (Jean-Jacques Rousseau, *Oeuvres Complètes*, vol. IV, *Emile* (Paris: Editions Gallimard, 1969), p. 304).

6 See Rousseau, *Émile*, pp. 158–59: 'you want to make him fit for nothing but a lord, a marquis, or a prince; and some day he may be less than nothing. I want to give him a rank which he cannot lose, a rank which will always do him honour; I want to raise him to the status of a man.' The French text reads: 'qui voulez le réduire à ne pouvoir jamais être qu'un Lord, un Marquis, un Prince, et peut-être un jour moins que rien; moi, je lui veux donner un rang qu'il ne puisse perdre, un rang qui l'honore dans tous les tems, et quoique vous en puissiez dire, il aura moins d'égaux à ce titre qu'à tous ceux qu'il tiendra de vous' (Rousseau, *Émile*, p. 470).

7 Rousseau, *Émile*, p. 45. ('Le monde réel a ses bornes, le monde imaginaire est infini; ne pouvant élargir l'un retrécissons l'autre; car c'est de leur seule différence que naissent toutes les peines qui nous rendent vraiment malheureux' (Rousseau, *Émile*, p. 305).

8 Rousseau, *Émile* p. 48. ('L'homme vraiment libre ne veut que ce qu'il peut et fait ce qu'il lui plait. Voila ma maxime fondamentale' (Rousseau, *Émile*, p. 309); and Rousseau, *Émile*, p. 298 ('... c'est par la seule imagination que s'éveillent les sens. Leur besoin proprement n'est point un besoin phisique; il n'est pas vrai que ce soit un vrai besoin' (Rousseau, *Émile*, p. 662)).

9 See, for example, 'Imagination puts us more readily in the place of the miserable man than of the happy man; we feel that the one condition touches us more nearly than the other' (Rousseau, *Émile*, p. 182). ('L'imagination nous met à la place du misérable plustôt qu'à celle de l'homme heureux; on sent que l'un de ces états nous touche de plus près que l'autre' (Rousseau, *Émile*, p. 504).)

10 Wollstonecraft engages with precisely this issue in her first novel *Mary* where the heroine asks the following pertinent question: 'have I desires implanted in me only to make me miserable? ... My feelings do not accord

with the notion of solitary happiness. In a state of bliss, it will be the society of beings we can love, without the alloy that earthly infirmities mix with our best affections, that will constitute great part of our happiness' (*Mary*, *WW*, I, p. 46).
11 See, for example, Wollstonecraft, *Rights of Woman*, *WW*, v, pp. 93–94, where she refers to his 'overweening sensibility' and 'voluptuous reveries'.
12 Wollstonecraft, *Rights of Woman*, *WW*, v, pp.190, 107.
13 Wollstonecraft, *Religious Opinions*, *WW*, III, pp. 15 and 29.
14 Wollstonecraft, *Religious Opinions*, *WW*, III, p. 26.
15 Wollstonecraft, *Religious Opinions*, *WW*, III, p. 59.
16 For alternative accounts of Wollstonecraft's complex involvement with sensibility and its connection with the radical culture of the 1790s, see Syndy McMillan Conger, *Sensibility in Transformation: Creative Resistance to Sentiment from the Augustans to the Romantics* (London and Toronto: Fairleigh Dickinson University Press, Associated University Presses, 1989); J. Barker-Benfield, *The Culture of Sensibility: Sex and Society in Eighteenth-Century Britain* (Chicago and London: University of Chicago Press, 1992); Chris Jones, *Radical Sensibility: Literature and Ideas in the 1790s* (London and New York: Routledge, 1992), esp. pp. 85–107, where he addresses Wollstonecraft's redefinition of 'conservative sensibility'; Gary Kelly, *Revolutionary Feminism: The Mind and Career of Mary Wollstonecraft* (Basingstoke and London: Macmillan, 1992), and *Women, Writing, and Revolution 1790–1827* (Oxford: Clarendon Press, 1993).
17 Wollstonecraft, *Education of Daughters*, *WW*, IV, p. 7.
18 Wollstonecraft, *Education of Daughters*, *WW*, IV, p. 36.
19 See G. J. Barker-Benfield's chapter 'Wollstonecraft and the Crisis Over Sensibility in the 1790s', in *The Culture of Sensibility: Sex and Society in Eighteenth-Century Britain* (Chicago and London: University of Chicago Press, 1992), pp. 351–95. While recognising Wollstonecraft's distinction between good and bad sensibility, Barker-Benfield sees her as torn between them.
20 For an extended and intelligent account of Wollstonecraft's response to Burke, see Tom Furniss, 'Gender in Revolution: Edmund Burke and Mary Wollstonecraft', in *Revolution in Writing*, pp. 65–100.
21 Wollstonecraft, *Rights of Men*, *WW*, v, pp. 32.
22 Wollstonecraft, *Letters*, p. 263.
23 Wollstonecraft, *Rights of Woman*, *WW*, v, p. 145.
24 Wollstonecraft, *Rights of Woman*, *WW*, v, p. 238.
25 Wollstonecraft, *Rights of Woman*, *WW*, v, pp. 186, 108.
26 Wollstonecraft, *Mary*, *WW*, I, pp. 60, 59.
27 Wollstonecraft, *Rights of Woman*, *WW*, v, pp. 161 and 178 respectively.
28 Wollstonecraft, *Rights of Woman*, *WW*, v, pp. 160, 141, 121, 119, 301.
29 Wollstonecraft, *Rights of Woman*, *WW*, v, p. 201.
30 Wollstonecraft, *Education of Daughters*, *WW*, IV, p. 37.
31 Wollstonecraft, *French Revolution*, *WW*, VI, p. 62.
32 Wollstonecraft, *French Revolution*, *WW*, VI, pp. 229, 514, 521, 112. See also her

observation in the posthumously published *Hints*: 'Poetry flourishes most in the first rude state of society' (*WW*, v, p. 275).
33 Wollstonecraft, *French Revolution*, *WW*, VI, p. 110.
34 Wollstonecraft, *French Revolution*, *WW*, VI, pp. 110, 220.
35 Wollstonecraft, *Rights of Woman*, *WW*, v, p. 212.
36 Wollstonecraft, *Letters Written in Sweden, Norway, and Denmark*, *WW*, VI, pp. 325, 309.
37 Wollstonecraft, *Wrongs of Woman*, *WW*, I, p. 110.
38 Wollstonecraft, *Letters*, p. 345.
39 For recent accounts of this text which analyse its production of a new subjectivity in relation to sensibility and the form of the letter, see Mary Favret, *Romantic Correspondence: Women, Politics, and the Fiction of Letters* (Cambridge University Press, 1993), pp. 96–132; Gary Kelly, *Revolutionary Feminism*, pp. 171–95.
40 See Jane Moore, 'Plagiarism with a Difference: Subjectivity in "Kubla Khan" and *Letters Written During a Short Residence in Sweden, Norway and Denmark*', in *Beyond Romanticism*, pp. 140–59.
41 Wollstonecraft, *Letters Written in Sweden, Norway, and Denmark*, *WW*, VI, p. 316.
42 Wollstonecraft, *Letters Written in Sweden, Norway, and Denmark*, *WW*, VI, p. 309.
43 Wollstonecraft, *Letters Written in Sweden, Norway, and Denmark*, *WW*, VI, pp. 289 and 341.
44 For an alternative and powerful reading of these key passages in *Letters Written in Sweden, Norway, and Denmark* in relation to the maternal imaginary and Wollstonecraft's 'feminist melancholy', see Mary Jacobus, 'In Love with a Cold Climate: Travelling with Wollstonecraft', in *First Things: The Maternal Imaginary in Literature, Art, and Psychoanalysis* (New York and London: Routledge, 1995), pp. 63–82.
45 See Catherine Gallagher, 'The Body versus the Social Body in the Works of Thomas Malthus and Henry Mayhew', *Representations*, 14 (1986), pp. 83–106; and Sylvana Tomaselli, 'Moral Philosophy and Population Questions in Eighteenth-Century Europe', in Michael S. Teitelbaum and Jay M. Winter (eds.), *Population and Resources in Western Intellectual Traditions* (Cambridge University Press, 1988), pp. 7–29.
46 Wollstonecraft, *Letters Written in Sweden, Norway, and Denmark*, *WW*, VI, p. 288.
47 Disgust is a significant aspect of Wollstonecraft's text and it ranges from a mild distaste to a strong physical reaction, from a mild critique of manners to nausea induced by the smell of herrings. See Wollstonecraft, *Letters Written in Sweden, Norway, and Denmark*, *WW*, VI, pp. 246, 249, 259, 262, 278, 279.
48 Wollstonecraft, *Letters Written in Sweden, Norway, and Denmark*, *WW*, VI, p. 279.
49 See Ann Janowitz, *England's Ruins: Poetic Purpose and the National Landscape* (Cambridge, Mass. and London: Blackwell, 1990).

50 Wollstonecraft, *Letters Written in Sweden, Norway, and Denmark*, WW, VI, p. 279.
51 See Kenneth Smith, *The Malthusian Controversy* (London: Routledge and Kegan Paul, 1951).

PART II   IMAGINATION AND UTILITY

1 William Godwin, *Enquiry Concerning Political Justice and its Influence on Modern Morals and Happiness*, (Harmondsworth: Penguin, 1985; first published 1793), p. 395.
2 Godwin, *Enquiry*, pp. 394–95.
3 Godwin, *Enquiry*, p. 395.
4 See Mark Philp (ed.), *Political and Philosophical Writings of William Godwin* (London: William Pickering, 1993), vol. 6, p. 132, and vol. 5, particularly pp. 313–14, where, in his preface to *Bible Stories . . . for the Use of Children*, Godwin asserts that 'modern improvers have left out of their system the most essential branch of human nature the imagination . . . Imagination is the ground-plot upon which the edifice of a sound morality must be erected. Without imagination we may have a certain cold and arid circle of principles, but we cannot have sentiments: we may learn by rote a catalogue of rules, and repeat our lesson with the exactness of a parrot, or play over our tricks with the docility of a monkey; but we can neither ourselves love, nor be fitted to excite the love of others.'
5 See Patricia Ingham, *The Language of Class: Transformation in the Victorian Novel* (London and New York: Routledge, 1996), pp. 1–19, where she considers the complex 'linguistic codings' which structure the representation of British society at the beginning of the Victorian period. Among these she notes the conflict between 'Malthusian struggle and Benthamite Utilitarianism', paternalism, and the patriarchal family.
6 See F. E. L. Priestley (ed.), *Collected Works of John Stuart Mill*, 33 vols. (Toronto and London: University of Toronto Press and Routledge and Kegan Paul, 1963–91), vol. X, pp. 75–115 and 117–63; F. R. Leavis (ed.), *Mill on Bentham and Coleridge* (London: Chatto and Windus, 1950); Basil Willey, *Nineteenth Century Studies: Coleridge to Matthew Arnold* (Cambridge University Press, 1949); Raymond Williams, *Culture and Society 1780–1950* (Harmondsworth: Penguin, 1961; first published 1958), pp. 49–71.
7 See Elie Halévy, *The Growth of Philosophical Radicalism*, trans. Mary Morris (London: Faber & Faber, 1952), pp. 263–64. (Étienne Dumont, *Souvenirs de Mirabeau et sur les deux première assemblées législatives* (1832), pp. ix–x, fn.) See also Halévy, *The Growth of Philosophical Radicalism*, pp. 249–310.
8 Terry Eagleton, *The Ideology of the Aesthetic* (Oxford: Basil Blackwell, 1990), pp. 60–62.
9 David Simpson, *Romanticism, Nationalism, and the Revolt Against Theory* (Chicago and London: University of Chicago Press, 1993), pp. 142–48.

10 Jeremy Bentham, *A Fragment on Government,* J. H. Burns and H. L. A. Hart (eds.) (Cambridge University Press, 1988; first published 1776), pp. 8, 3.
11 Bentham, *Fragment on Government,* p. 3.
12 Bentham, *Fragment on Government,* pp. 22, 24.
13 Bentham, *Fragment on Government,* p. 20. The passage continues: 'We inhabit an old Gothic castle, erected in the days of chivalry, but fitted up for a modern inhabitant'.
14 Bentham, *Fragment on Government,* pp. 105, 108.
15 Bentham, *Fragment on Government,* p. 16.
16 For an extended philosophical analysis and justification of Bentham's mode of critique and, in particular, his critical tool of 'paraphrasis' and his attack upon legal fictions, see Ross Harrison, *Bentham, The Arguments of the Philosophers* series (London, Melbourne and Henley: Routledge and Kegan Paul, 1983), pp. 24–46.
17 There are instances, however, when Bentham, somewhat grudgingly, admits to the usefulness of the visual force of imagination. See, for example: 'Preach to the eye, if you would preach with efficacy. By that organ, through the medium of imagination, the judgment of the bulk of mankind may be led and moulded almost at pleasure. As puppets in the hand of a show-man, so would one be in the head of the legislator, who, to the science proper to his function, should add a well-informed attention to stage effect', Jeremy Bentham, *Rationale of Judicial Evidence, Jeremy Bentham's Works,* John Bowring (ed.), 11 vols. (Edinburgh: William Tait, 1843), v, p. 108.
18 Jeremy Bentham, *Anarchical Fallacies,* in *'Nonsense Upon Stilts': Bentham, Burke and Marx on the Rights of Man,* Jeremy Waldron (ed.), (London and New York: Methuen, 1987; first published 1816; first published in English 1843), pp. 68–69.
19 Jeremy Bentham, *Rationale of Reward, Jeremy Bentham's Works,* II, pp. 253–54.
20 See John Dinwiddy, *Bentham, Past Masters* series (Oxford and New York: Oxford University Press, 1989), pp. 28–29, 33–35, 112–13; James Steintrager, *Bentham* (London: George Allen and Unwin, 1977), pp. 16–17, 30–31, 104–5.
21 See, for example Geoffrey Scarre, *Utilitarianism* (London: Routledge, 1996), pp. 77–79.

4 HAZLITT AND THE LIMITS OF THE SYMPATHETIC IMAGINATION

1 John Barrell's chapter on Hazlitt in *The Political Theory of Painting from Reynolds to Hazlitt: 'The Body of the Public'* (New Haven and London: Yale University Press, 1986), pp. 315–16, contains a brief, but eminently sensible description of the dangers of composing Hazlitt's thought into a coherent view. See also Annette Wheeler Cafarelli, *Prose in the Age of Poets: Romanticism and Biographical Narrative from Johnson to De Quincey* (Philadelphia: University

of Pennsylvania Press, 1990), pp. 113–36, where she considers Hazlitt's deployment of discontinuous narrative to be a deliberate tactic in an age of cultural fragmentation; and Simon Dentith's interesting study of Hazlitt's deployment of rhetoric in the public sphere, *A Rhetoric of the Real: Studies in Post-Enlightenment Writing from 1790 to the Present* (Hemel Hempstead and New York: Harvester Wheatsheaf, 1990), pp. 65–91.

2 For an extended account of Hazlitt's associationist imagination in relation to organic sensibility and his appreciation of Romantic poetry, see James Engell, *The Creative Imagination: Enlightenment to Romanticism* (Cambridge, Mass. and London: Harvard University Press, 1981), pp. 197–214. For a more philosophically informed view of Hazlitt's imagination which qualifies its straightforward associationist identity, see Roy Park, *Hazlitt and The Spirit of the Age: Abstraction and Critical Theory* (Oxford: Clarendon Press, 1971); see also J.-C. Salle, 'Hazlitt the Associationist', *Review of English Studies*, 15 (1964), pp. 38–51; John M. Bullitt, 'Hazlitt and the Romantic Conception of Imagination', *Philological Quarterly*, 24 (1945), pp. 343–61; J. D. O'Hara, 'Hazlitt and the Functions of the Imagination', *PMLA*, 81 (1966), pp. 552–62.

3 See Jonathan Bate, *Shakespearean Constitutions: Politics, Theatre, Criticism 1730–1830* (Oxford: Clarendon Press, 1989), pp. 129–213, esp. pp. 152–66, where he offers a valuable celebratory account of the role of the sympathetic imagination in Hazlitt's drama criticism. My account, in contrast, focuses on the inherent problems and limits of Hazlitt's sympathetic imagination as a mode of knowledge.

4 See David Bromwich, *Hazlitt: The Mind of a Critic* (New York and Oxford: Oxford University Press, 1983), pp. 288–99; Jonathan Cook, 'Hazlitt: Criticism and Ideology', in *Romanticism and Ideology: Studies in English Writing 1765–1830* (London: Routledge, 1981), pp. 137–54; W. P. Albrecht, *Hazlitt and the Creative Imagination* (Lawrence: University of Kansas Press, 1965), pp. 57–58; Herschel Baker, *William Hazlitt* (Cambridge, Mass. and London: Harvard University Press, 1962), pp. 50–56; Terry Eagleton, 'William Hazlitt: an Empiricist Radical', *New Blackfriars*, 54 (1973), pp. 108–17. For a more expansive version of this section of the chapter, see my 'Hazlitt on Burke: The Ambivalent Position of a Radical Essayist', *Studies in Romanticism*, 25 (1986), pp. 465–81; and for a response to my article, see Mark Garnett, 'Hazlitt Against Burke: Radical versus Conservative', *Durham University Journal*, 49 (1989), 229–39. For a provocatively imagistic and interestingly masculinist reading of Hazlitt's appreciation of Burke which pushes Hazlitt towards the violent and physical pole of his aesthetic, see Tom Paulin, *The Day-Star of Liberty: William Hazlitt's Radical Style* (London: Faber and Faber, 1998), esp. pp. 138–61. For an intelligent account of the significance of Hazlitt's engagement with Burke in relation to the wider issue of the politics of print culture in the Regency, see Kevin Gilmartin, 'Burke, Popular Opinion, and the Problem of Counter-Revolutionary Public Sphere', in Edmund Burke's *Reflections on the Revolution in France, Texts*

Notes to pages 111–129

    in Culture series, John Whale (ed.) (Manchester University Press, forthcoming 2000).
5 Park, *Hazlitt and the Spirit of the Age*, p. 22.
6 William Hazlitt, *The Complete Works of William Hazlitt*, ed. by P. P. Howe, 21 vols. (London and Toronto: J. M. Dent and Sons, 1930–34), VII, p. 325, hereafter cited as *Works*.
7 Hazlitt, *Works*, VII, p. 319.
8 Hazlitt, *Works*, XII, p. 53.
9 See Cook, 'Hazlitt: Criticism and Ideology', p. 147.
10 Hazlitt, *Works*, VII, p. 303.
11 Hazlitt, *Works*, VII, p. 308.
12 This is the main thesis of Roy Park's valuable study.
13 Hazlitt, *Works*, XVII, p. 48.
14 Hazlitt, *Works*, XV, p. 71.
15 Hazlitt, *Works*, XIV, p. 84.
16 Hazlitt, *Works*, XVII, p. 10.
17 Hazlitt, *Works*, XVII, p. 39.
18 Hazlitt, *Works*, XVII, p. 68.
19 For an alternative account of Hazlitt's literary relationship with Coleridge conceived as Bloomean hero-worship, see Thomas McFarland, *Romantic Cruxes: The English Essayists and the Spirit of the Age* (Oxford: Clarendon Press, 1987), pp. 53–89.
20 Hazlitt, *Works*, XVI, p. 138.
21 Hazlitt, *Works*, XVI, p. 121.
22 Hazlitt, *Works*, XVI, p. 137.
23 Hazlitt, *Works*, XVI, p. 137.
24 Hazlitt, *Works*, XVI, p. 137.
25 Hazlitt, *Works*, XVI, p. 138.
26 Hazlitt, *Works*, XVI, p. 104.
27 Hazlitt, *Works*, XVI, p. 102.
28 The term is Coleridge's and it is taken up by Jon Klancher in his important study of the construction and rhetorical deployment of audiences in this period. See Klancher, *The Making of English Reading Audiences, 1790–1832* (Madison: University of Wisconsin Press, 1987), p. 153.
29 Hazlitt, *Works*, XVI, p. 101.
30 Hazlitt, *Works*, XVI, p. 100.
31 Hazlitt, *Works*, XVI, p. 101.
32 See Klancher, *The Making of English Reading Audiences*, pp. 150–70.
33 See Cafarelli, *Prose in the Age of Poets*, pp. 126–36.
34 See Park, *Hazlitt and the Spirit of the Age*, p. 76.
35 Paley's book provided a Christianised version of utilitarian ethics and was almost immediately adopted, to the horror of Coleridge, as a set text at the University of Cambridge. In a footnote to *A Lay Sermon* Coleridge credits Hazlitt with 'detecting the fallacious sophistry of the grounding principle of this whole system . . . with great ability and originality' in his *Essay on the*

Principles of Human Action. See Samuel Taylor Coleridge, *The Collected Works of Samuel Taylor Coleridge*, gen. ed. Kathleen Coburn, Bollingen Series LXXV, 16 vols. (Princeton and London: Princeton University Press and Routledge and Kegan Paul, 1969–), VI, pp. 186–87.

36 For an insightful account of Hazlitt's inheritance from French Enlightenment thinking, see Seamus Deane's *The French Revolution and Enlightenment in England 1789–1832* (Cambridge, Mass. and London: Harvard University Press, 1988), pp. 130–57.

37 Hazlitt, *Works*, XII, p. 382. For an account of Hazlitt's interaction with the so-called 'new reformers', see Stanley Jones's invaluable *Hazlitt: A Life from Winterslow to Frith Street* (Oxford: Clarendon Press, 1989), pp. 232–49.

38 The exception here is Roy Park, whose *Hazlitt and The Spirit of the Age* contains a chapter on Hazlitt's critique of Bentham. Park's valuable account treats Hazlitt as a metaphysician whose consistent philosophical position celebrates the power of a self-transcendent, disinterested imagination which operates according to a moral imperative. My account, in contrast, sees Hazlitt's writing as offering a much more strategic and contradictory set of ideas, and views his notion of imagination as a more polemical and embattled feature of his oppositional rhetoric. See Park, 'Morality and Science: Hazlitt and Bentham', *Hazlitt and the Spirit of the Age*, pp. 43–76. See also Paulin, *The Day-Star of Liberty*, pp. 231–43, 285. And for a contemporary assessment, see Leigh Hunt, 'Mr Hazlitt and the Utilitarians', in *Leigh Hunt's Literary Criticism*, L. H. Houtchens and C. W. Houtchens (eds.) (New York: Columbia University Press), pp. 275–81.

39 Hazlitt, *Works*, XII, p. 44.
40 Hazlitt, *Works*, XII, p. 45.
41 Hazlitt, *Works*, XII, p. 45.
42 Hazlitt, *Works*, XII, p. 45.
43 Hazlitt, *Works*, XII, p. 50.
44 For a brief analysis of this article in relation to Hazlitt and cultural difference, see my 'Indian Jugglers: Romantic Orientalism and the Difference of View', in *Romanticism and Colonialism: Writing and Empire, 1780–1830*, Tim Fulford and Peter Kitson (eds.) (Cambridge University Press, 1998), pp. 206–20.
45 Hazlitt, *Works*, XII, pp. 50.
46 Hazlitt, *Works*, XII, p. 51.
47 Hazlitt, *Works*, XII, pp. 51–52, 53.
48 Hazlitt, *Works*, XI, p. 15.
49 Hazlitt, *Works*, XI, p. 10.
50 Hazlitt, *Works*, XI, p. 10.
51 The phrase occurs in 'Self-Love and Benevolence' which appeared in the *New Monthly Magazine* in two parts in 1828. Here, at the end of his career, Hazlitt revisits many of the concerns of his *Essay on the Principles of Human Action*. See Hazlitt, *Works*, XX, p. 185.

52 Hazlitt, *Works*, XII, p. 53.
53 Hazlitt, *Works*, XII, p. 180.
54 Hazlitt, *Works*, XII, p. 192.
55 Hazlitt, *Works*, XII, p. 193.
56 Hazlitt, *Works*, XII, p. 194.
57 See Barrell, *The Political Theory of Painting*, pp. 314–38.

5 COBBETT'S IMAGINARY LANDSCAPE

1 I am thinking of Williams's entry for 'culture' in *Keywords: A Vocabulary of Culture and Society* (London: Fontana, 1976), pp. 76–82.
2 See Olivia Smith, *The Politics of Language, 1791–1819* (Oxford: Clarendon Press, 1984), pp. 202–51; David A. Wilson, *Paine and Cobbett: The Transatlantic Connection* (Montreal and London: McGill-Queen's University Press, 1988), pp. 97–192; Jon Klancher, *The Making of English Reading Audiences, 1790–1832*, pp. 113–29; Ian Dyck, *William Cobbett and Rural Popular Culture* (Cambridge Unversity Press, 1992); and Leonora Nattrass, *William Cobbett: The Politics of Style* (Cambridge University Press, 1995).
3 Leonora Nattrass offers an intelligent and cogent account of the problem of coming to terms with Cobbett's apparent contradictoriness as a sign of his strategic, rhetorical styles in the opening section of her important *William Cobbett: The Politics of Style*, pp. 1–30. Similarly, Jon Klancher responds to the divergent figures of Cobbett produced by the Victorians, G. D. H. Cole and Chesterton, as well as more recent accounts by Raymond Williams and E. P. Thompson, by addressing 'the different discourses within Cobbett'. Cobbett's 'inconsistency' thus becomes a means of 'traverse[ing] particular political and rhetorical modes within a peculiar personal style'. See Klancher, *The Making of English Reading Audiences*, p. 125. And in a fascinating chapter entitled 'Reading Cobbett's Contradictions' Kevin Gilmartin engages with Cobbett's attack on the system as a complex mixture of simplicity and complexity, of contradictions and single-mindedness; and in a very resonant phrase he refers us to Cobbett's 'countersystematic imagination' *Print Politics: The Press and Radical Opposition in Early Nineteenth-century England* (Cambridge University Press, 1996), p. 161.
4 Kevin Gilmartin hints at the imaginative utopianism informing Cobbett's radical assault upon the connection between language and things when he writes: 'Cobbett's struggle with the system was a struggle over the authority to issue the verbal decrees that would divide truth from fiction, vice from virtue, defeat from victory. The corrosive principle of "clear" expression "stripped statement and reasoning of the foppery of affectation" . . . and left in its aftermath the extensive rhetoric of corruption that filled the pages of the *Political Register* . . . *The Political Register* was . . . firmly under the spell of things, and struggled to bring language back into its original and perfect correspondence with the world' (*Print Politics*, pp. 174–75).

5 E. P. Thompson, *The Making of the English Working Class* (Harmondsworth: Penguin Books, 1980; first published by Victor Gollancz, 1963), p. 830.
6 Thompson cites a number of Cobbett's contemporaries, particularly Hazlitt, in order to separate him from 'the polite culture of the essayist'. See Thompson, *Making of the English Working Class*, pp. 820–37. As more recent studies have suggested, it is certainly not so easy to make this separation; and the evidence used by Thompson could, I think, be used to indicate the level of anxiety in those wishing to clarify the boundary between the vulgar and the refined.
7 William Cobbett, *Political Register*, January 5, 1805, col. 1. See also *Political Register*, July 14, 1810, cols. 20–21: 'I have stripped statement and reasoning of the foppery of affectation; and, amongst my other sins, is that of having shown, of having proved beyond all dispute, that very much of what is called "*learning*" is imposture, quite useless to any man whom God has blessed with brains.'
8 Cobbett, *Political Register*, January 5, 1805, col. 1.
9 Cobbett, *Political Register*, September 20, 1834, cols. 708–9.
10 William Cobbett, *Advice to Young Men, and (Incidentally) to Young Women, in the Middle and Higher Ranks of Life, in a Series of Letters Addressed to A Youth, A Bachelor, A Lover, A Husband, A Father, and a Citizen or a Subject* (Oxford University Press, 1980; first published 1830), pp. 296–97.
11 Cobbett, *Advice*, p. 305.
12 Cobbett, *Advice* p. 128.
13 Cobbett, *Advice*, p. 59.
14 William Cobbett, *A Grammar of the English Language, in a Series of Letters. Intended for the Use of Schools and of Young Persons in general; but more especially for the Use of Soldiers, Sailors, Apprentices, and Plough-boys* (Oxford and New York: Oxford University Press, 1984; first published 1819), p. 113.
15 Cobbett, *Political Register*, November 14, 1807, col. 751.
16 Olivia Smith takes a very different view of Cobbett's *Grammar*. She compares it, perhaps surprisingly, with Coleridge's *Biographia Literaria*, as a text which carries the signs of his conservatism in his paternalistic tone and in his continuing faith in class hierarchy (*The Politics of Language*, p. 248).
17 Cobbett, *Political Register*, November 14, 1807, cols. 750–51.
18 William Cobbett, *History of the Regency and Reign of King George the Fourth* (London: William Cobbett, 1830), para. 273.
19 Cobbett, *History*, para. 273.
20 William Cobbett, *Rural Rides*, 2 vols. (London: Dent 1912), I, p. 152.
21 Cobbett, *Rural Rides*, I, p. 44.
22 Cobbett, *Rural Rides*, II, p. 278.
23 Dyck, *William Cobbett and Rural Popular Culture*, p. 114.
24 See John Barrell, 'John Clare, William Cobbett, and the Changing Landscape', in *The New Pelican Guide to English Literature*, vol. 5, *From Blake to Byron* (Harmondsworth: Penguin, 1982), pp. 226–43. Barrell writes: 'For the most part his enjoyment of land as landscape is inseparable from his delight in its

productivity: when he writes of a landscaped park that "everywhere utility and convenience is combined with beauty" it is hard to imagine what sort of beauty, for him, might not be combined with convenience and utility... One might imagine, on reading the first passage, that Cobbett is simply endorsing a notion of beauty common in contemporary writings on aesthetics, that it arises from the experience of smooth or easy transition among elements of variety – an experience like that described in Burke's famous remark, of "being swiftly drawn in an easy coach, on the smooth turf, with gradual ascents and declivities". Yet, as we compare the two passages, it seems that this notion of beauty has to be combined with the evidence of productivity for the landscape to be truly delightful' (p. 239). In the same essay Barrell also astutely reminds us that 'Cobbett is never content simply to record and to exult in the sight of "views that a painter might crave"... He is always reading the landscape' (pp. 240–41).

25 Cobbett, *Rural Rides*, I, p. 5.
26 See Dyck, *William Cobbett and Rural Popular Culture*, p. 13: 'Where Cobbett stood apart from other Radicals was not in the broad subject matter of reform, but in his efforts to create a national reform platform that belonged as much to the countryside as to London and the industrial towns.'
27 For a detailed account of this period in Cobbett's life (which includes his falling out with Windham), see George Spater, *William Cobbett: The Poor Man's Friend*, 2 vols. (Cambridge University Press, 1982), pp. 137–56. Spater's conclusion to this chapter of Cobbett's life is that 'By mid 1806 Cobbett had definitely made a break with the past' (p. 156).
28 However, Cobbett cites Paine's *Rights of Man* as the origin of his economic critique of the funding system and paper money in *Paper Against Gold* (London: William Cobbett, 1817), p. 56. In his introduction to the same book he refers to the topic as 'the grand cause' of 'our miseries' (p. i) and the origin of 'all those sudden changes in the country, which have ruined the farmers, the tradesmen, the land-owners, and which have reduced the journeymen and labourers to such intolerable misery as that which they now endure, and which never was endured in England at any former period' (p. iii). He also dates his first efforts on the topic to 1804 (see p. iv). For an analysis of Cobbett's complex involvement with Paine, see Spater, *The Poor Man's Friend*, II, pp. 204, 313–16, 346–47, 575, and 576; and Wilson, *Paine and Cobbett*, pp. 146–83.
29 William Cobbett, *Selections from Cobbett's Political Works; Being a Complete Abridgement of the 100 Volumes which Comprise the Writings of 'Porcupine' and the 'Weekly Political Register'*, with notes, Historical and Explanatory by John M. Cobbett and James P. Cobbett, 6 vols. (London: Anne Cobbett, 1835–7), I, p. 25.
30 In the same work Cobbett also makes the following large-scale pronouncement on the importance of this issue:

we must now step back a little, and take a look at those money affairs, the management of which, during the career of PERCEVAL, laid the foundation of all those changes, all those troubles, all those important events, which have taken place since the year 1810. The restriction, as it was called, on the Bank of England, but which was, in reality, a stoppage of the bank, which took place in the month of February, 1796, had made paper money, that is to say bank-notes, the legal tender of the country; its sole medium of exchange; its sole measure of value. The history of the reign of GEORGE THE THIRD, up to the time of the commencement of the regency, will be found to contain a detail of the contrivances by which the circulation of gold was supplanted by that of paper money; the detail of all the acts of parliament; of all those numerous financial tricks by which the country was drained of its gold, and by which its money-affairs were kept going without any real measure of value. (Cobbett, *History*, p. 116)

31 Raymond Williams, *William Cobbett* (Oxford and New York: Oxford University Press, 1983), p. 37.
32 William Cobbett, *Cobbett's Two-Penny Trash; or, Politics For the Poor*, vol. I (July 1830–June 1831) (London: William Cobbett, 1831), no. xv (May 1831), pp. 241–42.
33 William Cobbett, *Journal of a Year's Residence in the United States of America* (Gloucester: Alan Sutton, 1983; first published 1819), p. 16.
34 Cobbett, *Political Register*, February 15 1834, col. 386.
35 Cobbett, *Journal of a Year's Residence*, p. 162.
36 Cobbett, *Rural Rides*, II, p. 253.
37 Cobbett, *Rural Rides*, I, p. 85.
38 Cobbett, *Grammar*, p. 44. See also *History of the Hundred Days of English Freedom* where Cobbett attacks Sir Francis Burdett on the issue of property: 'It used to be the importance of *the people*; the importance of the people's rights; the importance of men's rights, as *men* . . . Property does not consist solely in house and land, nor in goods and chattels; nor in certificates of Stock, like that of COUTTS's; nor in specie and bank-notes. Every man has property in the works of his hands, or in those of his mind . . . Civil society is built upon this basis, that the whole mass is to derive benefit from the *wisdom* which it contains' (Cobbett, *Selections from Cobbett's Political Works*, v, p. 270).
39 Cobbett, *Advice*, p. 318.
40 See Dyck, *William Cobbett and Rural Popular Culture*, p. 32, where he quotes *Political Register*, March 17, 1821, p. 780.
41 Williams, *William Cobbett*, p. 24.
42 Thomas Paine, *The Decline and Fall of the English System of Finance* (London: R. Carlile, 1826; first published 1796), p.14.
43 Dyck argues that Cobbett remains true to an idea of restoration rather than acceding to the demands of revolution or wholesale reform : 'Revolution, Cobbett argued, was the labourer's right in theory, yet he remained hopeful, right up until 1834, that country ideology could be restored, if not by the voluntary will of landlords and farmers, then by the permanent threat of periodic exercise of physical encouragement from below' (*William Cobbett and Rural Popular Culture*, p. 208). In *A Year's Residence* Cobbett makes the point about himself as a patriotic reformer and therefore as a reluctant revolutionary quite clearly: 'Having this powerful argument of experience before me, and seeing no reason why the thing should be otherwise, I have never

Notes to pages 158–164 221

wished for republican government in England; though, rather than that the present tyrannical oligarchy should continue to trample on king and people, I would gladly see the whole fabric torn to atoms, and trust to chance for something better, being sure that nothing could be worse' (p. 304).

44 Paine, *Decline and Fall*, p. 4.
45 For another account of Cobbett in relation to political economy and paper money, see John W. Osborne, *William Cobbett: His Thought and His Times* (New Brunswick: Rutgers University Press, 1966), pp. 111, 136–43.
46 Cobbett, *Rural Rides*, II, pp. 37, 52, 180, 280, and 37.
47 Cobbett, *Rural Rides*, II, p. 52.
48 William Cobbett, *Surplus Population: and Poor Law Bill. A Comedy in Three Acts. By William Cobbett, MP* (London, 1831). (The play is also published in no. XII of *Cobbett's Two-Penny Trash; or, Politics for the Poor* in June 1831, pp. 265–92.) At the end of his career as an MP Cobbett spoke frequently on the subject of the Poor Rate as it came up as part of the Poor Law Amendment Bill which became law in 1834. This tax was inspired by the philosophy of the utilitarian philosophers Bentham and Malthus. (See Daniel Green, *Great Cobbett: The Noblest Agitator* (Oxford University Press, 1985), p. 458; and Dyck, *William Cobbett and Rural Popular Culture*, pp. 103–4.)
49 Cobbett, *Surplus Population*, p. 3.
50 Kevin Gilmartin even goes so far as to consider this inversion of representation within Rural rides as a powerful and strategic elision of Cobbett the writer: 'The self-consuming energy of Cobbett's prose culminated in the Rides when the figure who disappeared before a polemical landscape conditionally resurfaced in a world free of corruption and mediation' (*Print Politics*, p. 193).
51 Cobbett, *Political Register*, July 21, 1810, col. 69.
52 Cobbett, *Political Register*, July 28, 1810, col. 106.
53 Cobbett, *Selections from Cobbett's Works*, I, col. 544.
54 *The Book of Wonders: In Fourteen Chapters containing In the Compass of eighty closely printed columns, a Mass of Information, more suited to the Present Moment, and better calculated to open the Eyes of the People of England, than any Work of a similar nature, that has hitherto appeared*, 2 parts (Leicester-Square, London: H. Stemman, 1820 and 1821), and *The Beauties of Cobbett*, 3 parts (London: H. Stemman, 1820?). In the former, Cobbett is referred to throughout as 'the Great Enlightener'.
55 See, for example, Alice Chandler, *A Dream of Order: The Medieval Ideal in Nineteenth-Century English Literature* (Lincoln: University of Nebraska Press, 1970), pp. 59–82; and James Sambrook, *William Cobbett* (London and Boston: Routledge and Kegan Paul, 1973), pp. 29–30. Jon Klancher also endorses this view by claiming that Cobbett must always fall back on what Alice Chandler calls a 'feudal dream of order' to make historical sense of what he ineluctably perceives and writes about. (*The Making of English Reading Audiences*, p. 128). See also Karl W. Schweizer and John W. Osborne, *Cobbett in His Times* (Leicester University Press, 1990), pp. 144–56.

56 See Karl Marx and Frederick Engels, *Collected Works*, 3 vols. (London: Lawrence and Wishart, 1979), XII, p.189. The article was first published in the *New York Daily Tribune* No. 3826, July 22, 1853, p. 5. In the same article Marx claims that Cobbett failed to 'see the modern bourgeoisie' and that for all his trenchant social critique, 'He saw the machine, but not the hidden motive power.'
57 See Sambrook, *William Cobbett*, pp. 148, 159, and 164 respectively.
58 Osborne, *William Cobbett: His Thought and His Times*, p. 254.
59 Williams, *William Cobbett*, p. 31.

6 COLERIDGE AND THE AFTERLIFE OF IMAGINATION

1 S. T. Coleridge, *Lectures 1808–1819 On Literature, The Collected Works of Samuel Taylor Coleridge*, gen. ed. Kathleen Coburn, Bollingen Series LXXV, 16 vols. (Princeton and London: Princeton University Press and Routledge and Kegan Paul, 1969–), V, vol. 2, p. 193. All references to Coleridge's writings are to this edition, hereafter cited as *CW*.
2 See Nigel Leask, *The Politics of Imagination in Coleridge's Critical Thought* (Basingstoke: Macmillan, 1988).
3 See Jon Klancher, *The Making of English Reading Audiences, 1790–1832* (Madison: University of Wisconsin Press, 1987), pp. 150–70; and Lucy Newlyn, 'Coleridge and the Anxiety of Reception', *Romanticism*, 1:2 (1995), pp. 206–38.
4 Coleridge's definitions of imagination have generated an extensive and conflicting literature. See, for example: Carl Woodring, 'Coleridge: the Politics of Imagination', *Studies in Romanticism*, 21 (1982), pp. 447–76; Christine Gallant (ed.), *Coleridge's Theory of Imagination Today* (New York: AMS Press, 1989); Richard Gravil, Lucy Newlyn, and Nicholas Roe (eds.), *Coleridge's Imagination: Essays in Memory of Pete Laver* (Cambridge University Press, 1985); Kathleen Wheeler, *Sources, Processes, and Methods in Coleridge's 'Biographia Literaria'* (Cambridge University Press, 1980); Barbara Hardy, 'Distinction with Difference: Coleridge's Fancy and Imagination', *Essays in Criticism*, 1 (1951), pp. 336–44; Mary Warnock, *Imagination and Time* (Oxford: Basil Blackwell, 1994); Thomas McFarland, 'The Origin and Significance of Coleridge's Theory of Secondary Imagination', in Geoffrey Hartman (ed.), *New Perspectives on Coleridge and Wordsworth: Selected Papers from the English Institute* (New York and London: Columbia University Press, 1972); Leslie Brisman, 'Coleridge and the Supernatural', *Studies in Romanticism*, 21 (1982), pp. 123–59.
5 For Coleridge's attack on utilitarian thinking and his deployment of a 'Kant-like' distinction between 'Reason' and 'understanding', see John Colmer, *Coleridge: Critic of Society* (Oxford: Clarendon Press, 1959), esp. pp. 119, 131, 142; Laurence Lockridge, *Coleridge the Moralist* (Ithaca and London: Cornell University Press, 1977), pp. 244–50; and for Coleridge's deploy-

ment of this in *The Friend*, see Deirdre Coleman, *Coleridge and The Friend (1809–1810)* (Oxford: Clarendon Press, 1988), pp. 63–66.
6 Coleridge, *Table Talk*, *CW*, XIV, vol. 1, p. 479.
7 Coleridge, *Table Talk*, *CW*, XIV, vol. 1, p. 323. See also p. 45: 'a numerous party, who has already the ascendancy in the *State*; and which, unless far other minds and far other principles than the opponents of this party have hitherto allied with their cause . . . *will* obtain the ascendancy in the *Nation*'; and *CW*, XIV, vol. 2, p. 275: 'What between the sectarians and the political economists, the English are denationalized. England I see as a country, but the English nation seems obliterated'; and *On the Constitution of Church and State*, *CW*, X, pp. 68–69, where he lumps 'the parliamentary leaders of the Liberalists and Utilitarians' together and derides as spurious the manifestation of their philosophy in tract societies, conventicles, Lancasterian schools, mechanics' institutions, and 'lecture bazaars under the absurd name of universities'.
8 Coleridge, *A Lay Sermon*, *CW*, VI, p. 28.
9 Coleridge, *The Friend*, *CW*, X, p. 324. See also p. 108 for another attack on Paley, referred to as 'a writer of wider influence and higher authority' than Godwin and then followed by this devastating parody: 'But what are my metaphysics, merely the referring of the mind to its own consciousness for truths indispensable to its own happiness! To what purposes do I, or am I about to employ them? To perplex our clearest notions and living moral instincts? To deaden the feelings of will and free power, to extinguish the light of love and of conscience, to make myself and others worthless, soul-less, God-less? No! to expose the folly and the legerdemain of those who have thus abused the blessed machine of language'; and *On the Constitution of Church and State*, *CW*, X, p. 68, where Coleridge refers to Paley's prominence at Cambridge: 'The Guess-work of general consequences substituted for moral and political philosophy, adopted as a text book in one of the Universities, and cited, as authority, in the legislature.'
10 Coleridge, *CW*, IV, vol. 1, p. 497.
11 Coleridge, *A Lay Sermon*, *CW*, VI, p. 139.
12 For an interesting analysis of this anxiety and a helpful discussion of the conflicting arguments of Coleridge's critics on this subject, see Newlyn, 'Coleridge and the Anxiety of Reception', esp. pp. 224–28.
13 Coleridge, *CW*, VII, vol. 1, p. 44.
14 Coleridge, *CW*, VII, vol. 1, p. 38.
15 Coleridge, *CW*, VII, vol. 1, p. 57.
16 Coleridge, *CW*, VII, vol. 1, p. 38.
17 Coleridge, *CW*, X, p. 69.
18 Coleridge, *CW*, VII, vol. 1, p. 229.
19 Coleridge, *CW*, VII, vol. 1, p. 59.
20 Coleridge, *CW*, VII, vol. 1, p. 88.
21 Coleridge, *CW*, VII, vol. 1, p. 82.
22 See Leask, *The Politics of Imagination in Coleridge's Critical Thought*, pp. 9–77.

23 *The Westminster Review*, January 1830, p. 525.
24 *The Westminster Review*, January 1830, p. 527.
25 *The Westminster Review*, January 1830, p. 527.
26 *The Westminster Review*, January 1830, p. 559.
27 John Stuart Mill, *Collected Works of John Stuart Mill*, 33 vols., gen. ed. F. E. L. Priestly (Toronto and London: University of Toronto Press and Routledge and Kegan Paul, 1963–91), x, p. 121.
28 Mill, *Collected Works*, x, p. 122.
29 Mill, *Collected Works*, x, p. 127.
30 Mill, *Collected Works*, x, p. 129.
31 Mill, *Collected Works*, x, p. 136.
32 Mill, *Collected Works*, x, p. 138.
33 Mill, *Collected Works*, x, pp. 139–40.
34 Mill, *Collected Works*, x, p. 140.
35 Mill, *Collected Works*, x, pp. 96, 100.
36 Mill, *Collected Works*, x, p. 91.
37 Mill, *Collected Works*, x, p. 92.
38 Mill, *Collected Works*, x, p. 93.
39 Mill, *Collected Works*, x, p. 102.
40 Mill, *Collected Works*, x, p. 112.
41 Mill, *Collected Works*, x, p. 105.
42 Mill, *Collected Works*, I, p. 113.
43 Mill, *Collected Works*, I, p. 115.
44 Mill, *Collected Works*, I, pp. 139, 143.
45 Mill, *Collected Works*, I, p. 151.
46 Mill, *Collected Works*, I, p. 153.
47 For an account of Richards's critical position in relation to Arnold, as well as to the First World War, Cambridge, and practical criticism, see Chris Baldick, *The Social Mission of English Criticism 1848–1932* (Oxford: Oxford University Press, 1983), pp. 134–61.
48 'Our protection, as Matthew Arnold, in my epigraph, insisted, is in poetry. It is capable of saving us, or since some have found a scandal in this word, of preserving us or rescuing us from confusion and frustration' (I. A. Richards, *Poetries and Sciences* (London: Routledge and Kegan Paul, 1970; first published as *Science and Poetry*, 1926, revised edn. 1935), p. 78).
49 The full quotation reads: 'attempts to use poetry as a denial or as a corrective of science are very common. One point can be made against them all: they are never worked out in detail. There is no equivalent of Mill's *Logic* expounding any of them. The language in which they are framed is usually a blend of obsolete psychology and emotive exclamations' (Richards, *Poetries and Sciences*, p. 63).
50 Ruminating on the meaning of the words *instruction* and *usefulness* in his book *Speculative Instruments* (London: Routledge and Kegan Paul, 1955), Richards offers the following anecdote: 'What poetic and practical worlds! May I quote you a sentence I found this summer written up – above a door I used,

many years ago, to go through daily – by a hand which seemed to have been mine: I had forgotten. It is from William Godwin, that singular anarchist, author of *Political Justice*: "The remainder of my time I determined to devote to the pursuit of such attainments as afforded me the most promise to render me useful"' (p. 154).

51 In his revised edition of *Poetry and Science* Richards offers the following gloss on his idea of 'linguistic psychology': 'Psychology, to carry out such a duty, will have to absorb much of what is currently labelled linguistics. In return, linguistics, being thus absorbed, will have to become radically more empirical and humble than has of late been its wont' (*Poetries and Sciences*, p. 90). At the very beginning of his career he had worked with C. K. Ogden to produce a pioneering work on semantics, *The Meaning of Meaning: A Study of the Influence of Language upon Thought and the Science of Symbolism* (London: Kegan Paul, 1946; first published 1923).

52 This statement follows on from Richards's call for a scientific criticism: 'But apart from these answers, the assumptions which give rise to doubts as to the value of literary theory deserve attention, for they are connected with the general disparagement of intellectual and theoretical effort, in literature as in life, which has been characteristic of our time. They give us a convenient subsidiary field in which to examine the general revolt against reason, which shows itself most flagrantly in mid-European politics, but is to be noticed, in varying forms, everywhere' (*Coleridge On Imagination* (London: Kegan Paul, 1934, p. 38).

53 At one point Richards refers to the tone of critical writing having changed in the last third of the nineteenth century. After Pater, he suggests, 'We have since had intellectual snobs, spiritual snobs, taste-snobs . . . among our prominent critics far more often than candid inquirers' (*Coleridge on Imagination*, pp. 38–39).

54 Richards, *Coleridge on Imagination*, pp. 11–12.
55 Richards, *Coleridge on Imagination*, p. 18.
56 Richards, *Coleridge on Imagination*, p. 19.
57 Richards, *Coleridge on Imagination*, p. 21.
58 Richards, *Coleridge on Imagination*, p. 70.
59 Richards, *Coleridge on Imagination*, p. 70.
60 Richards, *Coleridge on Imagination*, p. 86.
61 Richards, *Coleridge on Imagination*, p. 19.
62 Richards, *Coleridge on Imagination*, p. 60.
63 Richards, 'Introduction' to *Viking Portable Coleridge* (New York: Viking Press, 1950), pp. 53–54.
64 I. A. Richards, 'The Vulnerable Poet and the Friend', *Poetries and Their Media and Ends*, ed. Trevor Eaton (The Hague, Paris: Mouton, 1974), p. 130. This article from 1974 is composed from a 1969 review of the *Collected Coleridge* volumes edited by Barbara Rooke containing *The Friend* and an essay from *The Harvard Review* in 1959.
65 See, for example: Paul Hamilton, *Coleridge's Poetics* (Oxford: Basil Blackwell,

1983), esp. pp. 58–121; Jerome J. McGann 'The *Biographia Literaria* and the Contentions of English Romanticism', in Frederick Burwick (ed.), *Coleridge's 'Biographia Literaria': Text and Meaning* (Columbus: Ohio State University Press, 1989), pp. 233–54; Stephen Bygrave, 'Land of the Giants: Gaps, Limits and Audience in Coleridge's *Biographia Literaria*', in Stephen Copley and John Whale (eds.), *Beyond Romanticism: New Approaches to Texts and Contexts 1780–1832* (London: Routledge, 1992), pp. 32–52.

66 Raymond Williams, *Culture and Society 1780–1950* (Hammondsworth: Penguin, 1961), p. 63.

AFTERWORD

1 William Wordsworth, *Wordsworth: The Prelude or Growth of a Poet's Mind (Text of 1805)* ed. Ernest de Selincourt, corrected by Stephen Gill (Oxford University Press, 1970), Book XIII, lines 52–65.

Bibliography

PRIMARY SOURCES

The Beauties of Cobbett, 3 parts (London: H. Stemman, 1820?).
Bentham, Jeremy, *Anarchical Fallacies*, in *'Nonsense Upon Stilts': Bentham, Burke and Marx on the Rights of Man*, ed. Jeremy Waldron (London and New York: Methuen, 1987; first published 1816; first published in English 1843).
A Fragment on Government, ed. J. H. Burns and H. L. A. Hart (Cambridge University Press, 1988; first published 1776).
Jeremy Bentham's Works, ed. John Bowring, 11 vols. (Edinburgh: William Tait, 1843).
Blake, William, *William Blake's Annotations to Richard Watson's 'An Apology for the Bible in a Series of Letters Addressed to Thomas Paine'*, ed. G. Ingli James, *Regency Reprints* (University College Cardiff Press, 1984; first published 1797).
The Book of Wonders: In Fourteen Chapters containing In the Compass of eighty closely printed columns, a Mass of Information, more suited to the Present Moment, and better calculated to open the Eyes of the People of England, than any Work of a similar nature, that has hitherto appeared, 2 parts (Leicester-Square, London: H. Stemman, 1820 and 1821).
Burke, Edmund, *Enquiry into the Origin of Our Ideas of the Sublime and Beautiful*, ed. J. T. Boulton (London: Routledge and Kegan Paul, 1958).
The Works of the Right Honourable Edmund Burke in Twelve Volumes (London: John C. Nimmo, 1899).
The Writings and Speeches of Edmund Burke, ed. Paul Langford, 12 vols. (Oxford: Clarendon Press, 1981–).
Claeys, Gregory (ed.), *Political Writings of the 1790s*, 8 vols. (London: Pickering and Chatto, 1995).
Cobbett, William, *Advice to Young Men and (incidentally) to Young Women in the Middle and Higher Ranks of Life in a series of Letters Addressed to a Youth, a Bachelor, a Lover, a Husband, a Father, and a Citizen or a Subject* (Oxford University Press, 1980; first published 1830).
Cobbett's Two-Penny Trash; or, Politics For the Poor (London: William Cobbett, 1831).
A Grammar of the English Language, in a Series of Letters. Intended for the Use of Schools and of Young Persons in General; but more Especially for the Use of Soldiers, Sailors, Apprentices, and Plough-boys (Oxford and New York: Oxford University Press, 1984; first published 1819).

History of the Regency and Reign of King George the Fourth (London: William Cobbett, 1830).
Journal of a Year's Residence in the United States of America (Gloucester: Alan Sutton, 1983; first published 1819).
Paper Against Gold (London: William Cobbett, 1817).
Selections from Cobbett's Political Works; Being a Complete Abridgement of the 100 Volumes which Comprise the Writings of 'Porcupine' and the 'Weekly Political Register', with notes, Historical and Explanatory by John M. Cobbett and James P. Cobbett, 6 vols. (London: Anne Cobbett, 1835–7).
Surplus Population: and Poor Law Bill. A Comedy in three acts (London, 1831).
Coleridge, S. T., *The Collected Works of Samuel Taylor Coleridge*, gen. ed. Kathleen Coburn, Bollingen Series LXXV, 16 vols. (Princeton and London: Princeton University Press and Routledge and Kegan Paul, 1969–).
de Condorcet, Antoine-Nicolas, *Sketch for a Historical Picture of the Progress of the Human Mind*, trans. June Barraclough (New York: Noonday Press, 1955).
Dumont, Étienne, *Souvenirs de Mirabeau et sure les deux première assemblées législatives* (Londres: Edward Bull, 1832).
Godwin, William, *Enquiry Concerning Political Justice and its Influence on Modern Morals and Happiness* (Harmondsworth: Penguin, 1985; first published 1793).
Political and Philosophical Writings of William Godwin, ed. Mark Philp, 7 vols. (London: William Pickering, 1993).
Hazlitt, William, *The Complete Works of William Hazlitt*, ed. P. P. Howe, 21 vols. (London and Toronto: J. M. Dent and Sons, 1930–34).
Hunt, Leigh, 'Mr Hazlitt and the Utilitarians', in *Leigh Hunt's Literary Criticism*, ed. L. H. Houtchens and C. W. Houtchens (New York: Columbia University Press), pp. 275–81.
Marx, Karl and Frederick Engels, *Collected Works*, 3 vols. (London: Lawrence and Wishart, 1979).
Mill, John Stuart, *Collected Works of John Stuart Mill*, gen. ed. F. E. L. Priestly, 33 vols. (Toronto and London: University of Toronto Press and Routledge and Kegan Paul, 1963–91).
Paine, Thomas, *Common Sense and The Crisis* (New York: Anchor Books, 1973).
The Decline and Fall of the English System of Finance (London: R. Carlile, 1826; first published 1796).
Rights of Man, ed. Henry Collins (Harmondsworth: Penguin Books, 1969).
The Writings of Thomas Paine, ed. Moncur Daniel Conway, 4 vols. (New York: Burt Franklin, 1969; first published 1902).
Richards, I. A., *Coleridge On Imagination* (London: Kegan Paul, 1934).
Poetries and Sciences (London: Routledge and Kegan Paul, 1970; first published as *Science and Poetry*, 1926, revised edn. 1935).
Speculative Instruments (London: Routledge and Kegan Paul, 1955).
(ed.), *Viking Portable Coleridge* (New York: Viking Press, 1950).
'The Vulnerable Poet and the Friend', *Poetries and Their Media and Ends*, ed. Trevor Eaton (The Hague, Paris: Mouton, 1974).

Rousseau, Jean-Jacques, *Oeuvres Complètes*, ed. Bernard Gagnebin and Marcel Raymond, 5 vols. (Paris: Editions Gallimard, 1969).
  The Social Contract and Discourses, trans. G. D. H. Cole (London: Dent, 1973; revised and augmented by J. H. Brummett and John C. Hall 1973; first published 1913).
de Volney, C.-F. *The Ruins* (translated from the French, first impression 1847, second impression, London 1853).
Wollstonecraft, Mary, *The Works of Mary Wollstonecraft*, ed. Janet Todd and Marilyn Butler, 7 vols. (London: Pickering and Chatto, 1989).
  Collected Letters of Mary Wollstonecraft, ed. Ralph M. Wardle (Ithaca and London: Cornell University Press, 1979).
Wordsworth, William, *The Prelude or Growth of a Poet's Mind (Text of 1805)*, ed. Ernest de Selincourt, corrected by Stephen Gill (Oxford University Press, 1970).

SECONDARY SOURCES

Albrecht, W. P., *Hazlitt and the Creative Imagination* (Lawrence: University of Kansas Press, 1965).
Aldridge, A. Owen, *Thomas Paine's American Ideology* (Newark, London and Toronto: Associated University Presses, 1984).
Arac, Jonathan, *Critical Genealogies: Historical Situations for Postmodern Literary Studies* (New York: Columbia University Press, 1986).
Baker, Herschel, *William Hazlitt* (Cambridge, Mass. and London: Harvard University Press, 1962).
Baldick, Chris, *The Social Mission of English Criticism 1848–1932* (Oxford University Press, 1983).
Barker-Benfield, G-J., *The Culture of Sensibility: Sex and Society in Eighteenth-century Britain* (Chicago and London: Chicago University Press, 1992).
  'Mary Wollstonecraft: Eighteenth-Century Commonwealthwoman', *Journal of the History of Ideas*, 50 (1989), pp. 95–115.
Barrell, John, *English Literature in History: An Equal Wide Survey* (London: Hutchinson, 1983).
  'John Clare, William Cobbett, and the Changing Landscape', in *The New Pelican Guide to English Literature*, vol. 5, *From Blake to Byron* (Harmondsworth: Penguin, 1982), pp. 226–43.
  The Political Theory of Painting from Reynolds to Hazlitt: 'The Body of the Public' (New Haven and London: Yale University Press, 1986).
Bate, Jonathan, *Romantic Ecology: Wordsworth and the Environmental Tradition* (London: Routledge, 1991).
  Shakespearean Constitutions: Politics, Theatre, Criticism 1730–1830 (Oxford: Clarendon Press, 1989).
Bialostosky, Don. H., *Wordsworth, Dialogics, and the Practice of Criticism* (New York and Cambridge: Cambridge University Press, 1992).

Blakemore, Steven, *Burke and the Fall of Language: The French Revolution as Linguistic Event* (Hanover and London: University Press of New England, 1988).
Intertextual War: Edmund Burke and the French Revolution in the Writings of Mary Wollstonecraft, Thomas Paine, and James Mackintosh (Madison, Teaneck: Fairleigh Dickinson University Press; London: Associated University Presses, 1997).
Boulton, J. T., *The Language of Politics in the Age of Wilkes and Burke* (London: Routledge and Kegan Paul, 1963).
Bourke, Richard, *Romantic Discourse and Political Modernity: Wordsworth, the Intellectual and Cultural Critique* (Hemel Hempstead: Harvester Wheatsheaf, 1993).
Brisman, Leslie, 'Coleridge and the Supernatural', *Studies in Romanticism*, 21 (1982), pp. 123–59.
Bromwich, David, *Hazlitt: The Mind of a Critic* (New York and Oxford: Oxford University Press, 1983).
Bullitt, John M., 'Hazlitt and the Romantic Conception of Imagination', *Philological Quarterly*, 24 (1945), pp. 343–61.
Butler, Marilyn, *Burke, Paine, Godwin, and the Revolution Controversy*, Cambridge English Prose Texts (Cambridge University Press, 1984).
Romantic, Rebels, and Reactionaries: English Literature and Its Background 1760–1830 (Oxford University Press, 1981).
Bygrave, Stephen, 'Land of the Giants: Gaps, Limits and Audience in Coleridge's *Biographia Literaria*', in Copley and Whale (eds.), *Beyond Romanticism*, pp. 32–52.
Cafarelli, Annette Wheeler, *Prose in the Age of Poets: Romanticism and Biographical Narrative from Johnson to De Quincey* (Philadelphia: University of Pennsylvania Press, 1990).
Chandler, Alice, *A Dream of Order: The Medieval Ideal in Nineteenth-Century English Literature* (Lincoln: University of Nebraska Press, 1970).
Chandler, James K., 'Burke's Mixed systems: the Political Economy of Burke's *Reflections*', presented at 'Our Present Discontents: A Conference to Mark the Bicentenary of Edmund Burke's Death', Goldsmiths College, University of London, July 1997.
Wordsworth's Second Nature: A Study of the Poetry and the Politics (Chicago and London: University of Chicago Press, 1984).
Christensen, Jerome, *Coleridge and the Blessed Machine of Language* (Ithaca: Cornell University Press, 1981).
Claeys, Gregory, *Thomas Paine: Social and Political Thought* (Boston: Unwin Hyman, 1989).
Coleman, Deirdre, *Coleridge and The Friend (1809–1810)* (Oxford: Clarendon Press, 1988).
Colmer, John, *Coleridge: Critic of Society* (Oxford: Clarendon Press, 1959).
Conger, Syndy McMillan, *Sensibility in Transformation: Creative Resistance to Sentiment from the Augustans to the Romantics* (London and Toronto: Fairleigh Dickinson University Press, Associated University Presses, 1989).
Cook, Jonathan, 'Hazlitt: Criticism and Ideology', in *Romanticism and Ideology:*

Studies in English Writing 1765-1830 (London: Routledge, 1981), pp. 137-54.

Copley, Stephen, and John Whale (eds.), *Beyond Romanticism: New Approaches to Texts and Contexts 1780-1832* (London: Routledge, 1992).

Deane, Seamus, *The French Revolution and Enlightenment in England 1789-1832* (Cambridge Mass. and London: Harvard University Press, 1988).

De Bolla, Peter, *The Discourse of the Sublime: Readings in History, Aesthetics and the Subject* (Oxford: Basil Blackwell, 1989).

De Bruyn, Frans, *The Literary Genres of Edmund Burke: The Political Uses of Literary Form* (Oxford: Clarendon Press, 1996).

Dentith, Simon, *A Rhetoric of the Real: Studies in Post-Enlightenment Writing from 1790 to the Present* (Hemel Hempstead and New York: Harvester Wheatsheaf, 1990).

Dinwiddy, John, *Bentham, Past Masters* (Oxford and New York: Oxford University Press, 1989).

Dyck, Ian, *William Cobbett and Rural Popular Culture* (Cambridge Unversity Press, 1992).

Eagleton, Terry, *The Ideology of the Aesthetic* (Oxford: Basil Blackwell, 1990).

'William Hazlitt: an Empiricist Radical', *New Blackfriars*, 54 (1973), pp. 108-17.

Egan, Kieran, and Dan Nadamer (eds.), *Imagination and Education* (Milton Keynes: Open University Press, 1988).

Engell, James, *The Creative Imagination: Enlightenment to Romanticism* (Cambridge, Mass. and London: Harvard University Press, 1981).

Essick, Robert N., 'William Blake, Thomas Paine, and Biblical Revolution', *Studies in Romanticism*, 30 (1991), pp. 189-212.

Everest, Kelvin, *Revolution in Writing: British Literary Responses to the French Revolution* (Milton Keynes: Open University Press, 1991).

and Alison Yarrington (eds.), *Reflections of Revolution: Images of Romanticism*, (London: Routledge, 1993).

Fairer, David, 'Organizing Verse: Burke's *Reflections* and Eighteenth-Century Poetry', *Romanticism*, 3:1 (1997), pp. 1-19.

Favret, Mary, *Romantic Correspondence: Women, Politics, and the Fiction of Letters* (Cambridge University Press, 1993).

Ferguson, Frances, *Solitude and the Sublime: Romanticism and the Aesthetics of Individuation* (London and New York: Routledge, 1992).

'Wollstonecraft Our Contemporary', *Gender and Theory: Dialogues on Feminist Criticism*, Linda Kauffman (ed.) (Oxford and New York: Basil Blackwell, 1989), pp. 51-62.

Foner, Eric, *Tom Paine and Revolutionary America* (Oxford and New York: Oxford University Press, 1976).

Friedman, Barton R., *Fabricating History: English Writers on the French Revolution* (Princeton University Press, 1988).

Furniss, Tom, *Edmund Burke's Aesthetic Ideology: Language, Gender and Political Economy in Revolution* (Cambridge University Press, 1993).

'Rhetoric in Revolution: The Role of Language in Paine's Critique of

Burke', in *Revolution and English Romanticism: Politics and Rhetoric* (London: Routledge, 1990), pp. 23-48.

'Stripping the Queen: Edmund Burke's Magic Lantern Show', in *Burke and the French Revolution: Bicentennial Essays*, ed. Steven Blakemore (Athens and London: The University of Georgia Press, 1992), pp. 69-96.

Gallagher, Catherine, 'The Body versus the Social Body in the Works of Thomas Malthus and Henry Mayhew,' *Representations*, 14 (1986), pp. 83-106.

Gallant, Christine (ed.), *Coleridge's Theory of Imagination Today* (New York: AMS Press, 1989).

Garnett, Mark, 'Hazlitt Against Burke: Radical versus Conservative', *Durham University Journal*, 49 (1989), pp. 229-39.

Gibbons, Luke, 'Customs in Contention: Burke, Ireland and the Colonial Sublime', delivered at 'Our Present Discontents: A Conference to Mark the Bicentenary of Edmund Burke's Death', Goldsmiths College, University of London, July 1997.

Gilmartin, Kevin, 'Burke, Popular Opinion, and the Problem of a Counter-Revolutionary Public Sphere', in *Edmund Burke's Reflections on the Revolution in France, Texts in Culture*, ed. John Whale (forthcoming from Manchester University Press).

Print Politics: The Press and Radical Opposition in Early Nineteenth-Century England (Cambridge University Press, 1996).

Gravil, Richard, Lucy Newlyn, and Nicholas Roe (eds.), *Coleridge's Imagination: Essays in Memory of Pete Laver* (Cambridge University Press, 1985).

Green, Daniel, *Great Cobbett: The Noblest Agitator* (Oxford University Press, 1985).

Halévy, Elie, *The Growth of Philosophical Radicalism*, trans. Mary Morris (London: Faber & Faber, 1952).

Hamilton, Paul, *Coleridge's Poetics* (Oxford: Basil Blackwell, 1983).

Hardy, Barbara, 'Distinction with Difference: Coleridge's Fancy and Imagination', *Essays in Criticism*, 1 (1951), pp. 336-44.

Harrison, Ross, *Bentham, The Arguments of the Philosophers* series (London, Melbourne and Henley: Routledge and Kegan Paul, 1983).

Heinzelman, Kurt, *The Economics of the Imagination* (Amherst: University of Massachusetts Press, 1980).

Ingham, Patricia, *The Language of Class: Transformation in the Victorian Novel* (London and New York: Routledge, 1996).

Jacobus, Mary, 'In Love with a Cold Climate: Travelling with Wollstonecraft', in *First Things: The Maternal Imaginary in Literature, Art, and Psychoanalysis* (New York and London: Routledge, 1995), pp. 63-82.

Janowitz, Ann, *England's Ruins: Poetic Purpose and the National Landscape* (Cambridge, Mass. and London: Blackwell, 1990).

Johnson, Claudia. L., *Equivocal Beings: Politics, Gender, and Sentimentality in the 1780s* (Chicago and London: University of Chicago Press, 1995).

Jones, Chris, *Radical Sensibility: Literature and Ideas in the 1790's* (London and New York: Routledge, 1992).

Jones, Stanley, *Hazlitt: A Life from Winterslow to Frith Street* (Oxford: Clarendon Press, 1989).
Jones, Vivien, '"The Tyranny of the Passions": Feminism and Heterosexuality in the Fiction of Wollstonecraft and Hays', in Sally Ledger, Josephine McDonagh, and Jane Spencer (eds.), *Political Gender: Texts and Contexts* (New York and London: Harvester Wheatsheaf, 1994), pp. 173–88.
'Women Writing Revolution: Narratives of History and Sexuality in Wollstonecraft and Williams', *Beyond Romanticism*, ed. Copley and Whale (London and New York: Routledge, 1992), pp. 178–99.
Kaplan, Cora, *Sea Changes: Essays in Culture and Feminism* (London: Verso, 1986).
Kearney, Richard, *The Wake of Imagination: Towards A Postmodern Culture* (London: Routledge, 1994).
Kelly, Gary, *Revolutionary Feminism: The Mind and Career of Mary Wollstonecraft* (Basingstoke and London: Macmillan, 1992).
Women, Writing, and Revolution 1790–1827 (Oxford: Clarendon Press, 1993).
Klancher, Jon P., *The Making of English Reading Audiences, 1790–1832* (Madison: University of Wisconsin Press, 1987).
Leask, Nigel, *The Politics of Imagination in Coleridge's Critical Thought* (Basing-stoke: Macmillan, 1988).
Leavis, F. R. (ed.), *Mill on Bentham and Coleridge* (London: Chatto and Windus, 1950).
Levinson, Marjorie, Marilyn Butler, Jerome McGann, and Paul Hamilton, *Rethinking Historicism* (Oxford and New York: Basil Blackwell, 1989).
Liu, Alan, *Wordsworth: The Sense of History* (Stanford University Press, 1989).
Lock, F. P., *Burke's Reflections on the Revolution in France* (London: Allen and Unwin, 1985).
Lockridge, Laurence, *Coleridge the Moralist* (Ithaca and London: Cornell University Press, 1977).
McCalman, Iain, *Radical Underworld: Prophets, Revolutionaries, and Pornographers in London, 1795–1840* (Cambridge University Press, 1988).
McDonagh, Josephine, *De Quincey's Disciplines* (Oxford: Clarendon Press, 1994).
McFarland, Thomas, 'The Origin and Significance of Coleridge's Theory of Secondary Imagination', in Geoffrey Hartman (ed.), *New Perspectives on Coleridge and Wordsworth: Selected Papers from the English Institute* (New York and London: Columbia University Press, 1972).
Romantic Cruxes: The English Essayists and the Spirit of the Age (Oxford: Clarendon Press, 1987).
McGann, Jerome J., 'The *Biographia Literaria* and the Contentions of English Romanticism', in Frederick Burwick (ed.), *Coleridge's 'Biographia Literaria': Text and Meaning* (Columbus: Ohio State University Press, 1989), pp. 233–54.
The Romantic Ideology: A Critical Investigation (Chicago and London: University of Chicago Press, 1983).
Mackie, J., *The Miracle of Theism* (Oxford University Press, 1982).
Martin, Philip, 'Romanticism, History, Historicisms', in *Revolution in Writing:*

British Literary Responses to the French Revolution, ed. Kelvin Everest (Milton Keynes: Open University Press, 1991), pp. 9–26.

Mee, Jon, *Dangerous Enthusiasm: William Blake and the Culture of Radicalism in the 1790s* (Oxford University Press, 1992).

Mitchell, W. T. J., *Iconology: Image, Text, Ideology* (Chicago and London: University of Chicago Press, 1986).

Moore, Jane, 'Plagiarism with a Difference: Subjectivity in "Kubla Khan" and *Letters Written During a Short Residence in Sweden, Norway and Denmark*', in Copley and Whale (eds.), *Beyond Romanticism*, pp. 140–59.

'Unseating the Philosopher-Knight', in *Political Gender: Texts and Contexts*, Sally Ledger, Josephine McDonagh, and Jane Spencer (eds.) (New York and London: Harvester Wheatsheaf, 1994), pp. 71–84.

Nattrass, Leonora, *William Cobbett: The Politics of Style* (Cambridge University Press, 1995).

Newlyn, Lucy, 'Coleridge and the Anxiety of Reception', *Romanticism*, 1:2 (1995), pp. 206–38.

O'Hara, J. D., 'Hazlitt and the Functions of the Imagination', *PMLA*, 81 (1966), pp. 552–62.

Ogden, A. K. and I. A. Richards, *The Meaning of Meaning: A Study of the Influence of Language Upon Thought and the Science of Symbolism* (London: Kegan Paul, 1946; first published 1923).

Osborne, John W., *William Cobbett: His Thought and his Times* (New Bruns-wick: Rutgers University Press, 1966).

Park, Roy, *Hazlitt and The Spirit of the Age: Abstraction and Critical Theory* (Oxford: Clarendon Press, 1971).

Paulin, Tom, *The Day-Star of Liberty: William Hazlitt's Radical Style* (London: Faber and Faber, 1998).

Paulson, Ronald, *Representations of Revolution (1789–1820)* (New Haven and London: Yale University Press, 1983).

Philp, Mark, *Paine*, Past Masters (Oxford and New York: Oxford University Press, 1989).

Pocock, J. G. A., *Politics, Language and Time: Essays on Political Thought and History* (New York: Atheneum, 1971).

Virtue, Commerce and History: Essays on Political Thought and History, Chiefly in the Eighteenth Century (Cambridge and New York: Cambridge University Press, 1985).

Poovey, Mary, *The Proper Lady and the Woman Writer: Ideology as Style in the Works of Mary Wollstonecraft, Mary Shelley, and Jane Austen* (Chicago and London: University of Chicago Press, 1984).

Pyle, Forest, *The Ideology of Imagination: Subject and Society in the Discourse of Romanticism* (Stanford University Press, 1995).

Reid, Christopher, *Edmund Burke and the Practice of Political Writing* (Dublin and New York: Gill and Macmillan, 1985).

Reiss, Timothy J., 'Revolution in Bounds: Wollstonecraft, Women, and Reason', in *Gender and Theory*, ed. Linda Kauffman (Oxford and New York: Basil Blackwell, 1989), pp. 11–50.

Richardson, Alan, *Literature, Education, and Romanticism: Reading As Social Practice 1780–1832* (Cambridge University Press, 1994).
Salle, J-C., 'Hazlitt the Associationist', *Review of English Studies*, 15 (1964), pp. 38–51.
Sambrook, James, *William Cobbett* (London: Routledge and Kegan Paul, 1973).
Sapiro, Virginia, *A Vindication of Political Virtue: The Political Theory of Mary Wollstonecraft* (Chicago and London: University of Chicago Press, 1992).
Scarre, Geoffrey, *Utilitarianism* (London: Routledge, 1996).
Schweizer, Karl W. and John W. Osborne, *Cobbett in His Times* (Leicester University Press, 1990).
Simpson, David, 'Coleridge on Wordsworth and the Form of Poetry', in *Coleridge's Theory of Imagination Today*, Georgia State Literary Studies 4, Christine Gallant (ed.) (New York: AMS Press, 1989), pp. 211–25.
  Romanticism, Nationalism, and the Revolt Against Theory (Chicago and London: University of Chicago Press, 1993).
  Wordsworth's Historical Imagination: The Poetry of Displacement (New York and London: Methuen, 1987).
Siskin, Clifford, *The Historicity of Romantic Discourse* (New York and Oxford: Oxford University Press, 1987).
Smith, Kenneth, *The Malthusian Controversy* (London: Routledge and Kegan Paul, 1951).
Smith, Olivia, *The Politics of Language, 1791–1819* (Oxford: Clarendon Press, 1984).
Spater, George, *William Cobbett: The Poor Man's Friend*, 2 vols. (Cambridge University Press, 1982).
Stanlis, Peter J., *Edmund Burke and Natural Law* (Ann Arbor: University of Michigan Press, 1958).
Steintrager, James, *Bentham* (London: George Allen and Unwin, 1977).
Taylor, Barbara, 'Mary Wollstonecraft and the Wild Wish of Early Feminism', *History Workshop Journal*, 33 (1992), pp. 197–219.
Thompson, E. P., *The Making of the English Working Class* (Harmondsworth: Penguin Books, 1980; first published Victor Gollancz, 1963).
Tomaselli, Sylvana, 'Moral Philosophy and Population Questions in Eighteenth-Century Europe', in Michael S. Teitelbaum and Jay M. Winter (eds.), *Population and Resources in Western Intellectual Traditions* (Cambridge University Press, 1988), pp. 7–29.
Turner, John, 'Burke, Paine, and the Nature of Language', *Yearbook of English Studies*, 19 (1989), pp. 36–53.
Warnock, Mary, *Imagination and Time* (Oxford: Basil Blackwell, 1994).
Whale, John, 'Hazlitt on Burke: The Ambivalent Position of a Radical Essayist', *Studies in Romanticism*, 25 (1986), pp. 465–81.
  'Literal and Symbolic Representation: Burke, Paine and the French French Revolution', *History of European Ideas*, 16 (1993), pp. 343–49.
  'Indian Jugglers: Romantic Orientalism and the Difference of View', in *Romanticism and Colonialism: Writing and Empire, 1780–1830*, Tim Fulford and Peter Kitson (eds.) (Cambridge University Press, 1998), pp. 206–20.

Thomas De Quincey's Reluctant Autobiography (Beckenham and Totowa New Jersey: Croom Helm and Barnes and Noble, 1984).
Wheeler, Kathleen, *Sources, Processes, and Methods in Coleridge's 'Biographia Literaria'* (Cambridge University Press, 1980).
Willey, Basil, *Nineteenth Century Studies: Coleridge to Matthew Arnold* (Cambridge University Press, 1949).
Williams, Raymond, *Culture and Society 1780–1950* (Harmondsworth: Penguin, 1961; first published 1958).
Keywords: A Vocabulary of Culture and Society (London: Fontana, 1976).
William Cobbett (Oxford and New York: Oxford University Press, 1983).
Wilson, David A., *Paine and Cobbett: The Transatlantic Connection* (Kingston and Montreal: McGill-Queen's University Press, 1988).
Wood, Marcus, *Radical Satire and Print Culture 1700–1822* (Oxford: Clarendon Press, 1994).
Wood, Neal, 'The Aesthetic Dimension of Burke's Political Thought', *Journal of British Studies*, 4 (1964), pp. 41–64.
Woodring, Carl, 'Coleridge: the Politics of Imagination', *Studies in Romanticism*, 21 (1982), pp. 447–76.
Worrall, David, *Radical Culture: Discourse, Resistance, and Surveillance, 1790–1820* (Hemel Hempstead: Harvester/Wheatsheaf, 1992).

Index

Abrams, M. H., 4
Althusser, Louis, 8
American independence, 57
American revolution, 67
aristocratic culture, 3, 15, 34, 40, 41, 42, 79, 91
Aristotle, 7
Arnold, Matthew, 187, 193
assignats, 36
Athenaeum, 177
Auden, W. H., 191

Baldick, Chris, 224n47
Barker-Benfield, C. J., 208n3, 210n19
Barrell, John, 151, 213n1, 218n24
Bate, Jonathan, 4, 214n3
Bentham, Jeremy, 99, 100, 101 102–9, 133, 134, 169, 177–78, 181–82, 188, 190
  Anarchical Fallacies 105–06
  Fragment on Government 102–05
  Rationale of Reward 106
Blackstone, William 102–3
  Commentaries 102–3
Bloom, Harold, 4, 11
Bonaparte, see Napoleon
Bourke, Richard, 6
British constitution, 21, 25, 28–30, 32–33, 35
  Appeal from the New to the Old Whigs 31, 37
  Enquiry into . . . the Sublime and Beautiful 19–23, 26, 113, 151
  Reflections 15, 19, 20, 23–26, 28–30, 33, 35, 37, 39, 40, 42, 47–51, 56, 77, 196
  Speech on Conciliation with Colonies 32
  and the constitution 28–30, 32–34
  and Coleridge 30–33
  and difficulty 27–28
  and necessity 24–25
  and the organic 12, 32–33, 39
  and Paine 47–52, 56–58, 64
  and religious opinion 31
  Romanticism 30–31
  and Wollstonecraft 77, 79

'Burke and Hare' murders, 136
Butler, Marilyn, 4

Campanella, Tomasso, 22
Cartesian dualism, 9
Cartwright, Major John, 101
Castlereagh, Robert, Viscount, 146
Chandler, James, 40
chivalry, 15, 20, 24, 28, 37, 39, 41
Claeys, Gregory, 205n9
Cobbett, William, 3, 11, 12, 63, 97, 100, 140–65, 195, 196
  Advice to Young Men 143, 154
  The Beauties of Cobbett 164
  The Book of Wonders 164
  Cottage Economy 149, 153
  Grammar of the English Language 144, 157
  Journal of a Year's Residence in the US 156–57
  'Observations on the Emigration of Priestley' 154
  Paper Against Gold 219n28
  Political Register 142
  Rural Rides 147–49, 151, 152–53, 157, 158, 160–61
  Surplus Population 160
  on paper-money 155
  on 'the system' 3, 159
Coleridge, S. T., 1, 3, 7, 8, 13, 30, 31, 32–33, 38, 40, 41, 66, 92, 97, 100–1, 166–93, 195–96
  Biographia Literaria 124, 128, 167, 171, 172, 174, 175, 178, 190, 192
  On the Constitution of Church and State 167, 174, 177–78, 180
  'Dejection: an Ode' 183
  The Friend 30, 168, 170, 190, 223n9
  'Kubla Khan' 92
  Poetical Works 177
  Lay Sermons 124, 126, 128, 167, 171, 180
  Statesman's Manual 167
  Table Talk 167, 223n7

237

'Work without Hope' 183
  and Burke 30–33
  and the organic 31, 33
  Hazlitt on 124–29
  idea of 'One Life' 5, 12
  'the Idea' 167, 176, 183,
Condorcet, Marie Jean Antoine Nicolas
  Caritat, Marquis de, 53, 55
  Progress of the Human Mind 55
Conger, Syndy McMillan, 210n16

Damien, Robert Frances, 22
De Bolla, Peter, 5
De Man, Paul, 8
De Quincey, Thomas, 3
Dickens, Charles, 100
  Hard Times 101
Dyck, Ian 149, 220n43

Eagleton, Terry 5, 31, 101, 201n3
  The Ideology of the Aesthetic 5, 31
Edinburgh Review 126, 131, 138
Eliot, George, 126
  Middlemarch 126
Eliot, T. S., 191
Empson, William, 191
Engell, James, 197n1
Engels, Frederick, 63
English revolutionaries, 33

Fairer, David, 204n56
Favret, Mary, 211n39
Ferguson, Frances, 208n1
Foucault, Michel, 7, 22
Fox, Charles James, 112, 118
Fox, W. J., 177
French constitution, 19, 30
Furniss, Tom, 200n1, 210n20

Gibbons, Luke, 202n9
Gilmartin, Kevin, 214n4, 217n4, 221n50
'Glorious Revolution', 24, 26
Godwin, William, 98–100, 108, 130, 175
  Bible Stories 212n4
  Caleb Williams 98
  Political Justice 98–99
Goethe, Johann Wolfgang von, 172

Halévy, Elie, 101
Hartley, David, 179, 188
Hartman, Geoffrey, 4, 11
Hazlitt, William, 1, 3, 12, 33, 38, 40, 41, 61, 97,
  101, 106, 108, 110–39, 173, 176, 179, 195,
  196
  Liber Amoris 110

Life of Napoleon 118, 122
The Plain Speaker 111, 113, 130, 132
Spirit of the Age 111, 127, 128, 134–35
'On Benevolence' 110
'On the Character of Burke' 115, 117
'On the Character of the Country People' 123
'On the Spirit of Partisanship' 130
'The Late Murders' 135
'The New School of Reform' 137
'Parliamentary Eloquence' 121
On the Principles of Human Action 110
'On the Prose Style of Poets' 112 3
'On Reason and Imagination' 132, 134–35
'What is the People?' 111
on Burke 111–24
Heinzelman, Kurt, 1–7, 8
Helvétius, Claude-Adrien, 130
Herder, Johann Gottfried von, 174, 180
Hobbes, Thomas, 8
Horace, 28
Hume, David, 8, 10, 93

Imlay, Gilbert, 69, 93
Ingham, Patricia, 212n5

Jacobus, Mary, 211 n44
Johnson, Claudia L., 208n1
Jones, Vivien, 208n1

Kant, Immannuel, 4, 5, 188
  post-Kantian aesthetics 5
Kaplan, Cora, 208n1
Kearney, Richard, 4, 8, 198n5
Kelly, Gary, 21 11n39
Klancher, Jon, 127, 167, 217n3, 215n28,
  221n55

Law, John, 36
Leask, Nigel, 5, 176
  The Politics of Coleridge's Imagination 5
libertinism, 15, 69, 97
literalism, 3, 12, 42, 66, 141
Liu, Alan, 4
Livy, 24, 35
Longinus, 45
Louis XV, (King of France), 22
Lovat, (Simon Fraser), Lord, 22, 26
Lyotard, Jean-Francois, 4
Lyrical Ballads, 12

Magna Carta, 100
Malthus, Thomas, 7, 97, 108, 119, 130, 160,
  166, 167, 168, 192
Mandeville, Bernard, 130

Index

Marx, Karl, 8, 63, 164, 222n56
McGann, Jerome, 5, 8, 201 M
Memoirs of Granville Sharp, 133
Michelet, Jules, 80
Mill, John Stuart, 13, 91, 100, 101, 108, 133, 139, 176-82, 184-92
  Autobiography 101, 183-84
  Logic 187
  crisis 183-4, 186
Milton, John, 82, 169
Moore, Jane, 211n40

Napoleon Bonaparte, 101, 120, 122, 145, 146, 163
Nattrass, Leonora, 217n3
Necker, Jacques, 74
  De L'Importance des Opinions Religeuse 74
Newlyn, Lucy, 223n12
New Monthly Magazine, 110

Osborne, John W., 221n45

Paine, Thomas, 3, 11, 12, 14-16, 41, 42-67, 76, 140, 155, 153, 158-59, 195, 196
  Age of Reason 45, 48, 51-55, 57
  Common Sense 67
  The Crisis Papers 59
  Decline and Fall of the English System of Finance 153, 158-59
  'On Dream' 43
  'The Eighteenth Fructidor' 63
  'First Principles of Government' 60-61, 63
  'The Forester's Letters' 37-38
  'Letter to Abbe Raynal' 45
  'Letters to American Citizens' 59
  'The Magazine in America' 45-47
  'Prospects on the Rubicon' 56, 65
  Rights of Man 48, 49, 50, 51-52, 56, 58, 67, 82, 159, 161
  and the body 62-63
  and Burke 47-52, 56-58, 64
  and commerce 16
  and deism 52-55
  and slavery 62-63
Paley, William, 130, 166-67, 168, 169, 175, 215n35
  Principles of Moral and Political Philosophy 130
Paulin, Tom, 214n4
paper-money, 36, 155, 158, 161
Park, Roy, 216n38
Peacock, Thomas Love, 129
Philp, Mark, 205n9
Pitt, William, 112, 153
Plato, 125, 190
political economy, 7, 69, 89

Poovey, Mary, 208n1
postmodernity, 4
Price, Richard, 34
Pyle, Forest, 6-8

rationalism, 16, 48, 67, 82, 85
Raynal, Abbé Guillaume-Thomas-Francois, 51
Reagan, Ronald, 67
Reynolds, Joshua, 35
Revolution Society, 34, 37
Ricardo, David, 7, 131
Richards, I. A., 13, 100, 176, 186-93
  Coleridge on Imagination 187-88
  Science and Poetry 187
  Speculative Instruments 224n50
  The Viking Portable Coleridge 190
Richardson, Alan, 6
Roebuck, John Arthur, 185
romantic aesthetics, 30, 39
romantic ideology, 5, 8, 20
Rousseau, Jean-Jacques, 6, 42, 57, 66, 69, 70-73, 74, 77, 80, 84, 130, 131, 132, 154
  Confesssions 72
  Discourse on Political Economy 66
  Du Contrat Social 66
  Emile 70-72
  and Wollstonecraft 68-73, 84

Sapiro, Virginia, 209n4
Shakespeare, William, 111
Shelley, Percy Bysshe, 125, 129
Simpson, David, 30, 102
Siskin, Clifford, 197n4
Smith, Adam, 7, 95, 182
Smith, Olivia, 218n16
Snow, C. P., 3
Southcott, Joanna, 126
Southey, Robert, 128
South Sea Bubble, 36, 39
sublime, 4, 5, 20, 31, 39, 45, 85, 86, 91, 92
  and beautiful 22-23, 34
  Burkean sublime 16, 19-21, 56, 113, 151
  rational sublime 15, 42
Swift, Jonathan, 20, 79
  Gulliver's Travels 78

Tantalus, 70
Thompson, E. P., 141, 217n3, 218n6
Taylor, Barbara, 208n1

United States of America, 93

Virgil, 35

Volney, Constantin Francois de Chasseboeuf, 52

Warnock, Mary, 8–10
Watson, Richard (Bishop), 65, 205n10
  Apology for the Bible 65
Whitbread, Samuel, 121
Williams, Raymond, 100, 140, 156, 157, 165, 191
  Culture and Society 191
Williams, William Carlos, 7
Windham, William, 153
Wollstonecraft, Mary, 3, 12, 14, 15, 16, 41, 68–97, 102, 195, 196
  Historical and Moral View 87–90
  Mary 82–3
  Rights of Men 69, 72–75, 78, 81
  Rights of Woman 69, 72, 76–78, 80, 81, 83–85

  Sweden, Norway, and Denmark 69, 79, 81, 89, 91, 92, 93, 96
  Thoughts on the Education of Daughters 75–76, 77, 86
  and Burke 77, 79
  and Christianity 83
  and commerce 16, 69, 78, 90, 93
  and genius 69, 81, 87
  and libertinism 69
  and Rousseau 68–73, 84
  and sensibility 41, 73, 75
Wordsworth, William, 6, 10, 127, 150, 169, 184–85, 186, 194
  'Immortality Ode' 184
  'Preface to Lyrical Ballads' 184
  The Prelude 150, 194

Yeats, W. B., 191

CAMBRIDGE STUDIES IN ROMANTICISM

General editors
MARILYN BUTLER
University of Oxford
JAMES CHANDLER
University of Chicago

1. *Romantic Correspondence: Women, Politics and the Fiction of Letters*
   MARY A. FAVRET

2. *British Romantic Writers and the East: Anxieties of Empire*
   NIGEL LEASK

3. *Edmund Burke's Aesthetic Ideology*
   Language, Gender and Political Economy in Revolution
   TOM FURNISS

4. *Poetry as an Occupation and an Art in Britain, 1760–1830*
   PETER MURPHY

5. *In the Theatre of Romanticism: Coleridge, Nationalism, Women*
   JULIE A. CARLSON

6. *Keats, Narrative and Audience*
   ANDREW BENNETT

7. *Romance and Revolution: Shelley and the Politics of a Genre*
   DAVID DUFF

8. *Literature, Education, and Romanticism*
   Reading as Social Practice, 1780–1832
   ALAN RICHARDSON

9. *Women Writing about Money: Women's Fiction in England, 1790–1820*
   EDWARD COPELAND

10. *Shelley and the Revolution in Taste: The Body and the Natural World*
    TIMOTHY MORTON

11. *William Cobbett: The Politics of Style*
    LEONORA NATTRASS

12. *The Rise of Supernatural Fiction, 1762–1800*
    E. J. CLERY

13. *Women Travel Writers and the Language of Aesthetics, 1716–1818*
    ELIZABETH A. BOHLS

14. *Napoleon and English Romanticism*
    SIMON BAINBRIDGE

15. Romantic Vagrancy: Wordsworth and the Simulation of Freedom
CELESTE LANGAN

16. Wordsworth and the Geologists
JOHN WYATT

17. Wordsworth's Pope: A Study in Literary Historiography
ROBERT J. GRIFFIN

18. The Politics of Sensibility
Race, Gender and Commerce in the Sentimental Novel
MARKMAN ELLIS

19. Reading Daughters' Fictions 1709–1834
Novels and Society from Manley to Edgeworth
CAROLINE GONDA

20. Romantic Identities: Varieties of Subjectivity, 1774–1830
ANDREA K. HENDERSON

21. Print Politics
The Press and Radical Opposition in Early Nineteenth-Century England
KEVIN GILMARTIN

22. Reinventing Allegory
THERESA M. KELLEY

23. British Satire and the Politics of Style, 1789–1832
GARY DYER

24. The Romantic Reformation
Religious Politics in English Literature, 1789–1824
ROBERT M. RYAN

25. De Quincey's Romanticism
Canonical Minority and the Forms of Transmission
MARGARET RUSSETT

26. Coleridge on Dreaming
Romanticism, Dreams and the Medical Imagination
JENNIFER FORD

27. Romantic Imperialism
Universal Empire and the Culture of Modernity
SAREE MAKDISI

28. Ideology and Utopia in the Poetry of William Blake
NICHOLAS M. WILLIAMS

29. Sexual Politics and the Romantic Author
SONIA HOFKOSH

30. *Lyric and Labour in the Romantic Tradition*
    ANNE JANOWITZ

31. *Poetry and Politics in the Cockney School
    Keats, Shelley, Hunt and their Circle*
    JEFFREY N. COX

32. *Rousseau, Robespierre and English Romanticism*
    GREGORY DART

33. *Contesting the Gothic Fiction, Genre and Cultural Conflict, 1764–1832*
    JAMES WATT

34. *Romanticism, Aesthetics, and Nationalism*
    DAVID ARAM KAISER

35. *Romantic Poets and the Culture of Posterity*
    ANDREW BENNETT

36. *The Crisis of Literature in the 1790s
    Print Culture and the Public Sphere*
    PAUL KEEN

37. *Romantic Atheism: Poetry and Freethought, 1780–1830*
    MARTIN PRIESTMAN

38. *Romanticism and Slave Narratives
    Transatlantic Testimonies*
    HELEN THOMAS

39. *Imagination Under Pressure, 1789–1832
    Aesthetics, Politics and Utility*
    JOHN WHALE